Unfulfilled Expectations

Unfulfilled Expectations:
Home and School Influences on Literacy

Catherine E. Snow

Wendy S. Barnes

Jean Chandler

Irene F. Goodman

Lowry Hemphill

HARVARD UNIVERSITY PRESS
Cambridge, Massachusetts
London, England
1991

Library of Congress Cataloging-in-Publication Data
Unfulfilled expectations : home and school influences on literacy
    Catherine E. Snow . . . [et al.].
            p.   cm.
        Includes bibliographical references and index.
        ISBN 0–674–92110–0
        1. Literacy—Evaluation. 2. Home and school. 3. Reading—Parent
participation—Case studies. 4. Education—Social aspects.
    I. Snow, Catherine E.
    LC149.U49   1991   90–4814
    302.2'244—dc20   CIP

Contents

Unfulfilled Expectations

Chapter 1

Determining the Sources of Literacy

The most basic expectation for children attending school is that they will learn to read and write. Sadly, this expectation is not always fulfilled for schoolchildren in the United States, far too many of whom fail at the basic school task of literacy acquisition. Although few children leave American elementary schools completely unable to read, an alarming proportion enter and ultimately graduate from high school with the ability to read at only a late elementary level. At this level of literacy, they cannot comfortably read newspapers or popular magazines. They do not know the meanings of many words used on nightly newscasts or in popular adventure fiction. On the job, they may be unable to read equipment manuals, file reports, or understand the vocabulary of technical instructions. Students with levels of literacy this low on entry to high school are at risk of dropping out because the schoolwork they are expected to do is too hard for them. Even if they manage to graduate, they are, while not technically illiterate, insufficiently literate to participate fully in American economic and political life.

Why do some students fail to achieve these sorts of literacy skills while others succeed? A substantial proportion of those who fail to achieve adequate levels of literacy are students from financially disadvantaged families. It was estimated in 1977 that fewer than 50 percent of adult members of families with incomes under $10,000 per year were competent in literacy skills (Adult Performance Level Study, 1977). Eight years later, the National Assessment of Educational Progress (NAEP) reported that less than 50 percent of young adults from disadvantaged urban backgrounds had acquired reading skills to the intermediate level (Applebee,

Langer, and Mullis, 1988; National Assessment of Educational Progress, 1985). The findings are doubly troubling: they suggest that the literacy deficits of adults in poor families are being replicated among the children. Furthermore, the children who fail to learn to read today can hardly aspire to more remunerative jobs or to higher levels of education than their parents have achieved.

While children of poor families are at greater risk of literacy failure, some children from financially disadvantaged families do well in school and in acquiring literacy. We cannot, then, invoke income or social class as a simple explanation for failure of literacy development, though the existence of social class differences may suggest some hypotheses about the causes. The study reported here was undertaken in order to develop our understanding of the factors that relate to achievement in literacy among children in low-income families. On the basis of this understanding, we can seek better ways to help low-income children who achieve less than they should.

Our study's primary objective was to study the effects of experiences in low-income children's lives, at home and at school, on their literacy achievement. Many studies have been conducted to answer the question of why some children fail to learn to read and write as well as others their age. Conclusions of these studies have implicated inappropriate teaching methods, low academic standards in schools attended by poor children, insufficient language stimulation at home and at school, and a variety of individual child characteristics. Books previously written on this topic have ranged widely: from endorsements of quick-fix teaching methods to indictments of schools for failing to maintain standards, reproaches to families for failing to stimulate, enrich, or discipline their children, and condemnations of society for replicating inequality of access to resources through institutionalized discrimination and cultural insensitivity. While many of these studies have succeeded in explaining some aspects of poor achievement among low-income children, the problem is still far from solved. Why do we feel we have anything to add to this long-studied and still unresolved issue?

The study which forms the basis for this book differs from previous research in a number of important ways, both in its basic theoretical framework and in the resulting decisions about what children to study and how to study them. We discuss here the factors that differentiate the present study from previous ones addressing the same problem.

Low-income families. A starting point for a very large part of the work previously carried out has been the evidence of social class differences in reading achievement. More than two decades ago, American public attention was forcefully drawn to evidence that socioeconomic status was related to differences in school achievement. In a monumental study, *Equality of Educational Opportunity,* based on a survey of thousands of children throughout the United States, it was found not only that children of low-income families did significantly worse than those from families of middle and higher incomes, but also that the differences in achievement by socioeconomic status (SES) became greater as students advanced through school (Coleman et al., 1966).

These findings have been confirmed by other more recent studies. The 1981 NAEP report, for example, indicated consistent and significant differences in reading achievement between children in affluent suburban schools and those in "disadvantaged" urban schools—with the urban schoolchildren lagging behind those in the affluent suburbs. The most recent NAEP report on reading (1985) found that although the gap between advantaged and disadvantaged nine-year-olds seems to be lessening, the low-income seventeen-year-olds could read only at a high elementary school level, a level achieved by advantaged students at age thirteen. Differences such as these have generated most of the hypotheses that have guided previous research efforts on how home factors contribute to school success. The assumption has been that any factor present in middle-class homes is likely to be positive for school learning, whereas factors present in working-class homes have negative consequences for achievement.

In fact, though, it is difficult to isolate the factors that may actually be producing an effect simply by comparing middle-class with working-class children. Social class is a package variable, a summary label for an intricate complex of related variables including parental education, occupational status, income, housing conditions, time allocation, attitudes toward school and schooling, experiences with school, expectations for future educational and occupational success, nature of the family's social network, and style of parent-child interaction. Replicating findings of social class differences in school achievement brings us no closer to understanding the mechanisms by which those differences develop because it is rarely possible to sort out the separate effects of the wide array of factors packaged together as "working class" or "middle class." The most provocative findings concerning the contribution of home variables to school achievement have isolated factors such as "thrust" or "push" for education (Bloom, 1976) or "curriculum in the home" (Walberg and Marjoribanks, 1976). These summary terms, which refer to activities such as buying books for children, taking children on excursions, and supervising their schoolwork, may be correlated with social class, but they can vary widely in middle-class as well as in low-income groups.

Our approach, therefore, was to eschew comparisons by social class in favor of a within-class comparison. We chose to limit our sample to children from low-income families. By contrasting low-income families that had produced successful school learners with those that had produced below-average learners, we felt we could isolate more easily the home factors that contribute to school success. Furthermore, with this approach we were not presupposing the as yet unproven hypothesis that the factors contributing to success for low-income children are exactly the same as those that determine success among children of richer families.

The strategy of focusing on low-income children enabled us, moreover, to collect information on what may be the most neglected subgroup of schoolchildren—low-income children who do well. Above-average readers from low-income families can show us how their families differ from those whose children are less successful in reading and writing achievement. Dolores Durkin (1982) has used this research strategy as well in studying black low-income children who were highly successful at school. She found that successful children had books at home, got help with their homework from a parent or someone else at home, and had parents who expected them to go to college. Most significantly, perhaps, many of the successful children in Durkin's sample had been able to read before kindergarten, evidence that an adult had provided books, interest, attention, and teaching early on.

Literacy as a set of skills. An important component of our view of literacy is that it includes a set of related but not perfectly correlated skills (Snow and Dickinson, in press). Accordingly, literacy cannot be defined by a single endpoint or measured by a single score on a single test. Rather, literacy involves skills at using print and language in ways that change as the skills develop. Since literacy includes both reading and writing, it is entirely possible, depending on one's instructional history, that one can read and write at different developmental levels. Furthermore, both high-level reading and sophisticated writing require an age-appropriate knowledge of vocabulary, which means that knowledge of word meaning as well as reading and writing must be assessed in order to reflect a child's literacy level.

In becoming literate, one must acquire skills that are only remotely related to print as well as those that are directly related. In addition to learning about letter-sound correspondence, one must learn quite a lot about word roots and about the complex rules that assign stress to English words, if one is to become skilled at word recognition. One must learn to relate what is being read to already acquired world knowledge, if one is to become skilled at reading comprehension. Fully literate persons can write correctly and interestingly, and can also adjust aspects of their writing style to different genres and audiences. Indeed, fully literate persons talk in a way that is influenced by their literate activities, using vocabulary items and some syntactic structures not found in the speech of the nonliterate.

This componential view of literacy required us to assess a full range of literacy skills, writing and language skills as well as reading. Instruments were selected that assessed separately four different components of literacy, enabling a more analytic view of distinct influences on achievement in each area. Since school achievement was a central concern of our investigations, instruments of a type commonly used in school settings were chosen (see Chall, Jacobs, and Baldwin, 1990, for complete details of all the instruments used). For purposes of the analyses reported in this volume, we looked at two components of reading—word recognition and reading comprehension—using subtests of the Diagnostic Assessment of Reading and Teaching Strategies (Roswell and Chall, in press). We also used the Wechsler Intelligence Scale for Children—Revised vocabulary subtest as a measure of vocabulary. And we selected word production in narrative and expository writing samples produced by the children as a measure of writing. Obviously, there were many other separable components of literacy we could have assessed. But we felt that the four we looked at were the most closely related to school achievement and were the most likely to suggest patterns of influence between home and school.

A developmental theory. Literacy is not a single skill that simply gets better with age or instruction, as a sprinter's running times get better with practice and conditioning. Being literate is a very different enterprise for the skilled first grader, fourth grader, high school student, and adult, and the effects of school experiences can be quite different at different points in a child's development (see, for example, Alexander and Entwisle, 1988). The tasks that can reasonably be set at the various levels of literacy are different, and the resources available to approach those tasks are different as well. Accordingly, the factors influencing literacy achievement may also be different.

Treating the ability to read as a developmental process had important implications for our research decisions. It led to our decision to include three cohorts of children, students originally in grades 2, 4, and 6, and to follow these students for two years, extending our data collection to grades 3, 5, and 7. We hoped that including children over this age range would help explicate earlier findings that SES differences in reading achievement increase in the intermediate and higher grades (Chall, 1983). Although the research literature tells us that differences in achievement between middle-class and working-class groups start to become quite large only in the middle and higher elementary grades, most of the research on SES differences has been done on children in the early grades.

Normal range of variation. We were interested in "average" low-income children for whom home and school experiences could be assumed to generate a large part of the variance in how quickly or slowly they were learning to read. In order to assure ourselves sufficient variability in literacy skills in a relatively small sample, we tried to choose children who ranged from somewhat above to somewhat below average in reading. We attempted, furthermore, to select better and poorer readers from the same classrooms, in order to maximize the variability due to home factors. The children selected by our tests and by teacher recommendations matched our requirements fairly well and enabled us to do analyses that involved correlating home and school factors to literacy achievement across a fairly wide range of literacy levels. The fact that we tested each child twice, at one-year intervals, meant that we could also assess whether the gains the children made were above or below the one-year gain in reading skills that would be expected during that time.

Home and school. Studies of failure in literacy achievement have tended to shift the blame back and forth between home and school, in cycles of about twenty years. Those who look to the home as the main cause of poor literacy skills tend to cite as factors leading to poor achievement a low level of parental literacy, a low level of parental education, instability of the home, absence of books in the home, and low parental aspirations for children's achievement. Those who look to the school as the main cause point to such factors as limited school resources, the questionable quality of administrative leadership, inadequate or inappropriate teacher preparation, low expectations for the children's achievement, poor quality of the curriculum and materials in urban schools, limited special services provided, a mismatch in discourse patterns and behavioral expectations between home and school, and the use of inadequate teaching methods.

Starting in the 1960s, major research efforts were directed toward identifying the role of home variables in predicting school achievement. This research is reviewed in some detail in Chapters 4 and 5. In general, income and education of parents were found to have the highest association with children's achievement, higher than school and classroom factors. Indeed, once the social factors were used in the statistical prediction of achievement, what the schools were or did seemed to add little to achievement. During the sixties, many of the programs instituted as part of the New Frontier and the Great Society were attempts to remedy what were seen by policymakers as the inadequacies of low-income, working-class, and non-mainstream homes. Head Start was designed to provide for preschoolers what low-income families did not provide for their children. And for school-age children, Title 1 and later Chapter 1 were established to provide extra help in reading for children of low-income families.

Understandably, total success in eliminating social class differences in school achievement did not result from the approach of the sixties. The early eighties saw the predictable reaction: the pendulum's swing to its other extreme, implicating school factors as primary in accounting for students' achievement.

Occasionally in the 1970s, and more frequently in the 1980s, studies began to appear that focused on the positive effects of school on achievement, particularly among children from lower-income families. Most of these, referred to as "school effectiveness studies," found that low-income children can, and indeed many do, achieve at or above grade level on national norms, and it is the school that "makes the difference" in their achievement (see for example, Brookover et al., 1982; Fleming, 1985; Pecheone and Shoemaker, 1984). These studies have found that certain characteristics of the schools in poor urban areas tend to be associated with higher achievement—for instance, a "strong" principal, high expectations for achievement, direct teaching, frequent testing, and the like. Recently researchers in the "school reform" movement have documented the characteristics of good versus poor schools (Rutter et al., 1979) and have also provided recommendations for improving school practice (Boyer, 1983; Goodlad, 1984; Lightfoot, 1983; Sizer, 1984).

Many people have suggested that a major source of children's school failure lies not so much in the home or the school per se but in the mismatch between home and school. For children who come from non-mainstream cultures that do not share many of the seemingly benign assumptions of Western schooling, schools can indeed be extremely alien environments in which the rules for how to act and how to talk are difficult to learn, precisely because they are never made explicit, and because mainstream children seem to know them already. Although there are well-documented cases in which this sort of home-school mismatch can be a source of academic problems (Heath, 1983; Philips, 1983; Scollon and Scollon, 1981), we selected a research site and a group of research subjects that would not give rise to this sort of problem. The children in our study were from low-income families but not from separate or homogeneous ethnic groups that differed in their basic rules for social interaction from more affluent mainstream families. In many ways, in fact, the families we studied and the classrooms we observed were more similar than different (Chandler et al., 1986; see also Chapter 6). Thus, while it is important to consider the possibility of home-school mismatches as one source of academic failure, it is also necessary to look elsewhere to understand the differences between the children who did well and those who did poorly in our sample.

A basic assumption of our research, in contrast to that of the two groups of studies mentioned above, is that neither home nor school is likely to be entirely responsible for either success or failure of literacy achievement. We believe that persistent patterns of failure most likely involve lacks both at home and in school, and some success in remediation is likely to be achieved by changes either at home or at school.

Accordingly, we sought relationships between success in literacy and both home and school factors. Unlike previous studies which had focused on the nature of children's lives at school (Goodlad, 1984; Rutter et al., 1979) or at home (Medrich et al., 1982), we attempted to get a comprehensive view of children's activities both at home and at school, and to relate these to each other. The possibility that the relationship between home and school is one explanation for success is discussed in Chapter 6. In Chapter 7, we consider whether home or school factors are more powerful in explaining the patterns of success and failure displayed by the children.

Our goals of collecting data from both the home and school imposed certain constraints. We had to secure the cooperation of a school system, and of many principals and teachers within that school system, in order to be able to collect data within classrooms. The teachers who volunteered to recommend subjects to us were generally happy to have us observe and were generous with their time in giving us supplementary information about the subjects. But when we followed each child into a second year and a second classroom, we found some of the second year teachers were less eager to welcome us into their classes than the teachers who had volunteered the first year. (There were other differences between these two groups of teachers as well; see Chapter 6).

The families who were recruited to participate, based first on teacher recommendation, showed a similar range of openness and willingness to participate. In some, all the family members were eager to participate and generous with their time. In others mothers were glad to be interviewed but fathers refused. (In the widely cited 1980 study of the children of divorce by Wallerstein and Kelly, more mothers than fathers also participated.) In yet others, appointments were frequently broken or postponed. Nonetheless, because we did want to include a full range of typical families in our sample, we persisted even with those who were less eager, despite the difficulties this created by reducing the size of the sample for our quantitative analyses.

No simple explanations. A final presumption of our research effort was that it was extremely unlikely that any simple explanation for reading success or reading failure, in the "normal range" we were considering at least, would be correct. We were not looking for a single variable that would differentiate the homes of better readers from those of poorer readers, nor for a single magic ingredient in the classrooms of the children making the greatest gains in literacy skills. Literacy is too complicated a developmental domain to be susceptible to simple explanations, and the patterns of literacy success and failure are too complex for one or a few variables to explain them.

We were prepared, on the contrary, to find both subtle and complex relationships between the selected home and school factors and the literacy skills of the children. We developed models of the interrelationships we believed would exist and prepared to collect data relevant to as many aspects as possible of the models. These models were theoretically driven—each tested a different hypothesis about the ways in which parents contribute to their children's literacy development. We selected from the array of data available to us about the families in the study those six to ten variables that were most closely linked to each of the models. We then used regression analysis, a statistical technique designed to assess the size and significance of the relation between the predictor variables in each model and the outcome literacy measures. We tested three different models, each consisting of an array of variables, precisely because we did not expect to find that any single variable nor even any single model would account by itself for the differences among the children in literacy achievement.

A consequence of our research strategy was that we were committed to collecting a wide range of data in a wide variety of ways from as many people as possible in the children's lives. More details of the data collection will be given in the next two chapters, but it is important here to consider the motive behind the data collection procedures chosen. First, three major types of data collection were combined: interview (including questionnaire), observation, and tests. Second, not just the focal children were sources of data; their teachers, parents, and siblings were as well. Finally, many different domains of the child's and family's life were probed for information about literacy skills, school experiences, and literacy practices, but also about such matters as free time activities, the family's social network, its susceptibility to economic and psychological stress, its use of rules and schedules, family members' perceptions of each other, and the emotional tone of family interactions. Collecting all these different sorts of data seemed to us crucial if we were to appreciate the process of literacy development and the home and school factors contributing to it.

The goal of this study, then, was to consider the ways in which both home and school experiences affect the literacy achievement of a group of elementary school children from low-income families. Having stated the rationale behind many of our research decisions, we turn in Chapters 2 and 3 to a description of how the research was carried out. Chapter 2 describes the community where the research took place, some of the families we studied, and the schools their children attended, and gives an overview of the kinds of information we collected about the children at school and at home. Chapter 3 supplies greater detail about our data collection methods, about the demographics of our subject sample, and about the structure of our quantitative analyses. Chapters 4 through 7 present our hypotheses and results concerning the various ways in which home and school factors accounted for the children's patterns of literacy achievements. Chapter 4 assesses the "Family as Educator" model for home influences, which relates most strongly to children's abilities in word recognition and vocabulary. In that same chapter we also present information on the school factors that explain gains in word recognition and vocabulary. Chapter 5 assesses the "Resilient Family" model, which we found to be related to children's writing. Chapter 6 presents the "Parent-School Partnership" model and reports on the many ways in which schools and families make contact with one another and how these contacts affect children's achievement. Chapter 7 focuses on reading comprehension, the home and school determinants of reading comprehension status, and the relative importance of home versus school factors in predicting gains in reading comprehension. Considerably greater detail about the literacy development of these same children is presented in Chall, Jacobs, and Baldwin (1990). Chapter 8 summarizes the major findings and conclusions together with implications for policy, curriculum, school, and family intervention. Finally, in Chapter 9 (the epilogue) we follow up on many of the children in the study as they continued through elementary school and went to high school. We present a picture of how these children turned out, not just in terms of their literacy skills, but also in terms of their plans for further education and future employment, and the life events that were impinging upon those plans.

Chapter 2

The Children, Neighborhoods, Schools, Classrooms, and Families

The Norwich Neighborhoods and Schools

Norwich is a small city located in the industrial Northeast of the United States.[1] Its population of about 100,000 represents a mix of working- and middle-class families. Over half the children in the school system are eligible for free lunches and are therefore considered low-income by federal standards. The median household income of Norwich families with schoolchildren in the early 1980s was $14,200; only three towns in the state had a lower median household income. Although Norwich is composed of relatively well-defined neighborhoods, a minority of these are homogeneous, white, middle-class residential areas. Most are racially and ethnically mixed and include financially secure working-class families as well as poorer families. In the years of our study, the school system was 52 percent white, 35 percent black, 9 percent Hispanic, and 4 percent Asian.

The children in our study resided in one of three low-income neighborhoods in Norwich: Righetti Field, the Flats, and Norwich Corner. Righetti Field is an area that includes about six square blocks of quiet streets with small, pleasant, owner-occupied homes, another ten square blocks of small multifamily houses and triple deckers, and two public housing projects. The projects, which are ethnically and linguistically much more mixed than the other residential areas of Righetti Field, provide rather large apartments

---

1. To ensure the anonymity of the children, families, neighborhoods, schools, and school officials, as well as of the town itself, we have given the town the fictional name of Norwich and have changed irrelevant details in presenting both the family case studies and the classroom portraits.

and adjacent outside play space for children. However, they are quite run down and considered dangerous by many residents. Most Righetti Project families can meet their needs close to home because of the proximity of discount stores, grocery stores, a public library, and a movie theater, and because of a clinic and Head Start program located near the projects. Fairly good bus service links Righetti Field to the center to Norwich and to the suburbs where many of our families' relatives lived.

The Flats is the only area in Greater Norwich that is primarily white. Housing consists of triple deckers and other small multifamily units on quiet streets with little traffic, but the houses are closer together than elsewhere, and there is no yard or play space visible from the street. Of the three neighborhoods, the Flats is the farthest away from shopping, movies, museums, and other amenities, and is the most poorly served by public transportation. A neighborhood school provides a health clinic, meeting rooms for social organizations, various lessons for adults, and a branch library.

Norwich Corner is a pleasant neighborhood of rather narrow, sometimes crowded tree-lined streets, with small single family houses scattered among low-rise multifamily apartment houses, triple deckers, and large old houses converted into apartments. The main shopping area of Greater Norwich is within walking distance of Norwich Corner, but so is Norwich Common, where muggings and drug dealing are common occurrences.

Families in our sample generally expressed satisfaction with their neighborhoods, a satisfaction attested to by remarkable stability in their residence patterns. Seventy-four percent of the families had lived in their current residences more than three years, and half more than five years.[2] Most (77 percent) said they would recommend their neighborhood to a friend moving to town.

2. In the chapters that follow, the exact numbers of children cited for various analyses differ slightly. There were 32 children originally selected for the study, from 31 families. Two of these children could not be tested again at the end of the year. Accordingly, the number (N) for any longitudinal or growth analysis is 30. However, most of the family and many of the school data were collected on all 32 children; thus, the N for these analyses is 32 children or 31 families. Occasional smaller N's indicate that we missed some data collection procedure with some families.

Eleven of the families had previously lived in another house in the same neighborhood, and only 4 had moved to Norwich from outside the metropolitan area. In Righetti Field especially, but also for some of the families in Norwich Corner and the Flats, a major advantage of the neighborhood is that the parents grew up there and their parents and siblings still live in the surrounding streets. The neighborhoods are familiar and relatively safe territory for parents and for children. Children could often visit grandparents or aunts and uncles alone, on foot or by bike, on a drop-in basis. The parents in these long-resident families were quite familiar with teachers and administrators at their children's school, not just because their older children had gone there but often because they themselves had attended the same school. Since many of the teachers were veterans of long service in the rather small Norwich school system and had their own roots in the surrounding neighborhoods, the gap between parents and teachers was bridged by considerable mutual familiarity.

The schools. The children in our study were part of a school system with a better-than-average reputation in the area. Norwich spends more per pupil in the elementary grades than all but five systems in the state, and its teachers' salaries are among the highest in the state. Still, like many other urban school systems, much of the budget must be spent on special and bilingual education. Twenty-one percent of the children come from families that speak languages other than English at home; only five towns in the state have a higher percentage of non-native English speakers. The dropout rate is viewed as an increasing problem. About 25 percent of the class entering high school will not graduate four years later. Only about 30 percent of students who do graduate from Norwich High go on to a four-year college or university. Although neighborhood schools with kindergarten through eighth grade classes have traditionally been the bedrock of the system, declining enrollment and pressures for greater racial balance have brought changes. In the first year of the study, nearly all our subjects attended elementary schools in their own neighborhoods (two black children took advantage of open enrollment policies and were bused to a school in an overwhelmingly white district). District lines for three of the four original schools in our study had just been redrawn, in some cases changing the neighborhood identity of the schools. Thus as the first year began, some children were in classes where teachers had taught their older siblings and even, in two cases, their mothers, while others were in schools that were new for them and unfamiliar to their families. It has long been recognized, by parents and teachers and by educational researchers, that schools have distinct identities, in Waller's (1932) words "separate cultures." The five schools involved in our study (four originally, and a fifth as a result of one school closing and reassigning its students) did, indeed, display their own, distinct character. In many ways, though, the schools looked quite similar, and individual classrooms within schools often varied more dramatically than did the schools. For example, sixth grade classrooms from school to school resembled each other more than they did second grade rooms in their own school. Schools that we characterized as very traditional included teachers who were among the most innovative in our sample, whereas in schools with generally low levels of parent involvement some teachers broke the pattern by contacting parents frequently. In the sketches of the schools presented here, we attempt to characterize the "school identity" of each school, while pointing out the range of variability within each school.

Hurley School. Hurley School is in many respects the most traditional of the schools we studied. Relatively unaffected by system-wide changes in assignments, Hurley School has strong community ties with its district, which includes a lower-middle-class white residential area and ethnically mixed streets of deteriorating housing. Several Hurley teachers live in the surrounding neighborhood, and a greater number grew up there. While about 40 percent of the children attending the school are black or other minorities, the staff is almost all white. Hurley School acts as a center of city services for the whole neighborhood, incorporating playing fields, a "tot lot," a public library, and a health clinic.

The Hurley School's classrooms, with few exceptions, were bleaker and less well equipped than focal children's classrooms in other Norwich schools. While the building was clean and pleasant, classrooms often lacked resources beyond the basics of texts, blackboards, and desks. Few Hurley classes had substantial classroom libraries; only two of the sixteen rooms we visited had activity centers. Children's work was displayed in the corridors, often quite formally in glass cases with teacher-made headings and decorations. Displays inside the rooms were usually limited to commercially produced posters and charts.

Focal children attending Hurley took fewer field trips than the children we observed at other schools but had more frequent class visits to the public library. The presence of a city branch library adjacent to the school may have facilitated this. Hurley teachers described classroom activities as adult-centered about 85 percent of the time, a higher average than most of the other schools in the study.

Mothers of focal children at Hurley gave teachers higher ratings than mothers with children at other Norwich schools; more than half of them rated their child's current teacher as "very good." They were more critical of buildings and equipment, with only one mother giving the Hurley a better-than-average rating.

Roosevelt School. Roosevelt School had maintained its distinctive style despite two years of changes in enrollment policies. In the first year of our study, focal children at Roosevelt were in classes in which 87 percent of the children were white and 23 came from non–English speaking homes. In the second year, Roosevelt merged with a largely black school, greatly increasing the racial mix. The transition to the merged district was quite smooth despite initial misgivings, and both parents and teachers eventually expressed guarded satisfaction with the new arrangement.

Roosevelt teachers, like those at the Hurley, described their lessons as "teacher-directed" at least 85 percent of the time. Reading instruction was more skills-based; all of the Roosevelt teachers (but only two-thirds of the other project teachers) mentioned having a specific skills focus like word meaning or literal comprehension. In the first year of the study, teachers reported that reading periods were also much longer, an average of 270 minutes per week at Roosevelt School, compared to 150 minutes or less at the other schools. (This was not the case in the second year, when all the schools in the study had a 150-minute norm.) Five of the seven classrooms we studied at Roosevelt had generous provision of materials beyond texts. These rooms included math and science activity centers, aquariums, classroom libraries, and teacher- and student-made charts and games. Focal children at Roosevelt visited the school's well-stocked and attractive library every week. They were also more likely to use trade books (that is, storybooks) in reading class than our other subjects: all teachers reported including these in their reading programs.

Mothers of focal children at Roosevelt School gave teachers and facilities average or better-than-average ratings, and more Roosevelt parents were active in school programs than parents elsewhere. Roosevelt School was also the only school in our study where every family was contacted at least once by the child's classroom teacher.

Sumner School. Sumner School also was affected by redistricting; at the end of the first year of our study it closed, reassigning most of its students to Alcott School, a magnet school established as part of the redistricting program. Sumner teachers relied primarily on basal readers, texts, and workbooks to organize their teaching. Relative to teachers at other schools, fewer Sumner teachers emphasized specific skills in their reading groups. Teachers described their lessons as adult-centered only 65 percent of the time on the average, the lowest proportion for the schools we studied. Parents with children at Sumner gave fewer positive ratings to teachers and facilities than did other families in our study.

Alcott School. Six of our target children moved to this school after Sumner was closed; it offered a program for middle-grade students that was markedly different than Sumner's, but an upper-grade curriculum rather like Sumner's. Two Alcott teachers described their lessons as adult-directed 85 or 90 percent of the time, while another two, both teachers of younger students, characterized theirs as more child-directed. All the Alcott teachers used trade books as materials for reading lessons and organized frequent and varied writing activities.

The transition to the new school was difficult for most of our Sumner subjects. Teachers at Alcott, perhaps used to dealing with middle-class students, gave children we studied lower skills ratings than the Sumner teachers had. They were less likely to expect our subjects to go on to college than the Sumner teachers, and had, according to their questionnaire responses, fewer contacts with focal children's families.

Bates School. Bates School serves an ethnically diverse neighborhood of two- and three-family homes and subsidized housing projects. Classes to which our children were assigned at Bates mirrored the racial mix of the system as a whole: about 50 percent white, 36 percent black, with the rest other minority groups.

Instruction for focal children at Bates was fairly standard for Norwich elementary schools. Teachers described their lessons as adult-directed about 80 percent of the time; reading was taught in ability groups using basal readers and skills workbooks. Although the rooms we visited at Bates had sizable classroom libraries, teachers did not consider trade books part of their reading program. Children took one or two field trips each year but made many fewer library visits than the norm for our study: Bates children averaged fewer than ten a year, according to teacher reports. Bates teachers also reported making fewer contacts with focal children's families than teachers at other schools.

Mothers of focal children at Bates School gave generally positive ratings to teachers, in line with the average for our sample. Their ratings of school buildings and equipment were much higher than the norm, evidence that parents appreciated the relatively modern and well-kept Bates facilities. Many more Bates parents included "discipline" as an important goal for schools than parents of children at other schools (57 percent at Bates, 18 percent elsewhere). Observers felt that Bates put more emphasis on discipline than the other schools in our study. Discipline problems were the only reason Bates teachers gave for contacting parents of focal children, and Bates classrooms we studied had more rules and more sanctions for rulebreakers than others did.

Schools' roles in fostering literacy development in particular center on the provision of varied and appropriate materials, the structuring of what Griffin (1977) calls "reading events" and the process and content of instruction in reading and writing. Individual classrooms varied more widely along these dimensions than schools in our study did, partly, but not entirely, because of the wide range of grades studied (from 2 to 7). Classrooms differed from one another enormously on such factors as resources available within the classroom, use of school library, frequency of field trips, organization and style of instruction, and parental opinions about the school and the teachers. But in some important respects, such as specific instruction in reading comprehension, there was *little* variation, either at the school or the classroom level. These differences and similarities are shown in the classroom portraits that follow. The portraits are composites that represent the types of literacy environments we encountered.

Mrs. Randolph's Third Grade Class

Kitty Randolph's classroom method resembled most others in our study: one that would be characterized as traditional and competent teaching in a fairly routine classroom environment. Mrs. Randolph's teaching was a skilled and well-practiced performance. The children knew exactly what was expected of them and they did it smoothly, often in unison, without hesitation. After completing independent work, for example, children filed their papers in different envelopes marked "math," "language," "spelling," and "phonics." Mrs. Randolph had an easy and cheerful manner with the children and often made learning activities into games or routines. For instance, she led the children in reciting multiplication tables while doing stylized calisthenics in unison—touching shoulders, waist, knees, and toes. The children were businesslike and task-oriented in Mrs. Randolph's room, as she was. In reading lessons she followed the teacher's guide in the basal series carefully. Yet she also went beyond the teacher's manual guidelines to engage in systematic checking of text comprehension. The children were involved in the activities and seemed to take pride in knowing the right answers.

Mrs. Randolph, a stylish black woman in her thirties, projected an attitude of competence and authority. When we entered her third grade classroom one day in February, she was seated at her desk, looking out over the twenty children sitting quietly in five rows of desks. Behind her was a long wall of windows with built-in shelves underneath. On the shelves were jigsaw puzzles and games like Scrabble, Boggle, and Quizmo; the countertop that ran the length of the room was empty except for a globe and an array of houseplants. Above some cupboards was a large bulletin board with commercially produced figures of snowflakes, snowmen and children pulling toboggans, and the caption "Winter Fun." In the cupboards were two different basal series at three different levels and a variety of workbooks for reading, phonics, spelling, language, and grammar, as well as math textbooks at the third grade level, twenty copies each of *Our Health and Us,* and Webster's *Elementary Dictionary.* The long wall opposite the teacher's desk had a coat closet and a bulletin board decorated with Disney characters illustrating consonant blends. Also on display were a chart listing "class helpers," an alphabet chart with script letters against a circus animal background, and a commercial phonics chart.

As we entered, Mrs. Randolph was saying, "Boys and girls, Mrs. Randolph needs a few minutes of peace to count these raffle tickets." She efficiently did this while the children practiced cursive handwriting, copying sentences she had written on the board about the weather. When the raffle tickets were counted and handed to a child monitor, Mrs. Randolph called the first reading group to come to the table. The seven children sat quietly with their books closed in front of them, while Mrs. Randolph reviewed the story they had started the day before. With the teacher's guide to the basal series open on her lap, she began,

"Yesterday we were reading a great story. What was the name of it, Ronny?"

"The Mystery of Goat Island."

"What is a mystery, Dan?"

"Something you try to solve."

"Good. Who tries to solve it, Denise?"

"A detective."

"Who was the detective in this story, Gail?"

"Mr. Bernard."

"Would you like to be his friend?"

"Yes" (said by all).

"Why, David?"

"Because he made pizza for all the children."

"What do you like on your pizza?"

David volunteered, "Pepperoni."

"What kind of pizza do you like, Lamar?"

"Sausage."

Mrs. Randolph smacked her lips and said, "Thursday was a strange day. What did Mr. Bernard put on the pizza?"

After ten more minutes of review, she instructed the children to read certain pages in the basal readers to themselves. Several children moved their lips as they read silently; Dan followed the text with his finger (third graders reading at grade level typically have ceased lip reading and finger pointing). When Mrs. Randolph went next door to ask Theresa's brother why Theresa was absent that day, the children all continued reading. After returning to the reading group and waiting for everybody to finish reading, Mrs. Randolph told the children to close their books and asked them a series of questions, all of which required factual recall of the story. Mrs. Randolph then had each of the children take a turn reading a paragraph out loud. When David had difficulty reading the word "suggest," the teacher waited while he sounded it out, syllable by syllable. Twice she asked children to define words, such as "leftovers" and "dough," and then to expand on these using their own experiences.

In a spelling lesson in which the whole class participated, Mrs. Randolph wrote spelling words on the board, and the children read them in unison, following the teacher's pointer. After eliciting a definition of a silent letter, the teacher nominated Julie to go up to the board and circle all the silent letters in the spelling words. Since Julie had done several correctly but omitted others, Mrs. Randolph prompted her. "What *don't* you hear in the word "night?"

"G-h."

"Good, honey. Circle it." After Julie sat down, the teacher said, "I'm looking for a word that is the opposite of low. If you know the word, raise your hand." All but two of the twenty children raised their hands. Mrs. Randolph called on Johnny to circle the word. The "game" continued in this vein with the teacher giving various cues including definitions like "something that helps tell time," antonyms like "the opposite of dark," and rhyming words. Even some of the more timid and less skillful children got caught up in the game format and waved their hands, eager to be called on. Then she said, "Okay. Mrs. Randolph is going to put ten words on the board. Your eyes are going to be little cameras. I'm going to erase one word, and then I want you to tell me which word I have erased. You'll have to spell the word that you think is missing."

After they had done this with all the words, the children had a spelling test. On a previous day they had copied the words three times each, composed sentences with each, and done workbook exercises involving the words. Thus, before taking the test, the children had practiced the words several times in various contexts.

This self-contained classroom seemed to provide a safe and predictable environment, a factor of particular benefit for one of our focal children from a chaotic home. The climate of this classroom also encouraged participation by children who may have lacked self-confidence and initiative. However, so much time was spent in Mrs. Randolph's classroom learning how to perform within her particular formats, much of what children were learning may not have transferred to other situations.

The view of literacy in Mrs. Randolph's class can be summed up as "literacy is what you do in school." The curriculum was largely determined by texts and workbooks. Each day's lesson was based on the next two pages in the spelling workbook, the math book, the readers, and so on. This was not an innovative classroom or one which provided a rich environment for literacy; there were no trade books and composition was not a frequent activity. But Mrs. Randolph used the material she had effectively. Conversation and especially her oral structuring of experiences became almost part of the "text," as in the reading lesson just described. Mrs. Randolph made the children feel secure and able to learn what her curriculum provided. She was concerned that they learned the spellings and the meanings of words encountered, and that they understood and enjoyed the stories they read. At the same time, children's written and verbal expression was elicited to serve fairly narrow goals, often those listed in the teacher's guide. Not only the aspects of the textbook Mrs. Randolph chose to discuss (pizza, leftovers, and so on), but also the general level of "culture" in the classroom (circus animals, snowy days, Disney characters) was pitched to the children's everyday life rather than extending their store of general knowledge.

Ms. Pasquale's Fourth Grade Class

Ann Pasquale's fourth grade class represented a different literacy environment from Mrs. Randolph's, and indeed from most in our study. Although her class was exceptional, seven others we studied had important features in common with it: generous provision of materials in addition to texts and workbooks, writing activities that went beyond filling in workbooks, and goals for reading that included enjoying books and communicating about them in diverse ways.

Ms. Pasquale's lessons combined fairly traditional instructional techniques similar to those Mrs. Randolph used with high standards for student participation and imaginative activities.

When we first visited her fourth grade class, it was late morning, a drizzly February day. Ms. Pasquale, a vivacious young woman of Italian descent, was standing in the center of the room; her nineteen students scattered at different tables were listening attentively.

"This is an exercise in writing directions, in using our memory to describe how carrots are peeled. It's an exercise in using your memory. We'll use real carrots tomorrow. It's really hard to do it perfectly, but this will be sort of a practice and later on we'll try doing it with peanut-butter-and-jelly sandwiches."

A child raised his hand.

"Yes, Darryl? Wait a minute, Jessica, put that radio away in your desk."

"Do we have to bring in our own carrots?"

"No, I'll bring in carrots."

Ms. Pasquale began walking around the room, handing out worksheets she had made, which first listed some questions and then left space for the children's carrot-peeling directions. She stopped at a table where a boy was sitting by himself.

"Do you understand what you have to do, Jerome?"

Jerome nodded without looking up and began writing an answer to the first question on his sheet.

Ms. Pasquale moved over to the large round table closest to the center of the room and sat down. From her seat she began scanning the class, monitoring who was working steadily and who seemed distracted or confused.

Three children were working in the library corner, either at desks or kneeling on cushions and using the tops of low bookcases as writing surfaces. Some six hundred books, mostly paperbacks, were arranged on makeshift shelves. Each book had a strip of colored paper taped to its spine, with a letter representing the first letter of its title. "A" books were all in one recycled milk case, "B" and "C" books were next to them in another carton, and so forth. Scholastic and Dell Yearling fiction were heavily represented, but the collection also included National Geographic children's books, Asterix comics, and books on crafts, basketball, biology, and the American Revolution. A battered old bookcase separating the library corner from the work area where Ms. Pasquale was sitting held multiple copies of dictionaries, a spelling guide, thesauruses, and almanacs. Two different children's encyclopedias, each missing a volume or two, rounded out the collection.[3] A teacher-made chart stapled to one end of the bookcase announced, "Book Theater: Now Appearing," and below that, "Ratings: *ok **good ***great." Brightly colored signs in children's writing were taped underneath. Each one included a title, sometimes misspelled, often in fanciful lettering, an illustration, a rating, and the name of the child who had made it. The signs here all named biographies, including *Anne Frank, John Henry, Harriat Tubbman* (sic), and *Bobby Orr*. Posted other places around the library corner were seventeen more of these signs announcing science fiction stories (*A Wrinkle in Time, The Grey King, Dragonfall*).

Over at the central work table, Ms. Pasquale was whispering to Tanya, "What do you need before you start?"

Tanya said, "A carrot? A peeler?"

Pointing to an unfinished sentence on Tanya's worksheet, Ms. Pasquale whispered, "Write it here."

Behind Ms. Pasquale there were Cuisenaire rods and abacuses stacked on the bookshelf. Next to these stood several publishers' reading kits and multiple copies of writing workbooks. Low cupboards against the wall were labeled "Science," and held microscopes, simple physics kits, and teacher-made activity cards. Commercial posters of the planets and of animals were hung on the wall here.

A blackboard separated this work area from another work area with a smaller round table and a row of four desks pushed together. Ms. Pasquale's side of this blackboard was decorated with origami sculpture, children's watercolors, and tissue paper collages. In this last work area, teacher-made and commercial math charts explained the names of seven-, ten-, and thirteen-digit numbers and beyond and rules for writing Roman numerals. More low shelves here held protractors, magnets, pocket com-

---

3. The richness of this collection of books and materials, as compared to that of Mrs. Randolph's third grade class, reflects in part the greater reading ability of fourth graders, and their associated capacity for independent reading and ability to deal with a wide range of reading.

passes, and commercial math kits. Two poems by children were posted along with van Gogh, Gauguin, and Degas prints with French labels in children's handwriting ("La nuit etoilée"). Large signs marked the four sides of the room: North, South, East, and West.

Ms. Pasquale got up from the table where she'd been sitting with Tanya and walked over to the girls sitting in the back of the room.

"Cheryl, Karen, you've got to be more quiet. I can hear you way over where I'm sitting. Does anyone need any help?"

The girls shrugged and the teacher moved on to another work area.

Behind the group of girls, children's winter overcoats and boots filled most of an old-fashioned coat closet, but there was also a typewriter, a phonograph, a collection of records, and art supplies with rules for their use posted. Yet another set of bookshelves here held boxes with viewing holes. Children had illustrated storybooks in the style of comics, and each of twelve boxes held a different story, which could be pulled through one frame at a time.

Darryl got up from his seat at the central work table and moved over to a group of five desks pushed together. Four boys were sitting here all writing quietly except for Andy. When Ms. Pasquale came by this group, she asked Andy to read the directions on the worksheet aloud to her and to respond orally to the first questions. She watched while he recorded these responses and then asked him what his first sentence of directions could be.

Behind the boys' seats was a teacher-made chart representing the Bermuda Triangle. Cut-out construction-paper planes attached to it at different points marked spots on a grid. Each plane was labeled with a child's name. A classroom helpers' chart nearby listed these occupations: communications expert, domestic engineer, horticulturalist, media specialist, assistant librarian. Job description cards were attached; for example, "The communications expert is the person responsible for keeping messages organized. They will also give out notices or bring messages for teachers to sign."

At eleven o'clock Ann Pasquale switched the lights off and on briefly and walked to the library corner. Children pushed the papers they'd been working on into folders in their desks and moved over to the library corner, where they sat in a semicircle on a rug around Ms. Pasquale.

"OK, I need to see Jennifer, Ayesha, Louanne, Robin, and Stacey. The table you left was not in good condition."

These girls returned to their seats, quickly straightened up piles of folders and papers and ran back to the group.

Ms. Pasquale was standing at an easel, holding a red marker in her hand.

"Nice job. I like the way those four guys are sitting. We should have nothing in our hands, we should be looking up at the board. Who remembers how to spell geometry? Ayesha?"

"G-E-O-M-E-T-R-Y."

"Who remembers what geometry *means?* Same two kids? How about someone else? Kevin?"

"Shapes."

"Right. It's the study of shapes. What's a shape we learned?"

As the children supplied "triangle," "square," "pentagon," "rectangle," Ms. Pasquale wrote these on the chart on the easel, including summaries of children's definitions for each one. She introduced the new term "quadrilateral" and asked several children to practice pronouncing and spelling it. She defined this term, wrote the definition on the chart, and asked different children to name shapes already given which are quadrilaterals.

"What did we learn about lines?"

"They have to be straight."

"Jerome, did you learn anything about lines yesterday?"

"Uh-uh."

"Mark?"

"They connect."

"What is the word for part of a line? Anyone remember?"

Four hands go up.

"Four people remember. How about you, Louanne?"

Louanne shrugs.

"Someone else?"

"A line segment."

"Right. Who remembers the difference between a line and a line segment?"

"It has two dots."

"Right, but what do we call those in geometry?"

"End points."

"Right, end points."

Ms. Pasquale drew a line connecting two dots on the easel chart.

"Now how do we tell one line from another?"

"You have letters."

"Right."

She drew an "A" next to one point on the chart and a "B" next to another.

"OK, for math today we're going to finish up the paper we started Monday with end points. These are due *tomorrow.* Find a nice quiet place to work and continue on your end point papers."

The children returned to desks around the room, pulling math folders out as they took their seats.

Although Ms. Pasquale's classroom might be called "open," children's activities were supervised more closely and she gave more explicit instructions, both to the whole class and to individual children, than in the majority of traditional rooms we visited.

Children in this class were bombarded with vocabulary, from the wall charts, from the novels Ms. Pasquale read aloud each day, and from subject area instruction, like the math lesson just recounted. Children were also exposed to a view of books that is quite rare and different from that of many other teachers; books provided experiences to be shared with other class members, through posters, story boxes, and book review cards, filed and indexed to the classroom library collection.

Ms. Pasquale's room provided background knowledge about worlds that may be unfamiliar to many students: Roman numerals, planets, French painters, famous people. Traditional elementary school classroom events, like the "helpers," were exploited as potential sources of new information and vocabulary. Standard texts and workbooks, although evident and sometimes part of Ms. Pasquale's lessons, did not dominate the curriculum the way they did in Mrs. Randolph's third grade classroom.

Mr. Barasch's Sixth Grade Class

Mr. Barasch's sixth grade class was typical of many of the upper-grade rooms we visited. The physical environment was fairly barren, with little of the wall displays or array of materials commonly found in primary classrooms. Lessons were text- or worksheet-centered, with a succession of scheduled periods for each subject area. Activities seemed very familiar to the students: They often anticipated the next step in an assignment and began doing it before the teacher finished explaining it to them, as in the reading lesson described below. The most noticeable contrast between the upper- and lower-grade rooms, however, was in children's attitudes. The enthusiasm and eagerness that was so characteristic of children in the primary grades in our study was replaced in many upper-grade rooms by boredom and even cynicism.[4]

Mr. Barasch seemed to have particular difficulty with his sixth grade students, as many do with this age group. He was ineffective in organizing routine classroom activities in ways that controlled his students' high spirits and tendencies to disrespect. Furthermore, he failed even to attempt to initiate challenging activities. Both his ineffectiveness in routine organization and his failure to provide sufficient challenge seemed to reflect his extremely low expectations for student achievement. Indeed, the tendency to expect little from students seemed characteristic of the teachers of upper-grade classrooms in our sample. Some, however, were more skilled at classroom management than Mr. Barasch.

We walked into Mr. Barasch's room on a sunny April day. The teacher, a dark-haired man in his early fifties, was distributing yellow paper to a class of sixteen students. Children's desks were arranged in a large U-shape, facing the front blackboard and the teacher's desk. The decorations in the room were a U.S. map attached to a front bulletin board and a commercial poster of the Grand Canyon between the rear windows. A U.S. flag and a printed set of fire drill instructions flanked the blackboard; homework assignments from the previous day were chalked in at one corner. Built-in cupboards held sets of textbooks in science, health, and reading. A side bulletin board displayed graded compositions by members of the class, one- or two-paragraph themes about occupational ambitions. Students were chatting to each other; one group was laughing out loud as Rene, a student, told a funny story.

Mr. Barasch looked stern. "You've got your assignment, it's time to start."

---

4. This change has been widely noted—both by researchers and by administrators and teachers—in all kinds of schools, whether of middle or low SES students.

Rene looked up at him. "I don't like yellow paper."

He replied, "Do you think I care!" and moved to the other side of the room.

Most of the class by now had opened their math textbooks to a section on addition and subtraction of fractions. Rene got up, walked over to another group of children, and asked, "Do you have any white paper?" She got a couple of sheets, brought them back to her seat and distributed them to the kids sitting next to her. She raised her hand.

"Hey, Mr. Barasch, I need help on number 16."

He walked over to her seat and looked over her shoulder at the problem.

"OK. We have one and two-thirds. How many thirds are there?"

"One?"

"At least! One has how many thirds?"

"Three."

He pointed to the fraction in her text. "And this has how many?"

"Two."

"So-oo, how many altogether?"

"Five."

He moved quickly on to help another student. Rene and her friends put down their pencils. Kerry, the girl sitting next to Rene, said, "Doesn't Pam go out with Joe now?"

"Yeah."

Pam said loudly, "No, I don't."

Kerry said, "Hey, Rene . . ."

Mr. Barasch looked up from the student he'd been helping. "OK, I'm gonna ask people to become more serious in their efforts."

Kerry, Pam, and Rene were still giggling together. The girl sitting next to Pam was steadily copying answers to the math problems from the back of her text.

Rene asked, "Hey, Mr. Barasch. Number 22 is sixth-fifths, right?"

"Right."

Rene started talking to Pam and Kelly again. When Mr. Barasch looked their way, they stopped for a second, then picked up their discussion of Pam's boyfriend.

Mr. Barasch returned, "I was locked into helping somebody, but you girls need to do better than that, OK?"

Valerie, who had been copying answers, sang a snatch of song in a mocking tone of voice. Rene, Pam, and Kerry burst into loud laughter. The teacher came over and stood behind Rene.

She looked up innocently. "Am I doing number 31 right?"

He looked at her paper. "How many thirds are there in one?"

Rene looked baffled. "I don't understand."

Mr. Barasch perched on the side of her desk. "If I take a candy bar and break it into three pieces, how many will I have?"

"Three."

"OK, how many thirds are there in one and one-third?"

Rene said, "I knew *that,* four."

He said, "Yeah."

She got up to sharpen her pencil. When she returned to her seat, the teacher was looking over her paper, circling problems with incorrect answers.

He said, "Look, I'll show you a picture." As he started to draw a strip divided into six boxes, Rene protested.

"I understand that."

He said, "What's your favorite candy bar?"

Rene said, "Snickers."

The teacher drew another strip next to the one he'd drawn already and divided it into eight boxes.

"I like Snickers, too, but I broke mine into eight pieces. How many pieces would I have to eat to have as much as you?"

Rene said, "I understand, it's four for three."

The girls sitting around her were laughing out loud.

Mr. Barasch looked up. "I'm going to have to end what I can put up with now, OK? I don't care if it *is* Friday."

He leaned over Rene's paper again. Rene said she understood the fraction equivalence he'd just explained.

"Do you think you can handle this?"

Rene nodded. Mr. Barasch walked over to his desk and Rene turned deliberately to Kerry to resume her conversation about Pam and Joe.

At ten o'clock the bell rang and Mr. Barasch announced, "Reading time." Children who were assigned to the lower of his two reading groups formed a line at the door and filed out into the hall, giggling, headed for the remedial teacher's room. The six remaining students took seats around one angle of the central U of desks. Mr. Barasch took a pile of reading texts from the corner cupboard and pulled up his chair so he was facing the group, while Kerry passed out the texts. Valerie got up from her seat and started whispering to Kerry.

Mr. Barasch started the lesson. "OK, page 186. What do you notice about this story?"

He waited while the students slowly flipped through their readers, looking for the page he'd cited. Valerie and Kerry were still out of their seats.

"What's *different* about the story?"

Valerie had sat down now but hadn't opened her book. Looking at Patty's text she suggested, "There are pictures of photographs and newspapers."

Mr. Barasch said, "Right, so they're not just drawings, they're about something factual. Before we read today, I want you to copy each of the new words from the story. I'll give you some of the definitions and the rest are for homework."

He moved to the board and began writing from a list of words: static, editorial, prophetic, ignite, analogy, horizontally. Next to each word he wrote the page number in the text where it appeared. The students made negative comments about the passage they were about to read as they copied the vocabulary list.

"This is dry."

"I hate science fiction."

"I bet we'll have to do questions."

Robin looked up. "I know what static electricity is."

Mr. Barasch replied, still writing on the board, "It's like a shock."

Donna added, "You know what happened to me when I was ironing? I touched the top of the iron and I got a shock."

The teacher asked, "Are you sure that wasn't a *burn?*"

"No, it was a shock, 'cause I just touched the top."

"Let's get the words finished, Robin, so I can give the definitions to you."

Robin copied the last word and said, "Oh, I know what 'puny' is. Very small." She and several of the other students began to write the words three times each.

Mr. Barasch stopped them. "Don't do that now, you're supposed to do that for homework, I don't want to have to wait while you finish. OK, here we go. 'Ignite,' start, like a car. 'Epic,' like an epic journey, historical."

Students began writing these definitions on their papers.

Mr. Barasch asked, "If descent is to go do-own, then ascent is to go . . ."

Patty said, "Up?"

"Right. OK, 'conceive' means to start or think of. 'Analogy'—we did some of those once—a dog is to a puppy as cat is to kitten. That's a com . . ."

Robin asked, "Combination?"

The teacher shook his head. "Uh-uh. Not exactly."

Robin tried, "Opposites?"

"No, comparison, comparing."

He sat on the edge of a child's desk and waited while the students finished writing down the ten definitions he'd already given. Several students were copying from Robin's notebook, which she had passed to them.

"I'm only going to give three more—the rest of the twenty-three you'll have to look up in the dictionary for homework."

One girl put down her pen and notebook and got up from her seat. She began demonstrating a dance for the other students. Mr. Barasch reprimanded her and announced that he wouldn't give any more definitions.

"You'll just have to look them all up yourselves. I want to start the story now. Is everyone open to page 186?"

Kerry asked, "Do we have to read aloud?"

"Yes. Robin, why don't you begin where it says, 'The crew was busy loading the command module.'"

"Can't we just read to ourselves?"

"Are we gonna have to do questions?"

Mr. Barasch improvised, "Why don't you just read silently, it's pages 186 to 209 and then . . ."

As he said that, the bell for the next period rang.

"We'll continue with our story tomorrow. Remember those definitions for homework."

Several things stand out about Mr. Barasch's class. The activities he organized were routine and predictable, perhaps because he felt such routine activities were less likely to be disrupted by these lively adolescents. Copying and recording dictated definitions took up most of one period (and the homework assignment that followed it would involve more of the same activity); simple computation took up another. The level of the work in math and in reading was not challenging. Simple fraction problems like those assigned in the math lesson observed were handled successfully by younger children in our study. The textbook being used by upper-ability sixth graders in Mr. Barasch's class was a controlled vocabulary reader designed for the average sixth grader—an arrangement not atypical in American schools.[5] Given the routine nature of these tasks, students in Mr. Barasch's class, like factory workers with production quotas to meet, avoided working too hard or too efficiently, since that would result in more of the same work being expected of them.

Children used elements of their own subculture to enrich classroom life. Rene and her friends had decorated the *insides* of their desks with photographs of friends and family and clippings from popular magazines. Valerie demonstrated a dance. Students carried on extended conversations and fit their work into the gaps and pauses in these, the more important parts of their day. Interactions with the teacher were used to relieve their boredom, or perhaps to challenge his authority. Whatever the reason, little meaningful work was accomplished. Mr. Barasch consistently underestimated the children's potential, so neither the one-on-one exchanges nor the lessons he planned challenged their abilities. He was concerned about the children being disruptive and therefore planned activities like reading aloud that were easy to supervise. Such an approach unfortunately failed to provide students with either motivation or techniques to control their own disruptive behavior, with all its destructive effects on their own academic progress. Although Mr. Barasch was among the least effective teachers in our study, the dynamics that characterized his classroom unfortunately were also found in a number of other classrooms, particularly at the sixth and seventh grade level.

Children at School and at Home

Classrooms, like homes and schools, vary in many factors which collectively have an impact on literacy development. Schools and

5. While the below-average reading level of poorer readers is typically taken into account by assigning them lower-level reading books, adjustments upward of the reading difficulty are not typically made for above-average readers. Many schools do not permit the use of books above the grade placement of the student.

classrooms can be judged as good, not just on the basis of the materials, the organization of lessons, the curriculum, and so on, but also on the basis of the interaction of the teacher's style, his or her strengths and weaknesses, with the particular children in the class. Ms. Randolph's class seemed perhaps lacking in opportunities for challenge and creativity, but its safe, predictable formats turned out to be an ideal learning environment for children from particularly disorganized homes. In the sketch of Mr. Barasch's classroom, we saw him interacting quite differently with Rene, the saucy, "class leader," and Robin, a quieter more academically oriented girl whose tested reading achievement was much higher than Rene's. Rene, in general, did quite well in Mr. Barasch's classroom, perhaps because his curriculum was directed to a low ability level. Rene's below-par reading and math skills were no particular hindrance to her success in Mr. Barasch's undemanding curriculum, particularly since Rene's informal role as "teacher's aide" meant that she was often out of the classroom running errands or engaged in projects during the lessons that might have revealed her academic failures. Robin, by contrast, was languishing under Mr. Barasch's treatment. She was noticeably bored in class and often put her head down and slept after finishing her seatwork. Mr. Barasch underestimated Robin's abilities severely, and thus did not see her boredom as a possibly natural response to an undemanding curriculum.

Rene and Robin are quite similar to one another in a number of ways, besides both being students of Mr. Barasch in sixth grade. They are good friends and often spend time together outside school. Both are black girls (these were two of the 12 black children included in our total sample of 32) who had achieved less than might have been expected of them in the Norwich schools, though neither disliked school or rejected literacy (both, in fact, owned and read Judy Blume books with great enthusiasm).[6] Rene and Robin represent well the range of children included in our study, in terms of demographic variables and literacy achievement, and their home lives are the subject of the sections that follow. Rene was being raised by her grandmother, Mrs. Grant, in a

---

6. The reading level of Judy Blume books has been estimated to be fourth or fifth grade—certainly these do not constitute challenging reading for above-average sixth graders.

largely nonliterate household, often with cousins, aunts, and more distant relatives around. Mrs. Grant knew the Norwich schools well and accepted them as adequate. Robin was being raised in a strict nuclear household by parents who had immigrated from Trinidad for economic reasons. They had high educational and occupational aspirations for their children and were critical of the Norwich schools. Robin was selected for the group of "above average readers" in the study; she scored well on our tests (at late seventh grade level on word recognition and mid-seventh grade level on reading comprehension, when tested at the end of sixth grade) and was considered an above-average reader even by Mr. Barasch, who underestimated her abilities by a good margin. Rene was a below-average reader, who scored 2 years and 1 month below grade level on the word recognition test, and 1 year and 3 months below on the reading comprehension test we administered at the end of seventh grade. Nonetheless, she was in the top reading group in Mr. Barasch's class; he rated her as a good reader and a good student.

The Grant Family

When asked to write a paragraph about the person she most admired, Rene described her grandmother: "The best person I look up to is my grandmother, because when I want something I get it. When I'm sick she takes care of me. When I want to talk to her about something she'll listen. She is like a mother to me." Rene had lived with her grandmother since she was two, and a few years later her two younger cousins, Sharon and Tanya, joined the household when their mother was divorced. The three girls and their grandmother formed a close family unit. They shared their house with two long-term boarders and an ever-shifting constellation of Mrs. Grant's relatives, who stayed for varying lengths of time. When we first visited the family, Mrs. Grant was somewhat disturbed by the recent arrival of a seventeen-year-old granddaughter (assigned to her by the court) who she felt was a bad influence on the three younger girls. During another visit, the front parlor had been converted to a temporary bedroom for Mrs. Grant's daughter (Rene's aunt) and the aunt's two daughters, age two and four.

Mrs. Grant was a warm, pleasant, responsive black woman who had raised five children of her own before taking responsibility for Rene, Sharon, and Tanya. She had lived in the same rented house for the past twenty-two years and was well acquainted with Rene's school, as all her own children had attended it before Rene. In fact, Rene's mother had had Mr. Barasch as a teacher, twenty years before Rene was enrolled in his class. Mrs. Grant dropped out of school herself when she was in third grade because she had no parents and "had to raise myself." At the time of our study she was learning to read in a class at work, which she said she loved because the "teacher is understanding." Throughout our interview with her, Mrs. Grant referred with some pride to one of her daughters as the "daughter who is in college." Rene selected this aunt as the smartest person she knew "because she went through college and answers a lot of questions."

Mrs. Grant worked evenings cleaning in a nearby office building. She had been working weekends until recently, when she told her boss that it was unfair to the children to leave them alone all day Saturday and Sunday, and that she wanted to be able to go to church with them, and he switched her to a weekday schedule. Mrs. Grant worked from 5:00 P.M. till midnight each day, although recently she had missed some work owing to a back injury and also a heart condition. Mrs. Grant was eager to return to work because her illness and lack of medical and disability benefits further strained the family's limited resources. Rene told us that despite her grandmother's long work hours, she and her grandmother went out several times a week on errands, to go shopping, or to restaurants. A meal at a restaurant was a typical reward when the girls brought home a good report card.

While Mrs. Grant worked, the girls took care of themselves, fixed their own dinners, washed the dishes, and cleaned up the kitchen. During the course of the week they were also expected to clean floors and do other chores. The children were not supposed to watch one of the several family televisions until their homework and chores were done. Then they could watch whatever they wanted, except R-rated movies, as late as 10:30 on school nights. They were allowed to watch Mrs. Grant's Home Box Office set if she was home, except when they were "out on punishment."

Mrs. Grant placed considerable emphasis on the children's obedience and politeness and on their not being fresh or sassy. Mrs. Grant told us, "Rene asks me why I have to beat on the kids, and I told her ain't no kid ever been brought up that ain't been beat on once in a while." Her expectations about what the girls were to do, when they were to be home, and how they were to act were very clear to all family members. This did not mean, of course, that the girls always did as they were told. During one of our home visits the three girls were being punished with "no television" for having gotten home late the previous day from a visit to their uncle's former girlfriend and her baby. Rene told us that "sometimes my punishment is no telephone and no TV and no going out or coming in late for saying things I'm not supposed to or something bad in school." Rene saw her younger cousin as somewhat of a tattletale and so she and Sharon talked about "things we're not supposed to—boyfriends and stuff like that"—only when Tanya was not around.

The emphasis on obedience extended into the girls' school life. Rene reported that her grandmother was displeased when a report came home from school mentioning that she talked too much. Generally, however, Mrs. Grant felt that Rene and her cousins were "very good, very easy, and don't get into trouble."

Rene had a casual, pragmatic attitude toward her schoolwork. She was one of the few children in the study who said they believed that homework was not important, although she did it so "I won't get into trouble with my teachers." She and her cousins shared their schoolwork like their other chores. Tanya told us that the girls "switch for each other, like Rene will do my homework if I sweep the kitchen floor for her." Despite the fact that Mrs. Grant was virtually illiterate, Rene said that sometimes she asked her grandmother for help with her homework. She drew upon other resources as well, and would telephone her cousin who lived across town or one of her classmates for help. She also got the head of the afterschool program to help her with her homework, according to her grandmother. At school, Rene played the leader's role among her classmates and maintained a jocular, somewhat egalitarian, relationship with teachers. As already noted, she tended to operate as a teacher aide, running errands, helping out in the library, and supervising other children; as a result, she frequently missed lessons by being out of the room or otherwise engaged.

The Grant household was one in which there were no books or magazines in evidence, and in which adults did not use literacy to any significant degree. The Grant girls needed to acquire their reading skills in school; their home would support the school's efforts, but school would be the primary source. Thus, Rene was particularly vulnerable to the low standards of Mr. Barasch's classroom, whereas, as we shall see, aspects of Robin's home helped mitigate the effects of a year in this classroom. The ultimate protection parents can offer against particularly poor teachers or schools is to move their children to other educational settings; such a possibility did not occur to Mrs. Grant, but it was a very real option for Robin's family, the Hendersons.

The Henderson Family

Robin lived in an extremely neat, clean three-bedroom apartment with her parents, two older brothers, Reginald and Ronald, and her little sister, Roxanne. Her mother worked full-time as a customer service agent in a savings and loan association—a position she had worked her way up to through various secretarial and bookkeeping jobs, after arriving in Norwich from Trinidad six years earlier. Robin's father worked as a security guard, and part-time for a janitorial service. He was a quiet man who sat in on the family interviews but said little, and in family decision making seemed to take a back seat to his much more dynamic wife.

The Henderson's small living room housed a television (which was always turned off during our visits), a bookshelf, and a coffee table with some magazines, prayer books, and a Bible on it. The other members of the Henderson household tended to be in their own rooms with their doors closed unless summoned to the living room, or unless they had asked permission to go out—in sharp contrast to the Grant household, where friends, family members, and neighbors drifted in and out, and where the children had to be tracked down by phoning around the neighborhood at the time scheduled for our interviews with them.

When Robin's family came to Norwich from Trinidad, she entered first grade in the Norwich Public Schools and experienced little difficulty in getting used to school or in learning to read, according to her mother (she had gone to nursery school in Trinidad, starting at age three). At the end of first grade her reading achievement scores were well above average, and her teacher reported that "she put a lot of effort in her work, although she is shy at first and tense with any new situation."

Robin's two older brothers were in second and third grades during the family's first year in the United States. As a second grader, Ronald was reported to be "a good student" by his teacher and was also reading well above grade average at the end of the year. In third grade, Reginald had more difficulty adjusting to school. His teacher reported difficulty understanding his Caribbean accent, he had problems with reading, and he was retained in third grade at the end of the year. His mother added retrospectively that he may have found it difficult to adjust to a school in which he was one of only a small number of black children. Because of Reginald's retention, the two older brothers were in the same grade at school, just a year ahead of Robin. Reginald's reading achievement remained considerably below the reading level of his younger brother and sister.

Mr. and Mrs. Henderson felt that the Norwich schools their children attended were disappointing. They believed that the schools were not demanding enough, that the teachers should expect more, and that the teachers did not provide enough individual attention to the children. Mrs. Henderson said, "The most important thing a school should teach a child is discipline, otherwise the parent's energy and investment in discipline is lost." She averred that a good teacher is one who "spends extra time with children and really cares, not about grades, but about the welfare of the child in school and out, one who, for example, calls up in the summer." Mrs. Henderson said the family had had good communication with the first Norwich school the three older children attended. When the children were reassigned to another school, her faith in the schools was so shaken that she considered keeping the children home in protest. As a consequence of this dissatisfaction, the Hendersons have sent their youngest child, Roxanne, on a scholarship to a private school where "the children are disciplined and there are standards." The Hendersons had also applied to other private schools in the area for the older children and were hoping that they would be accepted to private high schools that could provide scholarships.

There was an emphasis on proper manners in the family. Mrs. Henderson stressed that a good student not only got high grades but was also courteous. She made a point to introduce us formally to all the family members, and the children revealed their training in manners during our visits, shaking hands when introduced, knocking before entering rooms, and excusing themselves politely when they had to leave. Mrs. Henderson was highly deliberate in responding to our questions and very businesslike in scheduling our visits. She did not treat the interview as a social event, a chance to chat, as many of the mothers we interviewed did.

A great deal was expected of the children in the family. Household chores were divided among the children since both parents worked full-time or more, and the three oldest children helped care for their little sister. Robin was expected to clean up her room before school each morning, to pick up her younger sister from the baby-sitter each afternoon, to help with the dishes, and to be available to do household chores on Saturdays.

Robin had clarinet lessons twice a week and played in the orchestra at the high school every Wednesday afternoon. All three of her siblings took music lessons as well. During the school year she also baby-sat two afternoons each week. Robin told us that in addition to these regularly scheduled afterschool activities she went over to a friend's house or read in the afternoon before having supper, did homework, and then watched an hour or so of television. Robin attended confirmation class on Saturdays and church on Sundays with the rest of her family. Her older brothers were in the church choir.

During the years of the study, Robin continued to be a good reader. She said that reading was relaxing and that she frequently read before going to bed or in the afternoons. She reported reading many books for fun during her sixth grade year, including *Little Women, Charlotte's Web,* and *Charlie and the Chocolate Factory.* (These last two, and the Judy Blume books she favored, were well below her tested reading level, though *Little Women* was considerably above; one function of her teacher should have been to suggest more challenging books.) Robin was one of the few children in our study who said that she preferred reading to watching television and that she wished she had more time to read. She listened to stories her mother read to her younger sister several times a week. Mrs. Henderson bought books for the children she thought they would enjoy; Robin, for example, owned most of the Judy Blume books.

One of Robin's favorite leisure time activities was writing. She wrote stories and letters to relatives in Trinidad and got good marks in creative writing, according to her mother. Robin told us matter-of-factly: "I'm good at writing."

Mrs. Henderson said that she complimented her children when they brought home a good report card, but "I get furious and tell them about it" when they bring home bad grades. According to Mrs. Henderson, Robin got good grades but didn't work as hard as she should. Robin, interestingly, did not share this perception, reporting that her parents thought she worked hard enough. Robin's teachers generally had a lower than accurate perception of her school skills, perhaps because she displayed her boredom in class so openly.

Mrs. Henderson hoped that her children would go to college, but she was worried that they would have problems getting in if they attended Norwich High. She made efforts to get her children into enrichment programs and extra-curricular activities that would improve their academic chances. She felt that Reginald should be a pilot, Ronald a professional musician or computer programmer, Robin an executive secretary, and Roxanne a teacher. Her high expectations for her children went hand in hand with the high standards for their behavior that she demanded.

We can see that although Robin and Rene had similar school experiences, by sixth grade their reading levels diverged, and thus their chances for future educational success were equally divergent, should they conform to the predictions of many studies of education outcome. One major difference between them was their homes. The Grant household, although warm and loving, was not one in which high educational achievement was expected from all the children nor in which the resources to ensure such achievement existed. The Grant family set standards for behavior—assigning chores, limiting television use—but not for academic achievement or related domains such as music lessons, Sunday School, or extracurricular activities. The children in the Grant family spent much more of their time alone and in self-selected, unsupervised activities. Although the Hendersons worked long hours, thus leaving their children alone quite a bit, the children's time was much more heavily committed to activities with long-term goals. The access to literacy and the use of literacy by adults in the two families was different—many more books, and more use of books, characterized the Henderson household. The attitude toward the schools was also different in the two families. Mrs. Grant relied on the schools to provide her children's education, and had faith that they could do so. Mrs. Henderson adopted a much more critical stance, tried to supplement the school's educative function, and was prepared to consider alternatives to public schooling for her children. Thus, her children were less vulnerable to the variation in quality across classrooms and schools. Nonetheless, despite the strengths of the Henderson household, Reginald had had a less than ideal set of experiences in the Norwich schools, and Robin was in sixth grade starting to show a decline in her achievement (relative to national norms) that could, if it continued, predict academic problems in high school and college.

~ *Chapter 3* ~

Methods of Data Collection

Research designs inevitably reflect compromises, and ours is no exception. The design we chose is a compromise between qualitative and quantitative methods, between careful description and justifiable inference. We recognized in originally planning this project the advantages of in-depth ethnographic approaches to understanding the social sources of literacy achievement. Contemporary projects at the University of Pennsylvania (see Gilmore, 1983, 1986; Gilmore and Smith, 1982) and at Teachers College, Columbia (see McDermott, Goldman, and Varenne, 1984; Varenne et al., 1982), which were more purely ethnographic than ours, have contributed a great deal to our understanding of how literacy operates in low-income homes. Nonetheless, the limitations on sample size and generalizability from such studies meant that a truly ethnographic approach was inappropriate in answering our research questions. Furthermore, we needed access to quantifiable and comparable data on the literacy achievement of all the subjects. Whereas true ethnographers distrust test results, we believe they provide crucial information about children's performance; some outcome measures were obviously indispensable to our research design. Accordingly, we combined data collection techniques informed by ethnographic methods with more interventionist and test-based measures.

We have also been informed by large-scale, quantified literacy assessments, such as those provided by the NAEP (see the 1981 and 1985 reports), which support general conclusions about low-income children's literacy achievement. Clearly (at least in the absence of unlimited funding) large sample sizes impose relatively severe limits on the amount of data collected from each subject.

Our interest in collecting a wide array of family and classroom data about each child in the study precluded a large sample. Thus, our focus in data analysis is on relationships among the home and school factors, and relationships of home and school factors to literacy outcomes.

Finally, we recognize that "literacy" is a complex and multi-faceted topic, and that it is difficult to capture what children know about literacy in a short test session. The various "informal" and observation-based assessments of literacy have considerable value for some purposes. Nonetheless, since we were primarily in-terested in low-income children's literacy achievement as tradi-tionally defined by schools, we chose to use a familiar, standard-ized literacy achievement measure. Elementary schools define literacy to a large extent as performance on standardized tests of word recognition and comprehension, and as performance in lessons and activities designed to teach and practice those skills. The informal literacy activities children engage in (reading menus in fast-food restaurants, performing rap songs, exchanging notes in class, and so on) are worth describing and analyzing. It is impor-tant to point out that children have literacy skills that are not reflected in formal test situations. Such literacy skills might serve as a basis for more effective teaching, and more sensitive testing. At the moment, though, performing well on standardized tests is how children demonstrate achievement in school; standardized reading tests are a basis for grades, for being promoted, for being tracked, and for entrance to college. We feel that choosing such tests as our literacy outcome measures supports the relevance of the findings we present here to real-world educational decisions.

Subject Selection

Recruitment of classroom teachers. A number of criteria directed our procedures for recruiting subjects. First of all, we needed children reading slightly below or slightly above average at three grade levels—second, fourth, and sixth. We sought children whose families would be likely to participate in all phases of the eighteen-month data collection. We wanted families who met commonly understood standards of "low-income," defined practically as meeting federal income guidelines for free or reduced-price school lunches. We chose this definition because it was based on information about families that was already available to teachers and school administrators. We wanted (but were not totally successful in finding) children from exclusively English-speaking families. And we wanted to select both better and poorer readers from the same classrooms, so that the variation in reading ability would not be attributable primarily to school factors. Furthermore, we wanted children whose classroom teachers would agree to being observed during the school day.

Accordingly, we recruited families by selecting children within particular classrooms in which the teachers had volunteered to collaborate in the study. Teachers were recruited through the good offices of the Norwich School Department, after a number of letters were sent and meetings held to explain the purpose of the project. The school department recommended schools which served primarily working-class populations and were ethnically representative of Norwich. Within schools the project was brought to the attention primarily of the more skilled and enthusiastic teachers. Teachers in eleven classrooms agreed to participate; their participation involved (*a*) consulting with us to recommend likely children, (*b*) providing ratings for those children on various aspects of reading and math skills, (*c*) agreeing to let children be taken from the classroom for the administration of individualized literacy tests, (*d*) agreeing to let researchers spend several hours in the classroom to observe the children selected, and (*e*) agreeing to fill out a questionnaire about the sample children and about classroom practices. The cooperating teachers recommended a total of 91 children; we were successful in contacting 88 families to obtain permission to consult school records and administer the screening tests.

Selection of final sample. The vast majority of the families contacted agreed to the initial testing for screening purposes. Many of the children recommended by their classroom teachers for inclusion turned out to be ineligible for the final sample, mostly because they came from homes where a language other than English was the primary language spoken (19 children fell into this category). Another 16 children were not selected for further participation because of chronic absence from school, grades and/or test scores that placed them outside our target groups, or a mixed achievement record that made it difficult to classify them. An additional 14 families declined to participate in the full study. Ultimately, 31 families were selected which met most of the criteria for inclusion (1 family had 2 children in the study), though 5 of these families turned out to be not exclusively English speaking. We included them nonetheless because the children were monolingual speakers of English, though the parents did sometimes use another language with each other. In addition, these families were included to make our sample more representative of the diversity of low-income families in the Norwich schools. Because of problems in administering all the instruments to all family members and in retaining the full sample over a year, different analyses are based on slightly different numbers.[1] Analyses of family factors were mostly performed on all 31 families and 32 children, while analyses of school factors as related to gains in the children's literacy scores were performed only on the 30 children to whom the literacy battery could be administered a second time.

Characteristics of the sample. Table 3.1 gives the distribution of the sample by grade level and gender. Because of our procedures for selecting families to participate in this study, we ended up with a heterogeneous sample of families on most dimensions. Compared to many studies of families, especially those motivated by an interest in educational achievement of children, we had a sample of very "ordinary" families. On the one hand, there were dysfunctional families in the potential subject pool who would not or could not participate in the study for two years, given the demands we would have made on their time. On the other hand, we did receive cooperation from families with members in prison and in mental hospitals, with parents or older children in substance abuse programs, with a history of referrals for abuse or neglect, and with children who were often truant from school. We did not choose

---

1. A difficult aspect of a long-term, in-depth study such as this one is that the data collection involves scheduling appointments with many different members of each family (and the children's teachers), over a period of eighteen months. Inevitably, incomplete data were collected on some families. Nonetheless, we felt that we should include even these families in the final sample, simply adjusting particular analyses for the presence of fewer subjects, rather than risk biasing the sample by including only those families with whom it was easy to schedule appointments. See Appendix 1 for details of the missing data.

Table 3.1   Distribution of sample children

Grade	Male	Female	Total
Second	8	3	11
Fourth	7	5	12
Sixth	1	8	9
Total	16	16	32

families whose children were failing in school—on the contrary, the children at the bottom of their classes were excluded from our study. We did not choose families whose children were exhibiting any particular behavior problem. Nor did we choose families whose children had exhibited exceptionally high levels of performance in school—we excluded the best students in each class, as well as the lowest achievers, from consideration as subjects.

Given our way of selecting families, it should be no surprise that we ended up with large families and small, with single-parent families, intact families, and reconstituted families, with a considerable range in terms of financial security, with families where both parents worked, where the mother was a housewife, and where both parents were unemployed, and with variation on all the other demographic characteristics one might consider important. Tables 3.2 through 3.5 give the composition of our sample on some of the crucial demographic dimensions.

Data collection in the homes was concurrent with school research and assessment, each area being the responsibility of a separate research team. In addition to being the only practical solution to the problems associated with the size of the data collection effort, this separation of responsibilities enabled the team responsible for the home and family component to proceed without explicit knowledge of the children's reading status. Researchers were thus less likely to be biased in their collection and interpretation of data about the home.

Data were collected about the children's literacy skills in a series of individual test sessions at school (see Chall, Jacobs, and Baldwin, 1990, for further details). In a few cases these tests were administered at home in the second year, when a few of the children had

Table 3.2   Family constellation

Families	Number of children in family							
	1	2	3	4	5	6	7	8
With single parent	2	3	3	—	2	—	—	—
With two parents	—	6	7	5	1	—	1	1
Intact	—	6	4	5	1	—	1	1
Reconstituted	—	—	3	—	—	—	—	—
Total	2	9	10	5	3	—	1	1

Table 3.3   Parental education

	Years of schooling				
	< 9th	9th–11th	12th	12th–15th	> 15
Mothers	6	7	9	7	1
Fathers	1	9	6	1	6

Table 3.4   Employment status of parents

Status	Single-parent families	Two-parent families	All families
No parent working	4	2	6
One parent working	6	4	10
One working full-time, one part-time	—	1	1
Two parents working full-time	—	14	14

Table 3.5   Reported family income

Income range ($)	Number of families
5,000–9,999	8
10,000–15,999	4
16,000–26,999	7
27,000–30,999	7
Not available	5

transferred out of Norwich schools to other schools in the greater Norwich area.

Home and Family

The collection of data about the children's families and out-of-school experiences was designed to be comprehensive, multi-faceted, and eclectic. Although the ethnographic studies of low-income families that have been carried out are of great interest (see Heath, 1983; Miller, 1982; Varenne et al., 1982), we had neither the time nor the personnel to provide full ethnographic descriptions of 31 different families (let alone of 11 different classrooms in 4 different schools). Accordingly, we opted for a mix of methods: some direct observation as well as fairly intensive interviewing were our primary sources of information about the families. The interviews incorporated some standard instruments that had been developed by other researchers, as well as sets of questions designed to test the hypotheses that guided our own investigation.

All family members. One of the principles which guided our efforts to collect as complete a picture as possible of the children's out-of-school activities and environments was to include all willing family members. We felt that it was crucial to collect information from several different family members—the children themselves and their mothers and fathers, of course, but also their siblings and their resident male caretakers or nonresident biological fathers, when appropriate—because a considerable amount of research on family dynamics has shown that family members often have different perceptions of shared experiences and activities (Beavers, 1977; Framo, 1972; Goodman, 1984; Reiss, 1981). Although we were not always successful in scheduling interviews with all family members (fathers were especially hard to involve in the study: only 11 of the 23 fathers could be interviewed), we feel that in those cases where we were successful, the data base is enriched considerably.

The role of observation. A second decision about the nature of data collection came after considerable efforts were made to develop observation schemes and to carry out pilot observation sessions. We originally intended to supplement our interview data with direct observation and audiorecording of interaction between the focal children and their families at high-interaction times of the day, because of our hypothesis that the nature of interaction around books, homework, and topics of general interest could contribute crucially to children's acquisition of reading skills, vocabulary, world knowledge, and attitudes toward achievement and toward learning. During the initial interviews we collected information about the children's schedules, hoping to be able then to select times for doing observations that would be appropriate and comparable across children. We discovered, however, that given the wide age range and the relative independence of many of the fourth and sixth grade children from rigid schedules or parental supervision, it would be difficult to find any time for observation that was comparable across children. Furthermore, even when the children were at home and their parents and siblings were present, there was no identifiable time for many families when interaction was likely to occur. The majority of the mothers in the sample worked and were therefore not home or available immediately after school. Many of the families did not sit down to any scheduled meal that provided an opportunity for conversation. Many children had no homework or did their homework on their own without parental supervision. Thus, there was no time of day when we would within a feasible period be likely to observe the kind of language-, literacy-, or information-focused interaction we hypothesized would be influential. The density of interaction between parents and children in the age range studied here was often quite low, which is not to say that the brief and scattered exchanges the children had with their parents were unimportant. But children in grades 2 to 6 present a different and much more challenging case to the observer than do preschool children, with whom interaction is much more constant and dense. Much of what ten-year-olds are interested in goes on inside their own heads or during social interaction with peers and is not accessible to tape recorders, note takers, or adult observers. Furthermore, the school-age children we were studying were capable of learning a great deal from small amounts of interaction. Thirty seconds of help reading a hard word, a few sentences expressing interest in what had happened at school, or even just seeing Mom select a book rather than the television for fifteen minutes of relaxation, could constitute the source of important learning for the older child. Yet none of these events showed up as notable or frequent in pilot observations, and the chances that any of them would occur during a one-hour observation session were quite small.

Accordingly, we decided to rely primarily on our interviews as sources of information about the families but also to include an observation situation which was sufficiently structured to provide, within about a half-hour of observation time, an analyzable sample of literacy- and task-focused interaction. Since the role of homework and parental supervision of homework had by this point in the study emerged as an issue of considerable interest, we designed a task that simulated to some extent the nature of a homework assignment, and we asked the mother or father (in some instances both were present) to help the child complete the task. The task was to record a diary, using a form provided, for the preceding day, filling in all the activities the child had engaged in, where they had occurred, and who else was present. Two researchers were present for this homework-like task: one who was familiar to the family from previous interview sessions, and one who had never met any of the family members and was unaware of the child's reading status. The first researcher explained the task to the child and parent, and the second kept a running record of what happened, what exchanges occurred between child and parent, and other events of importance. The narrative records were later transformed into a standard form for analysis, and the second researcher also filled out a SYMLOG form for both participants in the interaction (Bales and Cohen, 1979). The SYMLOG rating is designed to assess two or more participants in an interaction on the degree to which each is positive or negative (friendly or unfriendly), dominant or submissive, and task-oriented or emotionally expressive. It can be used by an outsider, as we used it in the diary task, or by participants. We also asked all the family members to fill in SYMLOG ratings for themselves and each other, to give us information on how they felt the family functioned.

Time allocation diaries. In addition to providing a context (not to say pretext) for observation of parent-child interaction around a homework-like task, the one-day diary filled in during the observation session was designed as a way to instruct the child in filling in other diary forms. We asked each child to keep a diary for four weekdays on two different occasions: during the school year, when the diary form included a checklist for in-school activities as well as a supplementary out-of-school checklist, and during the summer, when only the out-of-school checklist was included. The diary format (see Appendix 2) required that the child first write down the activities, location, and companions, at the appropriate times, and then go through a checklist and mark any activities engaged in that day. The checklist was included to get a more complete record than the longhand diary, as well as to jog the children's memories—they were specifically told they could go back and add to the diary if the checklist reminded them of activities not filled in.

The diary content was then analyzed for the number and nature of activities engaged in, for the degree of predictability of children's schedules, for a profile of who they spent their time with, and for the quality of the writing in them as well.

The interviews. In accordance with the principle that all family members should be interviewed in order to get a complete picture of events, activities, rules, and attitudes within the family, we designed the interviews for different family members, especially for the mother, the father, and the focal child, to parallel one another as much as possible. The mother and father interviews were, in fact, identical, enabling us to make extensive comparisons within families on parents' perceptions of their children, their beliefs about child rearing, their attitudes toward their children's school experiences, and other matters on which one might expect agreement between them. The interview for the focal child covered the same major topic areas as the parent interview, but the ways in which the questions were asked and sometimes the nature of the questions were quite different. The child interview also incorporated two scales that had proven useful in previous work with children from low-income populations, the Swanson Child-Parent Relationship Scale (Swanson, 1950), and the Nurturance Scale (Saunders, 1977).

The interviews focused on the following content areas: (1) Basic demographic information; (2) Parental education and literacy practices; (3) Children's educational histories and literacy practices; (4) Views of schools and teachers, and nature of interaction with schools and teachers; (5) Educational aspirations and expectations; (6) Degree of financial and of emotional stress family members were subject to; and (7) Television use and other leisure time activities. During the interview sessions, as already noted, each family member was asked to fill out a SYMLOG rating form on each other family member. These SYMLOG measures were useful in getting a sense of how the family functioned in terms of three dimensions: friendliness, task orientation, and egalitarianism.

Teachers and Schools

We relied on three major sources of data about the children at school: their school records, interviews and questionnaires administered to the teachers, and classroom observation.

School records. School records were used to determine what children's grades and standardized test scores had been, how many times they had changed schools, whether they had been held back to repeat a grade, whether they had received special help of any sort, and whether there were any other special factors (such as comments from teachers about health problems, home conditions, high levels of absenteeism, behavior problems) that needed to be taken into account to understand the child's achievement level.

Questionnaire. Teachers were asked to fill out questionnaires about their teaching practices, their instructional emphases, their frequency of contact with parents, and their allocation of time to different types of instruction. In addition they answered questions about focal children's specific strengths and weaknesses. We asked teachers (as we asked parents) how far they hoped, and expected, focal children to get in school, and what kind of job they might end up holding.

Classroom observations. Each classroom in which a focal child was placed was observed during one hour of reading instruction, one hour of other teacher-led instruction (typically social studies or math), and one hour of less structured time, such as independent seatwork.[2] In the first year of the study, the 32 children were in 11 classrooms whose teachers had all volunteered to be in the study. Thus, one hour of classroom observation gave us information

2. We would like to express appreciation to Courtney Cazden for her extensive help in reviewing teacher interviews and designing classroom observation procedures.

about the instruction available to several children. In the second year, the children were dispersed over 25 classrooms, requiring many more hours of observation. While the switch from volunteer to nonvolunteer teachers reduced to some extent the level of cooperation and thus the amount of information we could get, it also gave us access to a much more typical group of Norwich teachers. The volunteers were, on the whole, superior teachers who were eager to have observers in their classroom. While the nonvolunteer group included some excellent teachers, it constituted much more of a random sample, and thus displayed considerably more variation in quality than did the volunteer group.

The nature of the data collected about both home and school will become clearer in Chapters 4–7, where we present findings on the relationship of home and school factors to school achievement.

Literacy Skills

Three different procedures were used to collect data on the three domains of children's literacy skills of particular interest: a diagnostic test for reading, two writing samples as a basis for assessing writing, and the Wechsler Intelligence Scale for Children—Revised (WISC-R) vocabulary subtest to assess vocabulary knowledge.

Reading. The test used to assess reading was the Diagnostic Assessment of Reading and Teaching Strategies (DARTS), an experimental version of an individually administered diagnostic test of reading and related skills designed to measure six components of reading (Roswell and Chall, in press). The entire test was administered to the children, but the results from only two subtests are reported here (see Chall, Jacobs, and Baldwin, 1990, for further analyses of these and the other subtests). In the Word Recognition subtest, students orally identify words of increasing difficulty. In the Reading Comprehension subtest, students silently read passages of increasing difficulty and answer four multiple-choice questions on each.

Writing. Two writing samples were completed by each child in the spring when they were in grades 2, 4, and 6, and again a year later when they were in grades 3, 5, and 7. The narrative writing sample was produced in response to a picture of an elderly woman

Figure 3.1 "Tomato Lady" picture used as a stimulus
in the narrative writing task.

in a supermarket holding a package of tomatoes (see Figure 3.1);
this picture had also been used in the NAEP. The instruction
given for the narrative sample was: "Here is a picture of a woman
with some tomatoes. Look at the picture for a while and think
about what is going on. When you have decided, write a story that
tells what is happening in the picture and what is likely to happen
next."

The expository sample was elicited by asking the child to write about someone he or she admired or looked up to, following this instruction: "Many of us have a special person whom we look up to or admire for reasons that are very special to us. For example, some people admire and look up to famous sports players, to TV or movie stars, to a person in a story, or to a relative or friend. Write about whom you admire or look up to; tell who the person is and explain why you look up to this person." Each child completed the writing samples in a quiet room apart from the classroom and was given ten minutes for each sample.

Although many assessments of a writing sample are possible, we chose, after considering the relation among the various measures derived from these samples, to use as our overall index of writing quality only the length of the sample in number of words. Length, for these samples, correlated highly with holistic scoring results, with measures of syntactic complexity, and with measures of quality of content. More information about the additional measures derived from the writing samples is available in Chall, Jacobs, and Baldwin (1990).

Vocabulary. Vocabulary was measured using the WISC-R subtest, following the standard instructions for administration and for scoring. The WISC-R vocabulary subtest was administered as part of a longer battery of language measures. Information about results from the additional language measures is also available in Chall, Jacobs, and Baldwin, 1990.

Plan of analysis. The analyses pursued were dictated in part by the nature of the data available. We had carried out one round of data collection about the children's families and out-of-school lives. This information, which in general reflected fairly stable factors in effect throughout the children's history, was related to information about the children's literacy scores at the time of the first literacy assessment. As discussed in Chapter 7, and in greater detail in the next three chapters, we used information from the interviews and home observations to test the strength of three models of home influence in explaining scores on each of the four literacy outcomes. The implicit logic of these analyses was that home factors are, while not unchanging, relatively stable, immanent determinants of a child's academic performance and can be used therefore to predict a child's status relevant to other children from the same population.

School data, like the literacy assessments, were collected in two sweeps—one for each year of the study. Clearly, the variability between one year's classroom and the next can be quite large within any child's life, and there is little reason to think that the quality of instruction in a classroom the child has been in only a few months can determine much about his or her general literacy status. We could, however, measure quite accurately the size of the gains made by each child during the second year of the study, since the two testing sessions occurred in successive springs. Characteristics of the instruction, the teacher's attitudes, and the literacy environment in the children's third, fifth, and seventh grade classrooms could therefore be related to gains in reading comprehension, word recognition, vocabulary, and writing. Analyses like these of gains form the basis for the results reported in the next chapters about classroom influences on literacy achievement.

~ Chapter 4 ~

The Family as Educator

Perhaps the simplest hypothesis concerning how families affect children's literacy and language achievement is also the most obvious one. Families are most effective when they function directly as educating agents. This hypothesis is not sufficiently concrete to lend itself to simple tests, however. Many points need clarification first. How do families function as educating agents? Exactly what skills relevant to school do families teach? Do some children do better at school because they've learned at home some or much of what school will teach? Or do some children learn at home how to be better learners at school, mastering procedures for learning rather than specific content? Whatever the nature of the family-based learning, do families exert these influences by explicit direct teaching? Or do they create the opportunities for children to learn as by-products of other aspects of family interaction? Do they establish and communicate high expectations for educational achievement? Or do they tend to engage in and display the kinds of behaviors (for example, reading, writing, and studying) the children will need in school? Such questions need to be asked before we can know what specific relationships to look for in order to determine whether, and to what extent, the "Family as Educator" model explains differences in children's reading, writing, and language performance at school.

Specific Predictions and Outcomes

Of the wide range of information available about the 31 families in our study, we selected the variables past research indicated should best reflect the role of the Family as Educator. Previous research with school-age children (Bloom, 1976; Bradley and Caldwell, 1984; Durkin, 1982; Henderson, 1981; Iverson and Walberg, 1982; Scott-Jones, 1984, and others discussed below) and with preschool children (Clark, 1976; Cousert, 1978; Laosa, 1978) led us to propose five factors as central to a definition of the model. Under each factor we give the specific variables from our interviews and observations that were used as indicators in our analyses. The past research evidence on which this selection of variables was based is discussed in greater detail in the next section.

Literacy environment of the home. Many researchers have found that high levels of literacy in the home environment are related to children's higher levels of school achievement (Bloom, 1976; Dave, 1963; Shea and Hanes, 1977; Walberg and Marjoribanks, 1976; Ware and Garber, 1972). Such variables as number of books in the home (Lamme and Olmstead, 1977; Parkinson et al., 1982), parents' expressed interest in reading (Coleman et al., 1966), and listening to stories told or read from books (Wells, 1985) have been found to correlate significantly with children's reading achievement scores. Marjoribanks (1980) found that "press for English," a composite variable that reflected a family's use of language as well as of literacy, related to children's word knowledge, especially for the lower-class and immigrant groups in his large and varied sample. The potential complexity of relationships between home literacy environment and children's school achievement is well reflected in Marjoribanks's work. He found that the relation of press for English to children's school achievement was affected by factors such as ethnic group, social class, and parental aspirations for the child.

A problem in interpreting results like these, though, is that there are a number of dimensions to home literacy. In our data collection and analyses, we attempted to distinguish different dimensions of home literacy. First, the parents' own literacy behaviors and preferences may have an effect on the child both directly (in that the parent is a role model) and indirectly (in that the parent who reads a lot may do other things that facilitate children's reading). Second, direct measures of parental provision of literacy to the child, which correlate highly but not perfectly with the parents' own literacy, may relate to children's achievement. Third, assessing parental provision of literacy for the child in grades 2, 4, or 6 (the grades we were observing) may be inadequate. Aspects of the children's pre-reading history may also affect their current literacy achievement; for example, Bradley and Caldwell (1984) found that parental selection of play materials at twelve months correlated .58 with reading in first grade. The combination of parents' own literacy practices, skills, and preferences with their current and previous provision of literacy to their children is the complex we refer to as "literacy environment."

Although previous researchers have often assessed home literacy by estimating or counting the number of books in view, we realized early in our interview process that such a procedure could severely underestimate our subjects. Many of these low-income families maintained neat and tidy living rooms by putting papers and books away in drawers and cabinets, by throwing out magazines and newspapers, and by giving away books once read. In many households we did not have access to bedrooms or other places books might be kept. Ms. Saunders, for example, told us, "I'd show you around but the beds aren't made." We relied, thus, primarily on interview material to assess parental literacy and provision of literacy. However, we also felt that no single question adequately reflected the degree to which the parents and children exploited, enjoyed, relied on, or expanded their lives through literate activities. Accordingly, we put the greatest emphasis on two summary variables: observers' ratings of parental literacy and observers' ratings of provision of literacy. Both incorporated all the information available about any family from formal interviewing and from informal observation and conversation. The mean of these two measures was used as a global estimate of the literacy environment in the home.

To preview our results briefly, they suggest strongly how important it is to differentiate among the dimensions of home literacy as we have done. Children's ability to recognize and understand new words was not explained by how many literacy experiences their parents provided, but was explained by how literate their mothers were. Clearly, then, a one-dimensional conceptualization of "home literacy" is incorrect. Iverson and Walberg's synthesis of home environment and school learning studies also concluded that "home factors are differentially related to different kinds of achievement" (1982).

Direct teaching. Parents who value their children's school success may choose to teach their children the skills they perceive to be a prerequisite to school achievement, as well as the skills they believe the children are not learning adequately at school. Few previous researchers have looked at amount of direct teaching when investigating the family's influence on literacy. However, ratings of amount of direct teaching (called "intellectual stimulation in the home") correlate .59 with children's school achievement in one British study (Parkinson et al., 1982). In addition, amount and style of maternal teaching have been found to differentiate middle-class from working-class families (Hess and Shipman, 1965; Schachter, 1979). Parental teaching style is, itself, influenced by a wide variety of other demographic and psychological variables (McGillicuddy-DeLisi, 1982), and in particular by socioeconomic status (Marjoribanks, 1979).

We included two measures of direct parental teaching. One, based on the parent interview, was an assessment of how frequently the parent helped with homework. The other was a rating of how positive, or conflict-free, the parent-child interaction was during the homework-like task we asked them to carry out.

Creating opportunities to learn. Beyond direct teaching, parents can indirectly facilitate their children's learning in many ways. A bias in research about family influence on children has been to look at the parents as the direct source of all effects, both positive and negative. But parents can also enrich children's lives and promote their literacy and language indirectly, by facilitating access to other people and activities (as in the case of the stereotypical middle-class child who attends music, ballet, swimming, and French lessons). Even parents whose full-time work and other obligations prohibit them from spending a lot of time with their children may ensure that their children spend time with other adults (friends of the family, extended family members, or tutors) who can function as role models and provide information, interesting conversation, knowledge about the world, aid with homework, and emotional support (Clark, 1983). We saw in the last chapter that Rene Grant's grandmother encouraged her interactions with extended family members, friends, and school personnel who served as important role models for her.

Furthermore, older siblings can be a valuable resource in the "educating family." A recent study (Norman-Jackson, 1982) finds that low-income black successful readers are distinguished from unsuccessful readers not by their access to verbal interaction with parents but by the amount of verbal interaction with older siblings. Heath (1983) provides a series of examples in which siblings appear to influence language development and school achievement. She notes that in a small working-class community in the South, older siblings sense what their parents don't—that young girls are at a disadvantage when they enter school—and then work with the preschoolers to prepare them for classroom interactions. Especially if the parents have a low level of education or are limited English speakers, and as the school-related tasks a child faces become more complex, a successful older sibling may be a better teacher than a parent.

Another way in which families facilitate their children's learning is by exercising control over their leisure time. For example, families can establish rules to limit time spent watching television (TV time correlates negatively with school achievement in the study by Parkinson et al., 1982), and can promote the child's participation in a wide variety of activities outside the home (activities show a significant positive correlation with school achievement, Parkinson et al., 1982). Parkinson and her coauthors also found significant correlations between school achievement and the variety of activities children engaged in with their mothers (.48), and their opportunities to participate in adult conversation (.50). Findings on the importance of access to adult conversation were replicated by Anderson, Wilson, and Fielding (1988), who noted that growth in reading proficiency between second and fifth grade was related to the amount of time children spent eating dinner—an opportunity for discussion with adults of topics of general interest.

In addition, parents who provide models of intellectual activity and who have a variety of interests themselves have children with higher school achievement. For example, Dave (1963) and Wolf (1964) found that the extent and content of a family's activities influenced the educational achievement of the children. More recently, Griswold (1986) reported that family outing activities predicted reading achievement among low-income fourth graders.

We included in our Family as Educator model three measures

that reflect the facilitative role of parents. We selected them from the great number of relevant variables on which we had data because they were relatively distinct from one another and showed considerable variance across families. From questions on the child interview, we assessed the number of outings with adults the child experienced in a typical week. From both parent and child interviews, we used information on whether the time children spent watching television was restricted. From the child interview, we also assessed whether the content of TV viewed was limited by family rules.

Parental education. Parental educational attainment is an important component of "family background." It is, of course, intrinsically related to social class and bears a statistically significant relationship to children's school achievement. Many studies, such as those by Blau and Duncan (1967), Coleman et al. (1966), Jencks et al. (1972), Parkinson et al. (1982), and Sewell and his colleagues (Sewell and Shah, 1968; Sewell and Hauser, 1976), show that parents' education is a major predictor of a child's reading ability and school success.

Parental education has been criticized by some researchers as a "surface" status characteristic, which does not consider the total form and substance of family life (Clark, 1983). Although parents' education, and particularly maternal education, has been found to be an important predictor of children's reading level and other school achievement, the question of precisely how better educated parents confer an advantage on their children remains open.

A number of studies have suggested that mother's education is related to how she thinks about and behaves toward her children, which may, in turn, have an effect on their school achievement (Durkin, 1966; Laosa, 1978). More educated mothers may provide their children with more materials and activities that promote literacy; in addition, educated mothers may become more directly involved in their children's education. By collecting data on these other aspects of parent-child interaction as well as on parental education, we hoped to be able to sort out the mechanisms by which parental education may have its effect.

Parental expectations. Parental aspirations and expectations about how long their children will continue in school can be transmitted directly to the children through demands, support, or encouragement (Sewell and Hauser, 1976), and can also influence other aspects of parental behavior which might affect children's achievement (Seginer, 1983). Researchers have distinguished between aspirations, which are "goal choices without consideration of real-life constraints" (Spenner and Featherman, 1978), and expectations, which reflect financial or other constraints. Socioeconomic status relates both to level of aspiration and achievement (see Hess, 1970). In an early study, parents of low socioeconomic status were found to emphasize the importance of a college education for their children much less than middle- and upper-class parents (Hyman, 1953). Conversely, substantially more lower- than middle-class adults recommended skilled labor positions for young people.

More recently, some researchers have argued that low-income parents may have educational and occupational aspirations for their children that are as high as middle-class parents' but hold lower expectations and tolerate failure to achieve the aspirations more readily than middle-class parents (see, for example, Rodman and Voydanoff, 1978). This phenomenon has been referred to as the lower-class "value stretch" (Rodman, 1963)—the greater differential in working-class homes between desired and expected achievement.

Although the Plowden Report (1967), Thorndike (1973), and Marjoribanks (1980) have confirmed the relationship of parental aspirations to school achievement in countries other than the United States, Coleman et al. (1966) and St. John (1972) found that parental expectations predicted the achievement of children in the United States, while aspirations did not. This pattern suggests that, on the one hand, in the United States the cultural model of democracy, equal opportunity, and classlessness is reflected in the aspirations expressed by poor and minority parents; on the other hand, unequal access to educational opportunities and more limited employment possibilities are reflected in their expectations. Thus, aspirations are less predictive in the United States because they vary less across classes. Expectations, which are more realistic, vary more across classes and predict actual outcomes better.

Testing the Family as Educator Model

A simple model of the effects of the variables defined above on child literacy would operate incrementally: Each variable contributes, and each contributes additively, to the likelihood of a child's success. We know, however, that such a model is too simple; for one thing, many of the variables likely to promote children's literacy are themselves interrelated. A mother with more education is likely to have a higher degree of literacy, would probably provide more extensive literacy experiences for her children, is likely to have higher educational aspirations for them, and is likely to marry a man with more years of schooling. Furthermore, many of these variables are rather nonspecific about mechanism of action; knowing that the mother has a higher educational level does not, for example, enable us to determine whether she is teaching her child to read, or whether she is modeling reading behavior. A more detailed analysis of a wider variety of variables will be necessary to understand how effects on the children's literacy are achieved. But the first question is, do the variables identified above as relevant to the Family as Educator model explain anything? Do the children whose families score higher on these variables read better? The answer is, yes, they do, but only on some aspects of reading skill, not on all of those measured. Specifically, the Family as Educator model explains large and significant amounts of the variance in children's word recognition skills (45 percent), and in their vocabulary knowledge (60 percent), but only smaller amounts of the variance on reading comprehension and writing.[1] The most powerful predictors of both word recognition and of vocabulary were: (*a*) literacy environment in the home, (*b*) moth-

1. We refer to "percentage of variance explained" in our discussion of results because it constitutes the best reflection of how important a correlational relationship is. A perfect correlation between two variables, indicated by a correlation coefficient of 1.0, reflects absolute predictability from one variable to the other, in other words, explanation of 100 percent of the variance on one variable from knowing the other. As the correlation coefficient between two variables declines, so too does the amount of variance explainable, but as a function of the square of the correlation. Thus, a correlation of .5 means that 25 percent of the variance is explained whereas a correlation of .7 means that almost half (49 percent) is explained. When correlations fall below .3, less than 10 percent of the variance on one variable is explainable from the other.

Table 4.1 Simple correlations between variables of the "Family as Educator" model and literacy outcome measures

Variable	Word recognition	Reading comprehension	Vocabulary	Writing production
Maternal education	.45[b]	−.05	.21	−.13
Paternal education	.18	−.16	−.13	.01
Mother's educational expectations	.54[b]	.19	.37[a]	.17
Father's educational expectations	−.10	−.10	−.14	.42[a]
Literacy environment of the home	.34[a]	.30[a]	.39[a]	.09
Homework help	.15	−.10	.17	.00
Parent/child interaction	.19	.12	.19	.37[a]

a. $p < .05$
b. $p < .01$

er's education, and (*c*) mother's educational expectations for the child.[2] The other variables listed in Table 4.1 related, as we had expected, to children's achievement but less strongly than these three. In addition, we found significant positive predictions of both word recognition and vocabulary measures from the following variables in our Family as Educator model: parental provision of literacy and father's education. These variables did not show up in the results of the regression analysis because they were too highly correlated with one of the three variables that did emerge. But they did correlate significantly with children's scores on word recognition and word meaning, and thus may be important in explaining how families function in promoting their children's literacy and language skills.

In a study like this one, with a relatively small number of families and a relatively large amount of information about each family, we

2. The assessment of the power of a "predictor," or of its power in explaining variance on criterion variables, was based on the specific regression model we used, which tried to find the best predictors that also had the least association with one another. Other regression models might attribute more power to other variables highly correlated with these as well as with the criterion variables.

should be more than satisfied with findings such as we have for word recognition and vocabulary: to be able to explain 45 to 60 percent of the variance is remarkable—the equivalent of saying we know how to raise a child's word recognition score from several months below grade level to a couple of months above grade level, just by manipulating a few aspects of his or her home environment. But these results fail to satisfy in two major ways: (1) If we look through the masses of data we have, we wonder why some variables that seem as if they should relate to the Family as Educator model do not predict children's scores on word recognition or vocabulary tests. We need to consider these unfulfilled expectations. (2) At the same time, there are some fairly strong relationships between certain other variables—not originally incorporated in our model of the educating family—and word recognition and/or vocabulary. These "unexpected relationships" must also be accounted for.

Unrealized Predictions

As stated in Chapter 3, we asked parents many questions about their own educational histories, their own educational aspirations, and their uses of literacy. The most striking and unexpected finding was the relative irrelevance of all the information about these matters collected from fathers. Mothers' educational level and their aspirations for their children seemed to matter more to children's achievement than did fathers'. This result is partially due to the fact that there were fewer fathers interviewed; smaller numbers make significant relationships harder to find. But it may also reflect the greater amount of contact between mother and child in the families we studied; in general, the mothers in our study were the ones who helped with homework, selected reading material, answered questions, read bedtime stories, enforced TV rules, and in many other ways served the educating family functions. (But see the case study of Christina Khoury in Chapter 6, for presentation of a particularly active and facilitating father.)

The difficulty of collecting information that accurately reflects how "literate" a person is may have prevented us from finding many of the relationships we expected. We used a four-point rating scale for maternal use of literacy (1 = nonreader, 2 = minimal reader, 3 = reader, 4 = "printworm"), which reflected all the interview information, our observations in the home, and our opinions from having gotten to know the mothers. This rating correlated significantly with children's word recognition scores, but of all the other maternal literacy measures, only two others also correlated with word recognition: the number of authors mentioned by name in response to the questions, "Who are your favorite authors?" and "Who were your favorite authors when you were a child?" (See Appendix 4 for correlations.) The level of the newspaper read by the mother correlated with the child's vocabulary knowledge; higher vocabulary scores were achieved by children whose mothers read the local or a national newspaper than by those whose mothers chose easier-to-read tabloids. These predictor variables show strong relations to children's reading. Of course, it was not the mothers' specific memories of childhood authors nor the level of the newspaper read that had a direct effect on the child's reading. What made a difference was undoubtedly the greater ability and interest in books shown by mothers who could remember authors' names, or who chose a higher level newspaper.

Why did we not obtain similar results from many of the other questions we asked the mothers—how many hours a week the mothers read, how much they liked reading, the kinds of books they read, the number and kind of magazines they read, their use of crossword puzzles, dictionaries, and many other literacy materials, and their preference for reading over other leisure time activities? One strong possibility is that these questions were affected by the subjects' attempts to satisfy the interviewers. The family members knew what our study was about, and it is quite likely that they assumed that Harvard researchers would approve of responses indicating considerable use of literacy materials. It is also difficult to estimate accurately the number of hours a week one reads, or how many books one has read in the past year. When asked to give such estimates, anyone is likely to guess high rather than low. The request to name favorite authors, though, is not subject to such effects; either one can think of some names, or one can't. Similarly, the name of the newspaper one reads regularly is not subject to errors of estimation. These questions may work because they are better than most as veridical indicators of literate activities.

Similarly, we expected that the number of literacy experiences the parents provided for their children would relate highly to reading achievement. What more obvious steps could the educating family take than buying books for the children or reading to them, writing notes to them, playing word games with them, telling them stories, discussing items from the newspaper? None of these individual measures related strongly to word recognition scores, though the composite "provision of literacy" rating did correlate significantly with word recognition.

Another area in which we expected to see much stronger relationships than emerged was the tone of the parent-child interaction during a homework-like task. Other researchers have found that parents of less successful school learners are more punitive and critical of their children during such tasks, while parents of successful children use more praise and create a more positive atmosphere (Hess and Shipman, 1965). We observed a parent helping each child to complete the diary for one day and used SYMLOG (Bales and Cohen, 1979) to rate various aspects of the interaction. The "positive-negative" scale of SYMLOG relies on observer's ratings of the applicability of descriptions like "friendly," "outgoing," "gives helpful suggestions," and "fun to be with." The presence of a positive atmosphere can be seen as facilitative of teaching, since children engaged in conflict with their parents are not likely to benefit from the help the parents are offering. Furthermore, a positive atmosphere during this task can be seen as an indicator that other teaching or homework-like interactions might also be positive. However, the degree to which the interactions were positive and conflict-free did not significantly relate to children's word recognition or vocabulary. Most of the interactions we observed were in general quite positive—perhaps more positive than they would have been without an observer. (The positiveness of the interaction did relate to our measures of writing, as we will see in the next chapter.)

The success of most parents in our sample at establishing a relatively positive atmosphere during the homework-like task contrasts with others' descriptions of homework scenes as conflict-inducing (McDermott, Goldman, and Varenne, 1984). In addition to being quite positive, the homework-like scenes we observed were characterized by the parents' skill in using the situation as an opportunity to help children succeed and to teach school and literacy skills. Most, though not all, of the parents structured, helped, and taught rather effectively, in ways that were quite similar to the ways teachers organized such seatwork activities in school (see Chandler et al., 1986). (The skill of the parents in this setting, and their similarity to teachers, will be discussed further in Chapter 6.) Our families may have displayed less conflict than other researchers have observed precisely because our task was not *real* homework—that is, it was not a worksheet or practice exercise for which the rationale or modus operandi was relatively unfamiliar to the parents. The task we set—filling out one page of a diary, so the child would "know how to do it alone" for the rest of the week—made sense to the parents and drew upon their knowledge of their children's lives and their own memories. This task contrasts both in meaningfulness and in the availability of relevant parental skills to more typical homework assignments like "color the balloons that contain words with long vowels orange and short vowels green," or "copy definitions for these twenty words out of a dictionary and use each word in a sentence." Furthermore, math, science, and social studies homework assignments to children in grades 6 and 7 may have been too challenging for some parents with relatively low levels of educational achievement.

Unexpected Relationships

To balance our unrealized predictions, we report some findings about relationships that we had not predicted but that are nonetheless interesting and interpretable. The number of activities the mother reported engaging in outside her work (social clubs, church groups, union groups, and so on) related strongly both to children's word recognition and to their vocabulary. This might seem paradoxical: after all, children who engage in more activities *with* their mothers also score better on these tests. Similar results have, however, been reported for upper elementary and junior high school students—that those who read more are also involved in more out-of-school activities (Marston, 1982). Where do some mothers find the time to do all those things, both at home with their children and out in the community? Whatever the answer, one source of children's learning may be the broader horizons provided by an energetic mother who engages in many social and community activities, and perhaps may engage her children in more enriching and interesting out-of-school activities.

Another unexpected finding was that for second graders especially, more contacts with extended family members related to higher word recognition. Such contacts may play the same role that an active mother does: indirectly educating the child simply by exposing him or her to new domains of action.

To give a better sense of these various aspects of the educating family, let us introduce two single-parent families with sons in the second grade: the Dixons, a family that scored among the highest in the sample on the variables associated with the Family as Educator model, and the Pagliuccas, who scored very low on the variables that characterized the educating family.

Derek Pagliucca and Jeffrey Dixon present a contrast in how their homes contributed to their literacy achievements, and in the gains in literacy they made from second to third grade. The contrast between the boys on these dimensions indicates the need to go beyond "package" variables like social class, ethnicity, and family constellation in explaining home influences. Derek and Jeffrey came from single-parent families in financially straitened circumstances and were in the same school. But Derek's literacy environment was meager, while Jeffrey's was relatively rich. Precisely because they were similar on many of the variables often cited as predicting reading achievement, the differences between their families in promoting and expecting educational achievement became quite powerful in helping to explain the difference in the children's reading levels.

The Dixon Family

Despite inadequate financial resources and difficult living conditions, some families, like the Dixons, managed to stimulate educational achievement on the part of their children. The Dixon household showed the three characteristics we found to be most important for word recognition and vocabulary development. Mrs. Dixon had more education than most of the mothers in our sample. She provided a rich literacy environment for her two sons, Jeffrey (age nine) and Lee (age seven). Furthermore, her educational expectations for her children were very high. She wanted both of her sons to graduate from college and believed that Jeffrey would be a good lawyer, though she also appreciated his artistic talents and expected that he might end up as a commercial artist.

The Dixon family faced not only economic problems but other difficulties as well. Mrs. Dixon has been separated from her husband for several years. Jeffrey and Lee had previously spent time with their father but had lost touch with him by the time Jeffrey was a second grader. The family had moved five or six times in the past few years, living in a series of shabby apartments, sometimes in dangerous neighborhoods. During our study the family moved from a federally subsidized housing project into several rooms of a house owned by Mrs. Dixon's stepbrother. The house was dark and in poor repair, and there was less space than the family had had before. A cousin did live downstairs, however, and nearby extended family included Mrs. Dixon's parents, who stopped in regularly and took the boys shopping, to the movies, or out for dinner. Mrs. Dixon called her apartment "Grand Central Station" because of the constant flow of friends and relatives. Although family resources were more available in the new apartment, life was still unstable for the Dixons. Mrs. Dixon was steadily employed at a responsible and skilled job, but her salary was too low to support a family of three adequately. Their phone had been disconnected several times, and Mrs. Dixon was not able to provide a baby-sitter for her young sons after school or to afford an after-school program even if the local school provided one. Instead, Jeffrey and Lee came home to an empty house, let themselves in, and watched television until their mother got home at 5:30 or 6:00 each day. Given her financial situation, absence of a partner, and lack of adequate after-school care in the community, it was not surprising that Mrs. Dixon said of her life with the boys, "At times it's really been rough."

Even though Mrs. Dixon was financially strapped, she wanted to do things for her sons to give them some enjoyment and to broaden their horizons. Jeffrey had participated in Pop Warner Football, and Mrs. Dixon had managed to get the money together for him to go to a summer arts program the previous three years. Mrs. Dixon believed it was important for her sons to be involved in out-of-school activities, to meet other children, and to have new kinds of experiences, an attitude which may have been fostered by her own high school years.

Mrs. Dixon had attended high school at a suburban parochial school on a special scholarship for black inner-city students. Although she had had a difficult time adjusting and had felt alienated from her white suburban classmates throughout her school years, she believed, in retrospect, that she had received a better-than-average education. After high school she attended junior college for one year, taking business and secretarial courses, before starting to work as an administrative assistant. She dreamed of becoming a legal secretary or a paralegal worker. She planned to go back to college when her sons were older and more self-sufficient because she realized how important further schooling would be for her professional advancement.

Mrs. Dixon provided many and varied literacy experiences for her sons and was an avid reader herself. Both the living room and single bedroom she shared with her two boys were full of magazines, newspapers, and books, including comics, coloring books, and old copies of the *New York Post*. Prominently displayed on one wall was a poster of a football player (a present from Mrs. Dixon to the boys) with the caption: "Mean Joe Green says: Team up with your teacher and TACKLE THOSE BOOKS."

Mrs. Dixon read several daily newspapers and also regularly read newsmagazines she brought home from her office (*Time, Newsweek, Ebony, Jet*). Reading newspapers and magazines was a habit she had picked up from her father, also an avid reader. She reported having read books a lot when she was younger and had more time. As a teenager, she had loved books, particularly romance and autobiographies. Mrs. Dixon still continued her practice of reading regularly to Jeffrey and Lee through their grade school years. In addition, when she saw newspaper articles she thought might be of interest to the boys, for example about animals, she clipped them to read and discuss with the children.

Mrs. Dixon's high expectations for her sons were evident in her assertion, "I hope nothing will prevent Jeffrey from finishing college. I can't imagine it as long as he wants to and I can help him." She rewarded good achievement from Jeffrey and Lee by taking the boys out to dinner when they brought home report cards with improved grades. The boys' drawings were posted on the walls of the apartment, evidence to the children that their work was valued. In Mrs. Dixon's view, a good student is someone who tries hard. As much as she was able, she stressed the importance of effort and persistence to Jeffrey and Lee.

Both sons were doing well in school. In second grade Jeffrey (the focal child in our study) was described by his teacher as "better prepared in reading than most of his classmates." At the end of second grade, he showed particular strength in the vocabulary and word recognition tests. A year later, at the end of third grade, Jeffrey had made impressive gains in reading comprehension. Evidently his strengths in word recognition and vocabulary had now been integrated with other reading skills. It is very likely that this integration was promoted by the many opportunities for practice at reading that his mother provided. The dramatic improvement in Jeffrey's reading during his year in third grade was echoed by a somewhat less pronounced improvement in his writing. His nonschool reading experiences coupled with the instruction from his strong third grade teacher could well have contributed to these gains.

The Pagliucca Family

In contrast to the Dixons, another single-parent family, the Pagliuccas, scored very low on all the factors that were associated with children's achievement in word recognition and vocabulary. Debbie Pagliucca had not completed high school and reported that she had not particularly liked school as a child and did not like to read as an adult; nor did she provide much in the way of literacy materials or interesting outside activities for her children—Paul (age ten), Derek (age 8, the focal child in our study), and Gina (age 4). Finally, unlike most of the parents in the study, Debbie Pagliucca's educational expectations for her children did not match her aspirations for them. She hoped her children would attend college but expected them only to complete high school. She expressed no job aspirations for Derek, although she thought him "smarter" than his siblings.

The Pagliucca household was considerably less rich in literacy materials than the Dixon household. The living room of their three-bedroom apartment in the Righetti Field projects was attractively though modestly furnished, but totally devoid of print materials. During our visits we saw no physical evidence of books, magazines, or newspapers. Ms. Pagliucca said she never read books and could not remember the names of any favorite childhood authors or books. She said she occasionally read the Sunday or daily local newspaper and looked at magazines when at the dentist's office. When asked who read *least* in her family, Ms. Pagliucca named her preliterate four-year-old and herself.

After school and on weekends Derek and his siblings played with friends in the project and watched television. All the children in this family spent a great deal of time watching television. They had no special chores or other responsibilities around the house and participated in no organized after-school activities. The only outings they mentioned were trips to visit the children's grandmother in a nearby community. At the time our study began, Derek has not seen his father for almost a year, although his father had taken him on outings when he was younger.

Ms. Pagliucca did not seem to be interested in what Derek was doing in school, what kind of homework he brought home, or what he was reading. She knew Derek went to the bookmobile weekly with either his older brother or with friends, but she never asked to see his books or talked to him about what he was reading.

Her lack of encouragement and laissez-faire attitude about Derek's learning was evident from her remarks about teachers and school. Although she lived close to the school and did not work outside the home, Debbie Pagliucca did not visit the school. She felt that teachers should take the initiative in contacting parents. She told us, "I tell them they can call me on the phone; it's hard to get down there." She complained about the school to which her older son had recently been assigned, "I don't get calls from the teachers. She [the teacher] should let me know if my child is acting up." Although parent-teacher conferences were scheduled regularly, Ms. Pagliucca said she never attended. When the school had wanted to consult about a possible hearing problem of Derek's shortly before our first interview, she responded with a phone call.

The family's income was very low and came from public assistance. Ms. Pagliucca had recently held a ten-hour-a-week job as a laundromat attendant. But she quit after two months because she "didn't really want to work even though the job was as easy as nothing." After leaving high school, she had worked sporadically as a waitress and as a clerk for a few weeks at a time. At home she spent most of her time taking care of her children, cooking, and watching television. Unlike many mothers in our study, she did not see or talk to any friends or relatives on a daily basis. Fatalism seemed to color many of Ms. Pagliucca's observations. She spoke of her housing problems saying, "I don't like raising kids in the projects but this is where they [the welfare department] stuck me." Her view of schooling was largely a negative one. A good student in her view was one who "doesn't fool around, does what he's supposed to." Derek received no special encouragement for good school-work, and Ms. Pagliucca seemed to have no strategies for intervening when there were problems.

Derek's reading skills at the end of grade 2 were only slightly below grade level, but they were fairly inconsistent: his word recognition scores were almost a year below grade level, while his comprehension scores were at grade level. During his year in third grade his overall reading score improved dramatically, reflecting many positive changes in Derek's school and home life, as well, perhaps, as his growing maturity. One change was his third grade teacher, who, when she became concerned about his progress, contacted his mother to enlist her help. This active teacher was especially important in light of Ms. Pagliucca's laissez-faire attitude toward her children's schoolwork. A second change in Derek's life was the arrival of his mother's new boyfriend, Dwight. Derek began to turn to Dwight for help with homework and more general support. Derek's third grade teacher felt that Dwight had made a real contribution to Derek's language skills in particular, and she singled out interaction with Dwight as a factor in his improved school achievement. This improvement was particularly noticeable in his comprehension and word recognition, but Derek also showed improvement on vocabulary in third grade.

Age Differences

Both Derek and Jeffrey were second graders when they were first tested. Children were selected from grades 2, 4, and 6 at the start of the study precisely because we were interested in determining whether the educating family's influence is equally strong at all three grades or whether family educative effects seem particularly powerful at a certain stage of development. Although our sample size was too small to test the Family as Educator model at each age (this would have required about 30 subjects at each age for the statistical analysis), we were able to look at the relationship between the individual variables central to the Family as Educator model and achievement at each grade.

Our data indicate that the home becomes an increasingly important variable in children's school success as the children get older and the school tasks they face become more challenging and complex. For each of three major variables implicated in the Family as Educator model, the age effects are identical: the relationship to children's achievement is stronger for the older children. The fourth and sixth graders seemed to benefit more than the second graders from the advantages of a more literate home environment, a more highly educated mother, and higher maternal expectations for their achievement. Thus, Derek might not yet have felt the full impact of his home environment, though his failure to improve on word meaning tests after grade 2 may be a first hint of future negative effects. Nor might Jeffrey be experiencing the full positive impact of a parent who bought books, read, shared, and commented upon articles in periodicals, and expected high levels of educational achievement from her sons. This finding should be of considerable importance to those planning home interventions to reduce the rate of educational failure.

Schools as Another Source of Variance

Even with our high level of prediction from the variables included in the family as educator model, 40 to 50 percent of the variance on word recognition and vocabulary remains unexplained. Can this remainder be accounted for? So far, we have limited our discussion to home variables, without considering the other obvious source of literacy skills, namely, school. Are there aspects of the school environment that could account for the differences among children that the Family as Educator model leaves unexplained? Are there particular classroom activities, teaching methods, or materials that make a significant difference in children's word recognition and vocabulary scores? Or are children entirely dependent on their parents to provide such learning?

Schools do, of course, make a difference. Results from our analyses of the classroom activities and materials our subjects experienced suggest that the strongest positive effects on word recognition resulted from the use of basal readers and workbooks, both in class and for homework. These are highly structured materials with controlled vocabulary, which provide practice and many explicit checks on learning. In addition to structure, the degree of challenge in the materials was important. Those children whose basal readers were at or slightly above their own reading level did better overall. Importantly, all the variables that help explain differences in development of word recognition abilities are indicators of use of a particular type of reading material. The results of our analysis suggest that use of structured materials, particularly ones at an appropriately challenging level of difficulty, contributed to our subjects' ability to recognize new words. It is striking that virtually none of the other kinds of classroom variables that we examined explained any of the variance in this area of literacy. Neither quality of teaching nor exposure to varied materials and activities predicted gains in word recognition skills, at least using our measures of these factors. It is also striking that, although positive relations between word recognition and school variables were found, the home variables were much stronger, explaining 45 percent of the variance whereas school variables explained only 10 to 12 percent.

Nevertheless, classroom variables accounted for almost 50 percent of the variance in children's ability to explain the meaning of words. The home factors that affected vocabulary were much the same as those that influenced word recognition. At school, by contrast, the development of word meaning was promoted by entirely different variables than those which are positively associated with the ability to recognize words. The variety of classroom materials available, and especially use of a wide range of reading materials of varying difficulty, including trade books, basals, and workbooks, was important for vocabulary development. Also helpful to low-income children's ability to define words was classroom emphasis on higher-level instruction, that is, use of inference questions in addition to factual questions, stressing reading comprehension and critical thinking as instructional goals. Thus, while practice using structured and challenging materials promoted children's development of word recognition skills, growth in vocabulary ability was related to enrichment in classroom materials and to instruction that emphasized the development of higher-level cognitive skills such as comprehension and critical thinking.

Jeffrey Dixon and Derek Pagliucca at School

Jeffrey and Derek's school experiences contributed to their strengths and weaknesses in reading. Both boys were in the same second grade classroom, one which observers characterized as "disorganized." Considerable class time in Ms. Carey's room was given over to discipline and transitions from one activity to another. Lessons were regularly interrupted by children chattering loudly to each other and by Ms. Carey stopping to scold and reprimand them. Although Ms. Carey seemed cheerful and good-natured, her attempts to maintain and restore order were often ineffective.

Jeffrey and Derek were in the same room, but their access to reading instruction and the amount of reading they themselves did differed considerably for two reasons. First, they were in different reading groups, Jeffrey in the highest and Derek in the lowest of three. Second, their abilities to concentrate during class instruction and seatwork periods were very different.

Ms. Carey described Jeffrey as "better prepared than average" when he entered her class. She characterized his classroom behavior as well organized, attentive, and competent. Although Jeffrey had very strong reading skills (for example, he was 1 year and 4 months above grade level on word recognition), his teacher had only modest educational expectations for him, predicting he would not go beyond high school.

As a second grader Jeffrey Dixon seemed to be in constant motion in the classroom, often the center of a circle of loud giggly students who were singled out by Ms. Carey for reprimands. During class lessons he often doodled and sketched. Although he appeared uninvolved and inattentive, Jeffrey monitored the progress of lessons closely and was frequently the first to volunteer answers to teacher questions, usually correctly.

Derek Pagliucca, in contrast to Jeffrey, was a loner, looking on silently while other children talked or played. Derek was animated and involved during his small reading group but tuned out during class lessons, on one occasion spending a whole spelling lesson quietly shredding a styrofoam cup on his desk. During math and phonics seatwork, Derek roamed around the classroom listening in on other children's conversations, watching the classroom aide test a small group with flash cards, getting pieces of paper from a supply closet, sharpening his pencil, and going back and forth to the water fountain.

Derek was assigned to the lowest of Ms. Carey's reading groups on the basis of poor reading scores at the end of first grade and what his first grade teacher described as a "short attention span." Because Derek had transferred schools at the end of first grade when his family moved, Ms. Carey worried that difficulties in adjusting to a new school were a problem for him.

Both Jeffrey and Derek received relatively small amounts of formal reading instruction, about fifteen to thirty minutes a day. In some of the other second grade classrooms that were observed, children received up to sixty minutes reading instruction daily. Although Jeffrey's reading group worked in the same two second-grade basal readers as Derek's group did, Jeffrey's group nearly finished both books in the course of the year, while Derek and his classmates in the bottom group were only starting the second book at the end of the year.

Derek and Jeffrey exhibited different reading behaviors. Classroom interruptions affected Derek's reading. When Ms. Carey would stop his oral reading to scold noisy children elsewhere in the class, he would lose his place and have to wait for her to start him over again. He read hesitantly, pointing with his finger at each word and regularly stumbling over more difficult words. Although Jeffrey's reading-group lessons were often interrupted as well, he could find his place again. In contrast to Derek, Jeffrey read fluently, and was able to answer the teacher's questions accurately.

Ms. Carey's class used assigned texts in the basic school subjects almost exclusively. Classroom work was organized around progressing through the commercial basal readers, math texts, spellers, and phonics workbooks. The formal reading instruction was based on oral reading of brief passages from Macmillan readers and completing corresponding assignments in supplemental multiple-choice worksheets. Students who had limited access to magazines, newspapers, storybooks, and picture books at home did not encounter these literacy materials in Ms. Carey's class either.

At the end of second grade Jeffrey scored well above grade level in word recognition but was weak in reading comprehension. Derek was slightly below grade level in both reading comprehension and word recognition. Students in our sample who were weakest in reading comprehension were those who had relatively small amounts of instruction in reading. Both the chaotic atmosphere in Ms. Carey's room and the comparatively small amounts of time she allocated for reading lessons worked against Jeffrey and Derek's progress in this area.

Neither the Dixons nor the Pagliuccas communicated with the school during the boys' second grade year. Ms. Carey had no contact with Jeffrey's mother during the school year and said it would have been difficult to arrange meetings because of Mrs. Dixon's work schedule. Like many teachers of black children in our study, Ms. Carey felt there was little support at home for Jeffrey's school progress. Although observers were aware of many ways that Jeffrey's mother supported his school achievement, Ms. Carey had no sense of these or of their importance. Ms. Carey sent several notes to Derek's mother because of his inattentiveness and inability to complete assigned seatwork, but Ms. Pagliucca never responded to these. At the end of the year Ms. Carey referred Derek for a special needs evaluation on the basis of his poor test scores and general immaturity.

The second grade year was thus a disappointing one for both Derek and Jeffrey. A discouraged, overwhelmed teacher was unable to capitalize on the strengths that Jeffrey's home provided or to make up for some of the deficiencies in Derek's home experience.

Jeffrey transferred out of the Norwich system at the end of the first year of our study when his family moved. During the third grade he was bussed out of his black community, as part of a racial balance plan, to a school in a predominantly white neighborhood. "NIGGERS SUCK" in six-foot-tall letters was spray-painted across the school's entrance.

Jeffrey's third grade teacher was Miss Coyne. In contrast to Ms. Carey's room, Miss Coyne's class was extremely quiet and orderly. Twenty-eight children, about half of them black, sat in rows at old-fashioned bolted-down desks. Homework was assigned every school night, generally from subject area workbooks that formed the backbone of the curriculum.

In addition to the reading instruction Jeffrey received in Miss Coyne's class, which centered on basals and completing multiple-choice workbook assignments, Miss Coyne's students also visited a well-stocked school library every week and were given time for weekly independent reading. Miss Coyne described her instruction as emphasizing vocabulary and both literal and higher levels of comprehension, though her use of basal readers and workbooks also revealed her emphasis on basic skills. Miss Coyne assigned Jeffrey to the top of her four reading groups, although she described his level of preparation as only average. Children in Jeffrey's new class received reading instruction together with children of similar ability in an adjoining third grade room, making groups of 12–15 students each. In part because of the large group size, Miss Coyne asked the students to write answers to questions about their basal reading passages as part of every reading lesson. Furthermore, Miss Coyne allotted an hour a day to Jeffrey's reading group, much more time than Ms. Carey had allocated to reading instruction, and he managed to finish four readers in the course of the year.

We interviewed Miss Coyne about her perception of Jeffrey's skills. Despite a relatively large class size, she was aware and appreciative of Jeffrey's interest in drawing and provided an estimate of his academic strengths and weaknesses that corresponded closely to our test results. Miss Coyne had had no contact with Mrs. Dixon and described Jeffrey's mother's contribution to Jeffrey's success as minimal.

Jeffrey made dramatic gains by the end of his third grade year in reading comprehension (6.0), and he made consistent progress in word recognition (5.3). This progress could be related to the steady conscientious attention of his third grade teacher. In common with other teachers in our sample whose students were relatively strong in comprehension, Miss Coyne set aside ample time for formal reading instruction, made frequent checks on students' understanding, and encouraged children's reading through frequent library visits.

Derek also blossomed during third grade when he was placed in a class that was much smaller because of the decreased enrollment at his school. Ms. Bergeron, Derek's third grade teacher, was young and energetic. Derek's reading group had an uninterrupted half-hour of reading instruction every day, with an emphasis, according to Ms. Bergeron, on both comprehension and critical thinking. In the reading lessons we observed, Ms. Bergeron frequently interjected questions designed to tap both literal and inferential levels of meaning. She gave explicit instruction in strategies for reading words (word attack skills), by assigning the same kind of workbook exercises as Ms. Carey had used and also by helping with difficult words in the passages being read during reading-group lessons.

Derek's class visited the library every week, and Ms. Bergeron supplemented the school's basal and workbook series with paperbacks, language experience charts, and teacher-written worksheets. Writing activities were a regular feature of Ms. Bergeron's lessons; students wrote story booklets and journals, and captioned pictures. Ms. Bergeron described Derek as someone who loved to draw and whose favorite lesson was composing stories to accompany his drawings.

After a third grade year with a teacher who encouraged reading and set aside plenty of time for it, Derek, like Jeffrey, showed dramatic improvement in reading comprehension (6.0) and word recognition (4.9). Derek's gains in vocabulary were especially striking. Ms. Bergeron, like other teachers in our sample whose students showed strength in this area, exposed her class to a wide variety of print materials and also emphasized expressive uses of language: talking and writing. Because Derek's family was unable to provide much exposure to print or to stimulate reading and writing, the teacher's influence was critical.

Our findings suggest that parents in the educating family promote their children's word recognition and vocabulary skills in a number of ways: by engaging in literate activities themselves, by spending time participating in a variety of activities with the children, and by maintaining high expectations for the children's educational achievements. The families in our study that did these things also shared other characteristics. Their children watched television less; the mothers were in general more active outside the home and bought their children books and provided other opportunities for the practice of literacy skills; their children arrived at school on time; and the children visited relatives frequently.

These children are especially fortunate if they end up in a classroom where reading instruction combines structured activity (the use of basal readers and workbooks that are at or just above the child's reading level) with challenging and stimulating activities (access to a variety of literacy materials including dictionaries and other reference works, availability of trade books at a wide range of difficulty levels, frequent visits to the library, and an instructional emphasis on inference, comprehension, and critical thinking). The child with this combination of home and school environment is likely to score well on both word recognition and vocabulary.

The educating family affects the development of both word recognition and vocabulary knowledge in much the same ways. It seems that word recognition and vocabulary knowledge are closely linked in development, at least as influenced by home and family variables. Why do these two skills show a strong association with one another, and dissociation from reading comprehension and writing, in terms of their susceptibility to home influences? Why are these two skills influenced by different factors at school?

The association between word recognition and vocabulary is not surprising. It is clear that recognizing a long word like "pedestrian" or "hippopotamus" is easier if one "knows" the word (has heard it, is familiar with it both as an acoustic and an articulatory pattern). Children with very small vocabularies will start at about fourth grade to encounter words in their reading books and on word recognition tests that they do not know. Even if the children's phonics skills are adequate, such words will be hard to sound out quickly and correctly the first few times they are encountered. Knowing which syllable in a long word should be stressed or knowing whether a vowel in the middle of a long word is long or short requires either knowledge of the particular word being read, or a sufficiently large vocabulary to be able to generalize about longer words. Thus, it may be that home influences on word recognition are mediated by home influences on vocabulary. Home influences on vocabulary include parental use of less frequent words, provision of literacy materials that provide exposure to infrequent words, and provision of access to a wide variety of activities, interlocutors, and spheres of action, such that a wider variety of topics is discussed.

In addition to vocabulary knowledge, word recognition requires the technical skills of print literacy. In our sample at least, these skills were typically developed through explicit teaching and provision of relevant practice activities by teachers in classrooms. The traditional ways of providing this practice in classrooms (workbook assignments, use of basal readers) do not typically function to stretch children's vocabularies—reading curricula, especially in the lower grades, are designed to ease the teaching of reading by staying *within* the average child's linguistic competence and vocabulary. Thus, at school, vocabulary growth is dependent on the teacher's exploitation of instructional strategies and materials that go beyond the basics of teaching reading.

An interesting aspect of our findings was that the Family as Educator model could explain variance on word recognition and vocabulary but not on writing and reading comprehension. This dissociation between word recognition and vocabulary on the one hand and reading comprehension and writing on the other also deserves comment. We will see in the next chapter why writing, at least for children in the Norwich school system, showed a rather different pattern from the other literacy skills.

Chapter 5

The Resilient Family

The educating family is only one model of how a family can contribute to its children's word recognition and vocabulary skills. Alternative models of family influences on children's learning derive, as does the Family as Educator hypothesis, primarily from analyses of social class differences. The assumption is that any characteristic that occurs more frequently in working-class families may be responsible for the greater educational risk of working-class children. One hypothesis generated from a comparison of middle- and working-class families might be called the "Resilient Family" model.

Working-class families differ as a group from middle-class families in the degree of stress to which they are subject. Low-income families are more subject to a wide variety of psychological stressors than middle-income families—for example, scarcity of financial resources, inadequate and crowded housing, dangerous neighborhoods, unemployment, and the lack of realistic expectations that one's life will improve. If additional stress-inducing conditions exist within a family, such as illness, alcoholism or drug dependency of a family member, marital discord, and absence of a marital partner, or if stress-inducing life events such as divorce, death of a family member, loss of a job, and loss of housing occur, then the family's ability to cope is severely strained. Of course, all families are subject to some stress, and it is likely that certain levels of stress produce few long-term bad effects on family members. But if the stress levels exceed a critical limit, and if the family members' coping strategies (seeking support and professional help, solving problems creatively, establishing affectionate intrafamily ties as well as social and familial networks, and so on) are inadequate, then the effects on the quality of family life are likely to be severe. Both higher stress levels and fewer resources for coping are more likely to occur in low- than in middle-income families. The Resilient Family model is meant to capture how much stress families experience, as well as how well they function in areas that might predict their ability to cope with greater stress and that reflect how they are responding to current levels of stress.

An extensive study of the determinants of stress in low-income families (and one which greatly influenced our own data collection) was the Families and Stress Project (Belle, 1982), which looked at many different indicators of stress in low-income families with young children. As a group, the low-income parents Belle studied had rather high goals for their children, and they had some understanding of the importance of family support for educational achievement. They differed, however, both from one another and from middle-class parents, in their ability to implement their own goals. Thus, some low-income mothers managed to create a pleasant home environment, spend time playing with their children, and devote some effort to teaching them in preparation for school, whereas others who placed equally high value on these goals did not achieve them. The major factor affecting the mothers' ability to work toward their goals was the degree of stress they experienced—social as well as financial. Clinical depression and a sense of futility brought on by stress led to a deterioration of the mothers' ability to provide their children with a positive, warm, organized home environment (Belle, 1982). The most highly stressed low-income women simply did not have the resources of time, money, contacts, or knowledge to provide their children with the time and attention they recognized as necessary.

Belle's finding supports conclusions from other research that the degree of stress working-class women experience differentiates them from middle-class women more effectively than either their goals and aspirations for their children or their understanding of their own role in the children's school success (Jeffers, 1967; Silverstein and Krate, 1975; Zelkowitz, 1982). Maternal stress has been directly associated with children's academic skills. For instance, a large scale study of British five-year-olds reported a strong relationship between maternal reports of stress and children's vocabulary scores (Osborn, Butler, and Morris, 1984). Although parental stress has not been directly related to older school-age children's cognitive development or academic achievement, there is evidence for two links in a causal chain relating stress to school failure: evidence that stress affects the nature of parent-child interaction and relates to lowered self-esteem in children; and evidence that the kinds of changes that result from stress negatively affect school achievement.

Children from families that are not coping effectively with stress are likely to show responses such as conduct disorders (Cadoret and Cain, 1980), and a lowered sense of self-worth and personal control (Friedman, 1973; Doyle and Moskowitz, 1984; Hess and Camara, 1979; Hetherington, 1984; Malone, 1963; Pavenstedt, 1965). Psychiatric disorders are more frequent among children from families that experience marital discord, residential overcrowding, paternal criminality, maternal psychiatric problems, and low socioeconomic status (Rutter et al., 1975a, 1975b). If these factors relate to psychiatric problems, they very likely relate at least as strongly to academic problems.

But even children from high-risk families are likely to achieve at school if they have a high level of self-worth and personal sense of control (Garmezy, 1981; Werner and Smith, 1982). Affective characteristics of the home, particularly adult approval of the child and training in independence skills, contribute to the development of children's self-esteem as well as to their achievement motivation (Weiss, 1969). Competent children were in one study also likely to come from homes that were neater, better organized, and in which role relationships of family members were appropriate and well defined (Garmezy, 1983). The emotional security that some families—despite poverty, slum environments, or natural tragedies—can provide for their children turns up again and again in studies carried out in various parts of the world as a factor linked to the development of a successful, competent child (Fraser, 1974; Garmezy, 1983).

Children often suffer negative consequences from emotional stresses associated with divorce and the reorganization of a single-parent family unit (Longfellow, 1979; Hetherington, Cox, and Cox, 1982). A major study of the effects of divorce on children (Wallerstein and Kelly, 1980) showed that the consequences vary with children's age and with the level of conflict the divorce resolves. Some (but not all) of the children in the Wallerstein and Kelly study were reported to suffer from at least temporary academic declines as a result of their parents' divorce, but teachers' reports rather than tests of the children were the basis for this conclusion.

Thus, while family stress can be assumed to have generally negative consequences for children's social and academic functioning, the exact nature and severity of the consequences vary depending on attributes of both the child and the family.

A number of different lines of research adumbrate the circumstances under which stress is likely to generate problems in families. We know, for example, that multiple stressors are more likely to lead to lasting negative consequences than single stressors (Rutter et al., 1979) and that family resources such as cohesion, adaptability, and problem-solving skills can mitigate negative effects of stressful events (Hetherington, 1984).

Consideration of the various studies of the familial and personal consequences of stress, and the factors that protect families and children from negative consequences, led us to construct our model of the resilient family. We had considerable difficulty in selecting a name for this model that might capture the full range of relevant factors and complex interactions among factors. We use the abbreviated term "Resilient Family model" to refer to the whole complex of economic, sociological, interactive, and psychological variables related to the ability of a family to cope with daily problems and yet reserve some resources for promoting its children's well-being and self-regard. This model is meant to distill aspects of the family's functioning that relate to its capacity to set and pursue goals effectively and to invest its children with the affective characteristics of good learners. We included measures of family functioning in the model that reflect both the family's ability to cope with current stress levels and the family's projected resilience in the face of further stress. In highly stressed families, even matters like cooking meals, having clean clothes, or getting the children to school can be difficult. Families which do manage to schedule meals and bedtimes, to share chores, and to adapt to demands from outside the home are demonstrating an ability to cope with simple problems that may predict their ability to cope with more serious stresses. We also included measures of the emotional climate in the family within this model because we assume that conflict among family members creates stress and may be exacerbated by their inability to deal with other stressors.

In less stressed and more resilient families, one expects to find clearer role assignments, more positive parent-child relations, fewer conflicts, less frequent punishment of the children, and a greater feeling of nurturance and self-confidence among the children.

Measures of the Resilient Family

The Resilient Family model, then, conceives of children's family environments as making a crucial contribution to their literacy achievement by creating a supportive climate for development— one in which children develop self-confidence and a positive self-image, have positive expectations about their relations with teachers and other adults, have experienced success after persistence at difficult tasks, and can set goals and regulate their own behavior. These are the characteristics of a good school learner. Rather than teaching the child directly, as the educating family does, the resilient family provides an environment within which the child can become a good learner, and is thus more likely to benefit from any teaching situation. Our assumption is that positive environments for children include adequate per capita income and no more than moderate levels of financial or psychological stress on the parents, since highly stressed parents often have less time to attend to children's individual needs. Homes in which rules and schedules are agreed upon by family members are likely to be characterized by lower levels of conflict and uncertainty (Minuchin, 1974). Reasonable rules about how long and what children may watch on television may also be a positive factor in the children's lives, contributing to their sense of being cared for and reducing conflicts with other family members (Goodman, 1984). Measures of how much time children actually spend watching TV may reflect their lack of access to more interesting activities. The absence of organization, predictable rules, or schedules in the family may contribute to conflict in interaction among family members, and leave the child with a sense of uncertainty. Children who feel they have poor relationships with their parents and who feel they are punished frequently see their own homes as places where they are unhappy, and may well approach school with lower expectations for success and achievement. Homes characterized by conflict and stress may lead children to feel helpless, frustrated, and joyless when confronted with learning tasks, thus hampering their ability to function at school. Three major factors determine a family's ability to create the organized, predictable, stable, and low-conflict environment that helps the good learner develop: the family's organizational style, the interpersonal relationships among family members, and the external stresses the family has to deal with. Accordingly, the measures we included in our test of the Resilient Family model reflect these three types of internal and external factors.

1. Measures of organization in the family include the presence of rules for behavior, some predictability in scheduling of daily events, reliability of family members in meeting responsibilities, punctuality, physical neatness, and cleanliness of the house. The variables reflecting organization in the family were derived from our observations, our interviews concerning scheduled activities, evidence from the children's diaries about daily routines and evidence from school records on truancy and tardiness.

2. Measures of emotional climate in the family include information on the children's views of their relationships with their parents, of how punitive or nurturant their parents are, and of how much opportunity for fun the children have, both with other children and with adults. We assessed emotional climate by using standardized scales in interviews with the children and by relying on interviewers' observations and children's diary reports of the opportunities for fun they had and the level of conflict in the home.

3. Measures of stress on the family system include not only financial stress but also stress associated with life changes and with demands on family members from outside the family system. Stress was assessed by interview questions about impact of available financial resources and stress, as well as by a summary rating of other sources of stress on the family.

The Resilient Family's Effects on Literacy

Do any of the measures of organization, emotional climate, or stress relate to children's literacy achievement? The model explains considerable amounts of variance in literacy but is most strongly and convincingly related to the children's writing; it explained 43 percent of the variance on writing production, our measure of writing skill.[1] Although the model also explained 28 percent of the variance on reading comprehension, and smaller amounts on vocabulary and word recognition, the most powerful single variable in these relationships was frequency of outings with adults. This variable was in fact common both to resilient and to educating families and seems to work much more as an opportunity for education than as a reflection of positive affect in the climate of the home. It did not correlate, for example, with how children felt about their parents. In contrast, the most powerful variables in explaining our measure of writing were the parent-child relationship scale, observer ratings of organization in the home, the presence of rules for television use, and the number of different activities listed in the diary the children filled out. All these measures were specific to the Resilient Family model. Significantly, the measure that correlated most highly with writing, the parent-child relationship scale, was a measure of the children's own perceptions of their relationships with their parents. While such perceptions are not entirely independent of the facts of family life, they need not have a simple or direct relationship to them either.

1. Results from analyses of the writing data showed that word production scores correlated highly with other measures of writing quality, and worked better for a whole sample analysis than holistic ratings because word production varied more independently of grade level (see also Chall, Jacobs, and Baldwin, 1990). We could not use holistic ratings as our measure of writing ability because writing samples from all the children in the study were compared to one another, yielding in most cases higher scores for older children. Writing ability, as measured by holistic scores, would have been confounded with grade level. In addition to correlating highly with other measures, word production seemed to be a stable characteristic for children in our sample. The number of words produced for the writing samples we elicited during the testing session correlated .64 (p < .002) with the number of words produced during an entirely different sort of writing task: filling in the diaries. Thus, "word production" is a highly usable and relatively stable measure of writing skill, at least for children like those in our sample. Nonetheless, we must point out that a long piece of writing with a good vocabulary is not necessarily technically very good. Indeed, the writing samples obtained, even the long and interesting ones, were full of errors of spelling, punctuation, sentence structure, and cohesion. Vicki Jacobs's help in the writing analysis was invaluable.

Table 5.1 Simple correlations between "Resilient Family" variables and literacy outcome measures

Variable	Word recognition	Reading comprehension	Vocabulary	Word production
Organization				
TV rules	.15	.24	.23	.44[a]
TV hours	.02	−.11	.06	−.09
Organization rating	.15	.01	.30[a]	.34[a]
Emotional climate				
Outings with adults	.24	.24	.35[a]	.22
Activities / diary	.20	.09	.11	.39[a]
Time with children	−.04	.07	−.08	.20
Parent-child relationship scale	.20	−.09	.12	−.51[b]
Punishment scale	.09	−.02	−.11	.02
Stress				
Income per capita	−.00	.18	.14	−.10
Mother's social stress	.00	−.01	.03	.06
Father's social stress	.08	.02	.15	.20

a. $p < .05$
b. $p < .001$

Contrary to our expectations of this sample, the financial and emotional stress experienced by the parents were not major factors relating to the children's literacy skills. The highest correlations obtained for stress variables were quite low (see Table 5.1).[2] In contrast, organization in the home, participation in activities, the presence of TV rules, and the parent-child relationship scale showed substantial correlations with writing production, indicating that the children who wrote longer essays came from more organized and active homes, with rules about TV, and had more positive relationships with their parents. The relative unimportance of stress variables may have emerged because we could not recruit parents experiencing extreme stress to our project; the commitment involved in participating, allowing all family members to be interviewed, and having us visit their homes several

2. Correlations as low as .20 mean that there is very little real relationship between the two variables; only 4 percent of the variance on one can be explained by the other.

times over two years may have excluded the families that felt the least able to cope with the demands of everyday life (Garmezy, 1988). A few families recommended by teachers as potential subjects revealed themselves during that first contact as unable to face the prospect of having outsiders visit their homes and interview family members. Two families who participated in the early stages of data collection dropped out of the study when family problems became overwhelming. Stress variables might have shown up as more important in a sample that included some more severely stressed families.

However, we should not leave the impression that our subjects led stress-free lives: five of the families had per capita incomes as low as $2,500, a level indicating severe economic stress; several homes were rated by observers as "dirty and disorganized," and several families as "severely emotionally distressed"; some families required as many as eight or nine visits, callbacks, and reminders before three interviews could be scheduled and completed; and a few children in the sample were chronically late to school, truant, and/or sick because of familial neglect.[3] These poorly functioning families contrast with the most resilient families in the sample, who continued to meet the demands of everyday life even in the face of severe stressors such as death of a parent or fatal illness of a dependent relative. The highly resilient families lived in homes that were typically relatively neat and clean, though often simply furnished. Family members we had requested to interview were home when we arrived. Children in the resilient families were much more likely to have scheduled out-of-school activities— music lessons, Little League, church-related activities—which they attended regularly.[4] We use the term "resilient families" rather

3. It should be noted that a larger percentage of the families in the sample would have been characterized as severely stressed at the time of the later follow-up. As will be documented in Chapter 9, a number of the families had experienced death or serious illness of a parent within four years of the end of the initial two-year study period, with resultant financial reverses. Thus, our sample may be considered one that was at high risk for stress but happened to be experiencing relatively low stress levels at the time of recruitment.

4. These highly resilient families had certain demographic characteristics which distinguished them from the other families in the sample as well: they had more children, they had at least one child younger than the focal child, and they were more likely to be recent immigrants.

than, for example, "stressed families" precisely because our findings suggest that differences stemmed more from families' resources for coping with stress than from the amount of stress they experienced.

Despite the absence of strong relationships between familial stress and literacy, more subtle indicators of the robustness of family functioning—such as the ability to set rules, to get children to school on time, to keep appointments, to keep the house fairly neat and organized, and to organize a variety of after-school activities for children—did relate strongly to our measure of writing ability.[5]

It is important to explore why the variables reflecting emotional and organizational dimensions of family life related so strongly to writing whereas their relationship to other components of literacy was negligible.[6] Vocabulary and word recognition were, for example, strongly influenced by cognitive aspects of family life but not by affective characteristics of the family's functioning. Why do writing and these other components of literacy respond so differently to family influences?

Of all our literacy measures, writing was the one in which performing well was most likely to be affected by the child's self-confidence, initiative, and organizational ability. Our reading tests were similar to tasks children had undertaken many times before at school, as tests and as exercises. The children knew the rules for doing well on such tests. The task of sitting down to write an essay or story was, in contrast, relatively unfamiliar to most of these

5. These relationships were even stronger for the fourth grade children than for the other two groups of children in the study; for the fourth grade sample alone we found significant correlations between word production and the degree of organization and cleanliness in the family's physical environment, the predictability of family rules and schedules, the family's emotional stability, and the father's reliability in appointment keeping. The extreme power of the Resilient Family model at fourth grade suggests that this is an age at which writing skill is particularly susceptible to family influences.

6. The possibility must be explored that this relationship was specific to our measure of writing—number of words produced in each of the two writing samples. Number of words produced may seem an unacceptably crude measure of writing skill; in fact, at least for this sample of children, it correlated highly (.84) with holistic ratings, the writing measure with the greatest face validity, as well as with measures of the sophistication of the vocabulary used (see Jacobs, 1986).

children and therefore one which strained their initiative more severely. (As will be discussed later in this chapter, the children did very little writing in school.) We might recall here Scarr's (1981) statement that "whenever one measures a child's cognitive functioning, one is also measuring cooperation, attention, persistence, ability to sit still, and social responsiveness to an assessment situation" (p. 1161). "Social responsiveness," "persistence," and "cooperation" become particularly important in a task the child views as challenging and novel. In such a task, the personality characteristics fostered by a resilient family may emerge as particularly important determinants of success.

A frequently cited characteristic of good writers is the sense that they "have something to say." In fact, many criticisms of traditional writing instruction point out that the red-pencil approach with its emphasis on neatness, spelling, and formal correctness deflects the teacher's attention from the child's message and therefore discourages young writers (Birnbaum, 1980; Shaughnessy, 1977). Furthermore, basic adult writers (Shaughnessy, 1977) and working class children (Britton et al., 1975) have been shown to produce shorter texts precisely to avoid negative evaluations by teachers. Recent approaches to teaching writing stress the centrality of letting children express their own ideas about matters familiar to them, and responding at least initially to the content rather than to the form of their writings, in order to strengthen their sense of themselves as writers with a message (Graves, 1982, for example). It seemed to us that many of the Norwich children were afflicted by the sense that they had little to say—a fact which would account for the brevity of the average essay (24 words in second grade, 67 in fourth, and 48 in sixth). The children were relatively strong on content but weak on form in their writing samples, a finding which might seem to conflict with the notion that the children had nothing to say. In fact, though, we do not see any conflict; the children did have good ideas which emerged when they were induced to write. They did not have any confidence in the value of their own ideas, and had not typically experienced instruction which revealed to them their strengths as writers with something to say. During the writing task, many of the children chewed their pencils, stared into space, wrote a few words, then erased them to start again. It may be that children in the resilient homes with more nurturant parents and more opportunities for enjoyable activities had a stronger sense that they had something to say. This interpretation is supported by the finding that children who had more to say in their essays also engaged in more activities outside school (they had more interesting lives about which to write) and by the fact that the children who wrote longer entries in their diaries had interactions with their parents during the diary task that were rated as more positive and pleasant (r = .39, p < .06). Resilient families may thus strengthen their children's sense that they have something to say in at least two ways: by giving them a chance to engage in more activities, so they do in fact have more to write about, and by giving them the sense that what they say or write is interesting and worth attending to.

A final hypothesis about the better writing performance of the children from more resilient families focuses on the unstructured nature of the writing task: the children were given a topic and ten minutes to write about it. Children who were not used to organizing their time to meet their goals were unlikely to write much in the time given. It may be that children from more scheduled and orderly home environments are better able, like their parents, to set goals and meet them in the time allotted, a crucial component of success in writing (Flower and Hayes, 1980).

We suggest then, that the children's own ability to plan, their self-confidence in the face of a novel task, and their sense that they had something to say may have been fostered by resilient family environments and may have resulted in more and better writing. We feel it makes good sense that the resilient family has its greatest effect on children's writing—particularly in Norwich, where writing received so little instructional attention in the schools. In the absence of much direct writing instruction, the aspect of the essays that distinguished among children was their length rather than their correctness or their quality, and the factors determining length were primarily affective rather than cognitive.

In order to give a sense of how the many variables that go into the resilient family relate to each other and to writing, we present here case histories of two children and their families. Beth Gallagher was a sixth grader from one of the most emotionally stable and well-organized families in the sample. Second grader Lisa Palmieri's family contrasted with Beth's on several dimensions, including physical environment, family emotional stability, and presence of rules and schedules. These two families illustrate the range of our sample on measures of stress, organization, and intrafamilial conflict.

The Gallagher Family

The Gallaghers were one of the families who best exemplified our Resilient Family model. Mr. and Mrs. Gallagher created for Beth and her four siblings an emotionally supportive, stable, orderly, and predictable environment—one in which there were high standards for the children's social behavior. Although this family of seven was financially stressed, especially after Mr. Gallagher became ill and had to stop working during the second year of our study, the Gallagher's limited resources were frequently directed toward providing activities for the children which were educationally enriching and fun.

Seven people lived in the Gallaghers' tiny but very neat house. The television set was the most prominent feature of the living room, and Mrs. Gallagher's sewing machine and craft materials were tucked into one corner of the dining room. Throughout the downstairs rooms there were small plaques with Irish sayings, such as "May the road rise to meet you, health and long life to you, land without rent to you, a child every year to you, and may you die in Ireland." The downstairs was nicely, albeit sparsely and modestly furnished, in marked contrast to the upstairs bedrooms and bath which were rather barren and cramped. Beth, age thirteen, shared a tiny bedroom with her sister, Margaret, fourteen. Her two younger brothers, Timothy, twelve, and Patrick, eleven, also shared a bedroom, while her older brother, Michael, sixteen, had his own room. The garden, Mrs. Gallagher's special joy, was beautifully tended, with constantly changing displays of flowers, in contrast to the exterior of the house, which badly needed painting. All the children helped with the planting and weeding. At the time he became ill, Mr. Gallagher was in his twentieth year as a municipal bus driver, and Mrs. Gallagher had worked the night shift as a supervisor in a nursing home for seven years, so that one of them could be home with the children all the time. Despite both working full-time, the Gallaghers were not able to afford everything they needed. Mrs. Gallagher told us that it had gotten harder to pay bills over the previous few years. The children had participated in many more extracurricular activities a few years earlier, until inflation hit them. Beth, for example, had taken guitar and gymnastics lessons and had participated in the school band, but she had to stop these activities because "they just got to be too much money."

Organization in the Gallagher family was exemplified by the ease with which family members could be interviewed by the researchers on our project. Despite their busy school and work schedules, the Gallagher family was receptive to our research project. They were consistently reliable in keeping appointments with us. Mrs. Gallagher skillfully orchestrated the comings and goings of the children to ensure privacy and cooperation during our interviews. She was a friendly, warm person, who welcomed us graciously each time we visited. After her husband fell ill, the eldest son, Michael, took on additional family responsibilities, working after school and supervising the younger children in the evening. "I sit in dad's chair and let them have TV until 9:00 P.M.," he told us.

Religion was important in this family. Everyone attended church every Sunday, and Beth attended confirmation classes during the week. Mrs. Gallagher belonged to the Women's Sodality, although her work schedule didn't allow her to be as active as she would have liked. Mrs. Gallagher told us she believed that in Sunday School the children were learning about compassion and how to get along better.

In keeping with this emphasis on appropriate social behavior, there were certain things that the children were and were not allowed to do in the Gallagher household. Observers felt that the rules and expectations in the household were clear, and that there was some flexibility in schedules. For example, Mrs. Gallagher expected the children to "occupy themselves quietly because the house is so small," to do chores, and to visit with their grandmother, who lived down the street. Although the children frequently squabbled over which TV shows to watch, they knew that their mother would turn off the TV if the arguing got out of hand. The children were expected to keep their possessions in their rooms and to play in the basement, which had recently been fixed up for them.

Mrs. Gallagher believed that a great deal of sibling rivalry resulted from the closeness in age of the five children; Beth in particular had to "fight for her own place in the family." When Beth was three or four, Mrs. Gallagher took her to the local mental health clinic because she was concerned about Beth's nail biting and competitiveness and the general rivalry among the children. Mrs. Gallagher described Beth at thirteen as temperamental and sensitive. Her brothers teased her a lot, and this still caused some problems and tensions for Beth.

Beth had a good relationship with both her parents. She felt that she could talk with them about things that were important to her, and that they helped her best with problems and worries. Beth went on errands with her father and frequently joked with him about her favorite soap opera characters and episodes. Beth was particularly close to her mother, who felt that Beth "doesn't hold in like the other kids" (Mrs. Gallagher's sensitivity to Beth may have been due to Mrs. Gallagher's being the "middle child" in her own family). Beth shared her mother's interest in sewing and doing craft projects and frequently would come and talk to her while she was engaged in these activities. Beth's good relationship with her parents may have contributed to her style of interaction with other adults. One member of our research group described her as self-composed, comfortable, and displaying a good sense of humor. And Beth's teacher said, "It is a pleasure to have Beth in class."

Beth watched less television than many of the children in our study, although she watched the soap opera "General Hospital" with her sister every afternoon. Two of Beth's favorite television shows—"Nancy Drew" and "Love Boat"—influenced her career aspirations: she said she'd like to be a detective or cruise ship director. Although Mr. and Mrs. Gallagher did not restrict the amount of television the children watched up until bedtime, they did restrict the kind of programs. Mrs. Gallagher expressed concern about Beth and Margaret baby-sitting at houses with Home Box Office television because this could expose them to "dirty movies."

Beth's school diary, kept for our study over a four-day period, indicated that her afternoons and evenings were filled with a wide variety of activities other than watching television: doing chores at home and for her grandmother; attending religious education classes; going shopping, to sports events, and to the library with friends; doing errands for her parents; listening to the radio; talking on the telephone; reading; and doing homework.

Mr. and Mrs. Gallagher set high standards for their children's school behavior as well as for their behavior at home. The parents expected their children to attend school regularly and get to school on time. Beth told us she was hardly ever late to school and was allowed to miss school only when she was sick or "for something real special, like when the President visited town." The children were also expected to get along with their classmates and to receive good marks for effort. Mrs. Gallagher told us, "I look at the effort mark. If the effort is good, that's what I care about." Despite her emphasis on effort, Mrs. Gallagher was proud of the fact that four of her children, including Beth, had been on the honor roll the previous year. She hoped that all her children would go through college.

Mrs. Gallagher tried to encourage Beth's and her siblings' interest in reading and writing. She had recently bought Beth *Little Women,* which became Beth's favorite book. Mrs. Gallagher said that she concentrated on buying books and toys for the children that would bring out their interests—"each thing I buy has a reason." Mrs. Gallagher herself was an avid reader. She talked in greater detail about favorite books and authors than any other mother we interviewed and said she regularly read all the magazines delivered to the nursing home, such as *People, Family Circle,* and *Ladies' Home Journal.* Mr. Gallagher regularly read the local newspaper, *Newsweek* magazine, and sports magazines, and on occasion mystery books. During several of our visits at their house, he asked one of the children to get his evening paper at the corner store.

The Gallaghers' high level of interest in school success and concern that their children show effort and good behavior in school no doubt encouraged their children to do well. Their sense of commitment to their children shone through in their conversations and was clear in their allocation of the family's scarce resources. Nonetheless, because they had not attended any parent-teacher nights, one of Beth's seventh-grade teachers thought the Gallaghers were fairly indifferent to Beth's schooling and were hard to establish contact with. Mrs. Gallagher, however, specifically said that she had "not gone up to meet the teachers this past year because the children were all on the honor roll." The Gallaghers felt that all was going well with Beth and they didn't need to intervene with her teachers. It would have been difficult for them to attend evening PTA meetings because Mr. Gallagher needed to stay home with the children while Mrs. Gallagher worked. But the year before, when Beth had been doing somewhat less well, Mrs. Gallagher had gone to the class meetings and the teacher singled out "support from home" as a factor in Beth's improved school-work that year.

Beth Gallagher at school. Beth made a strong start in school, finishing the first grade with reading achievement test scores a full year above grade level. In first grade she had one of the strongest primary teachers we observed, and, as many of her upper-grade teachers commented, the reputation of her bright and mannerly older siblings preceded her.

Beth's attendance record was good throughout her elementary school years, and teachers described her on report cards as "cooperative" and "a good worker." Although her reading scores were consistently above grade level, she characteristically earned B's, only an average mark at the Hurley School. Some middle-grade teachers wrote comments suggesting that Beth needed to try harder or to "apply herself" more, but Beth's teachers generally saw her as a competent, pleasant child.

Like most of the classrooms at Hurley, Beth's sixth grade room was organized traditionally. Basal series and skill workbooks dominated the reading curriculum. Oral round-robin reading was a popular approach used to organize children's attention in math and social studies as well as reading lessons. Few resources beyond subject area texts and workbooks were available for student use, although the class made biweekly visits to a nearby public library branch.

Mrs. Poulin, Beth's sixth grade teacher, described her as a "real plugger," "eager," and "anxious to please." Although Mrs. Poulin spoke very positively of the Gallaghers' commitment to education, and although Beth was in the top reading group, Mrs. Poulin only expected Beth to complete high school.

Academic standards seemed modest in Mrs. Poulin's room.

Homework was assigned three times a week and typically consisted of simple computation problems in math workbooks. Although Mrs. Poulin said she had assigned written research reports earlier in the year, the only written work we observed involved composing sentences for spelling words and copying definitions from the dictionary.

Observers described the atmosphere in this sixth grade room as "family-like," with lots of warm informal give-and-take between Mrs. Poulin and the children. Beth's time was usually pleasantly occupied, but we rarely saw her challenged academically.

In seventh grade Beth's schedule was broken into subject area blocks, with separate teachers for math, social studies, English, and reading. As in sixth grade, lessons frequently seemed organized so as to simplify the task of maintaining order and attention. We saw a social studies lesson that mainly involved copying long lists of questions (such as, "What is Grand Rapids known for?") from the blackboard into notebooks. An English lesson similarly revolved around copying from the blackboard, this time a letter with labeled parts (salutation, heading, and so on). Another social studies lesson had the children label midwestern state and city names on dittoed outline maps, using student atlases as sources of the information. As in sixth grade, Beth was not assigned any composition writing while observers were present except for the typical homework assignment of looking up words in the dictionary and composing sentences using them.

Beth's reading teacher said she tried assigning longer written homework but abandoned it because "the quality of the work returned was poor." This teacher, Mrs. Tagliaferro, occasionally conducted lessons involving creative writing; for example, we saw student collages with accompanying poems posted in her classroom. Although she was pleased with the results of this work, Mrs. Tagliaferro used class time for writing only once a month or so. Her reading lessons were built around round-robin reading from a text series of literature excerpts geared for "slow" seventh and eighth graders. Although Beth seemed to enjoy the selections and Mrs. Tagliaferro was gifted at drawing out and expanding on children's responses, the passages were written at a level several years below Beth's competence, and the content rarely extended beyond the everyday life of young adolescents.

Beth's seventh grade teachers called her "quiet" and "orderly," but some worried that she was too shy, failing to volunteer even when she "knew the answers." In spite of the fact that Beth's literacy skills were better than her classmates' and than national norms at the end of seventh grade, her seventh grade teachers—like her sixth grade teacher—did not expect her to go to college. It was typical for teachers of the older girls in our study to have low educational expectations for them.

Beth's literacy skills were strongest in the areas that were emphasized in her school and weakest in the areas that her school gave little attention to. Relative to her classmates, she was an excellent reader; her scores at the end of sixth grade were a year above grade level, and her scores at the end of seventh grade were two years above grade level. During the two years of our study Beth made her strongest gains in word recognition and oral reading. She showed less growth on tests of silent comprehension, spelling, and word meaning.

Many classes in Beth's school had relatively little success—as compared to others in our sample—in developing students' reading comprehension and vocabulary. Beth's sixth and seventh grade classes provided sufficient structured practice for progress in word recognition and oral reading but lacked the enriching or stimulating activities associated with word meaning and comprehension growth. In Beth's seventh grade class, for example, the approach to developing vocabulary was limited largely to having students look up the words in a dictionary, write them in a sentence, and be quizzed on them. Similarly, efforts at promoting students' reading comprehension were too often limited to having them answer literal comprehension questions in their textbooks.

Beth's writing was above average compared to other sixth and seventh graders in our study but weak in relation to national samples (National Assessment of Educational Progress, 1985). She produced more words on both her narrative and expository samples than the average sixth and seventh grader in our study, and was at or above grade average on each of the other ratings made of her narrative samples:

Sixth Grade: Tomato Lady. There was a lady who came from the super market. She bought some tomatos. She feels like someone is going to sneak up behind her and rob or do something to tomatos, She's nervous because she feels she paid alot of money for her tomatos and she doesn't like to waist money on something she's not going to eat or use.

Seventh Grade: Tomato Lady. She's holding the tomatoes and showing them to someone, asking if there ripe enough. She's arguing with the person. She says she wants them for half price, but she cant so shes very mad. The person is saying "buy them at full price, or dont buy them at all." The Lady doesn't have enough money, so she's not going to buy them, but she does say she needs them for her recipe. She put something else back and finaly bought the tomatos at half price.

Beth made special gains, relative to her classmates, in expository writing.

Sixth Grade: Who do you admire? Her name is Angie Takis she's my best friend in the class. When I get mad at her sometimes she says sorry write away she's very nice and she's not selfish, or rude to me. we've stayed friends along time. We've never had a big fight or quarrel because were nice to each other. I've got other friends but she's probaly one of the nicest persons I've ever met.

Seventh Grade: Who do you admire? The people I most look up to are my parents. Because they work for me to support me. they're very caring for al of us, my three brothers, and my sister. Both of my parents work for us to feed us and buy us the things we want. I love my parents because they help other people out too. My father is a nor. bus driver and my mother works in a nursing home. So besides me, they take care of other people too. so the people I most look up to are my parents.

As noted above, since the instruction in writing in most of the classrooms we observed was so infrequent, the home environment may have played an important role in a student's relative success in writing. Writing is valued in Beth's family, and she has been encouraged by her mother to be creative. Asked to think about a time Beth did something that pleased her a great deal, Mrs. Gallagher responded, "when she started making her own cards for Mother's Day and Christmas."

The Palmieri Family

The Palmieris lived in one-half of a two-family house, owned by Mr. Palmieri's mother, who lived next door. The house was located a few blocks away from the Righetti Field housing project in a low-income area. The house was in poor condition, both inside and out. It was not surprising that the house had such a lived-in look since many family members and friends circulated through the modest space at all times. Lisa's immediate family consisted of her parents, both twenty-eight years old, and an older sister, Cheryl, eleven. During our study, Mrs. Palmieri's sister and two cousins lived with the family for five months, after being evicted from their own apartment. In addition, a number of other cousins and teenage members of the hockey team that Mr. Palmieri coached frequently spent time there, watching television or just "hanging out."

Mr. Palmieri painted a rosy picture of family life, but Mrs. Palmieri sketched a much less blissful portrait, noting marital difficulties and offering a considerably lower family-income estimate than did her husband. She referred to her marriage as a source of stress, detailing three separations in the past three years. Some conflicts also seem to have precipitated from disagreements with in-laws. According to Mrs. Palmieri, a few members of her family disapproved of her husband and his lifestyle.

Lisa watched a great deal of television, not surprising in a household where much of the activity revolved around television viewing. Mrs. Palmieri commented that "95 percent of the time my husband is home, he's in the parlor with the TV." Lisa's school diary indicated that watching television was the only thing she did between coming home from school and going to bed on three days out of four. Asked if Lisa played games with her sister, cousins, or friends, Mrs. Palmieri responded: "Only if we can get them away from TV." During one of our home visits, two television sets were on constantly; several children watched in the bedroom while seven or eight adults viewed a basketball game on the parlor set. A kettle of macaroni was left on the stove, and during commercials people helped themselves to food in the kitchen.

There were some rules in the Palmieri household, but they were easily transgressed and schedules were unpredictable. According to Mr. Palmieri, there was some regulation of the children's television viewing; yet when asked how the rules were enforced, he responded, "I never check, my wife does." Although Mr. Palmieri said that the children had strict bedtimes, Mrs. Palmieri said her husband let the children go to bed whenever they wanted. During one of our home visits on a weekday night, nine-year-old Lisa, her sister, and preschool-age cousins were still up at 10:30 watching television, and none of the adults seemed aware or concerned about what program they were watching.

Lisa probably did not receive at home the level of emotional support and encouragement necessary to facilitate her willingness to persevere and take risks in a demanding task like writing. During our home visits we observed Lisa's parents teasing her in a generally playful, but still rather negative way. For example, during one home visit Mrs. Palmieri said to the observers, "I'd offer you some Hawaiian punch but I can't guarantee anything about it because Lisa made it." Mrs. Palmieri belittled and slapped Lisa during the homework-like writing task we created. She commented laughingly on how Lisa had filled in the first page of the form, "Boy, I've got to give the people credit who are going to read that!" Ultimately Lisa left the room in tears because of her mother's behavior.

Lisa and her sister evidently received little if any academic support from their parents. Mr. Palmieri, who regarded himself as the class clown when he was in school, left school in the ninth grade to begin working. He described his current job as a vinyl-siding installer as "the best job I've ever had," in part because the seasonal demands of the work enabled him to spend time coaching a hockey team, which he enjoyed. Mrs. Palmieri left high school after her sophomore year. She worked off and on after that, and had worked full-time for the previous four years on the production line in a candy factory.

Both Mr. and Mrs. Palmieri described Lisa, the youngest family member, as the most avid reader in their household. Mr. Palmieri read only the sports page of the newspaper. When asked about her reading habits, Mrs. Palmieri commented, "I'm not crazy about it. I read when I have to," adding, "I hate to write; I'd rather call." Some children's books were haphazardly jammed into a small chest next to Mr. Palmieri's weight-lifting equipment in the room designated by the family as the toyroom. According to her parents, Lisa enjoyed school and generally worked hard, usually bringing home better report cards than her older sister, Cheryl. The Palmieris did not have concerns about Lisa's schoolwork, although reports from the school suggested that some greater level of concern might have been appropriate.

Lisa Palmieri at school. Lisa had a difficult start in school. The Palmieris chose not to enroll her in kindergarten, and Lisa's first grade year was marked by frequent absences and problems adjusting to the demands of the curriculum. Lisa had a string of recurring ear infections that year, leading the school nurse to investigate possible hearing problems (none was diagnosed), and her troubles mastering the basics of decoding words resulted in a special education evaluation. She was classified as learning disabled and received extra help in phonics from a tutor three hours a week. Despite this help Lisa scored close to half a year below grade level on the school's standardized reading tests at the end of first grade.

In second grade, Lisa was assigned to Mrs. Tierney's class along with a large and rambunctious group of seven-year-olds, many of them with reading problems. The combination of a larger than normal class and massive cuts in the school system's budget had a demoralizing effect on this teacher. Funds for an instructional aide to help with reading groups were eliminated; money for field trips, library helpers, and pull-out classes in science, art, and music (which provided planning periods for the teacher) was cut. Mrs. Tierney herself received a warning of layoff notice early in the year and began taking night classes to prepare for a new career as an accountant.

With adequate support services Mrs. Tierney might have been able to help Lisa and her classmates through a good second grade year. Without them, classroom organization collapsed quickly and days in Mrs. Tierney's room were somewhat chaotic. Reading classes rarely lasted more than fifteen minutes. A reading lesson we observed with Lisa and the other members of Mrs. Tierney's bottom group was continually interrupted by squabbles breaking out elsewhere in the room, loud chatter, and demands for the teacher's help. Lisa lost her place in the reader repeatedly and finally gave up trying to participate in the lesson. Lisa's reading group spent the whole year completing the reader designed for the first half of second grade.

Higher standards may have governed Mrs. Tierney's room in the past; she apologized to observers for the general barrenness of the classroom, explaining that she hadn't felt motivated to display children's work or collect trade books or resource materials this year. The only literacy materials available in the classroom were texts in reading, math, language, and spelling, some rarely used science and social studies texts, workbooks, and a few commercial seasonal wall displays. Writing activity in Mrs. Tierney's class was limited to having children occasionally compose sentences with spelling words. The students had no homework, and class exercises typically involved circling, checking, coloring, or connecting lines in workbooks.

By the end of second grade, Lisa scored at about grade level in word recognition; continued pull-out tutoring and Mrs. Tierney's emphasis on this area of literacy both may have helped. In reading comprehension and vocabulary, Lisa was still a half-year or more below grade level. Mrs. Tierney saw Lisa as a child with low skills whose family showed little support for her school success. For example, when Lisa's glasses were broken, they were not replaced for several weeks. In addition, she was often sleepy in school, having stayed up too late the previous night.

Lisa was assigned to Mrs. Randolph's class for third grade. As described in Chapter 2, Mrs. Randolph was a highly competent traditional teacher. She often made activities into games or routines; for example, she led the class in reciting their multiplication tables while doing stylized calisthenics in unison, touching shoulder, waist, knees, and toes. Children were expected to work quietly and independently on seatwork and then file their exercises in different envelopes marked language," "spelling," "phonics," and so on.

Although the range of literacy materials in Mrs. Randolph's room was not much wider than in Mrs. Tierney's room, the room was cheerful and orderly with well-tended houseplants and constantly changing colorful wall displays. Reading-group lessons closely followed the script provided by the basal series' teacher's manual but Mrs. Randolph also created occasions for children to relate their own experiences relevant to new vocabulary or episodes in the texts. The partial restoration of funds for library services meant that Lisa and her classmates now had a weekly library visit. Mrs. Randolph assigned short creative-writing pieces every week, typically using commercial story starters.

In the secure and predictable environment of Mrs. Randolph's room, Lisa blossomed. She improved in word recognition, reading comprehension, and vocabulary by at least two grade levels. Lisa herself was a determined, task-oriented student, interested in reading, so she was able to take full advantage of Mrs. Randolph's structured classroom environment. At the end of the third grade, Mrs. Randolph described Lisa as a child who "needs to be encouraged to answer" in recitation or conversation. She saw Lisa as a "quiet, well-organized self-starter" who "opened up" during the year in her room. She predicted Lisa would graduate from high school.

Despite her interest in reading and her adequate performance as a reader, Lisa's writing was less skilled than that of most second and third graders we tested.

Second Grade: Tomato Lady.
Shes going to open it
Shes holding it up
Shes at a store and shes going to by it
shes going home and eating it

Third Grade: Tomato Lady. She has some tomatoes. And then shes going to open them and then she going to make her supper and then when there done shes going to eat the supper and then wash up and go and watch tv and then put her nighties on and go to bed.

Second Grade: Who do you admire?
God is special to us
God loves us
God is our farther

Third Grade: Who do you admire? I would like to admire Jane Fonda. on Golden Pond. because she is a good actor and shes very pretty and she seems like a good person. I would love to be her.

Influences on Writing Skills

The role of the classroom. More than reading, writing is affected by self-confidence and willingness to try, both by its very nature and by virtue of the tests available to measure it. Writing is also quite different from reading in terms of how it is dealt with in these Norwich schools. Every classroom we observed had regularly scheduled reading lessons, of no less than fifteen minutes per day, with thirty minutes per day being more typical; in contrast, formal teaching of writing was hardly ever observed. Nor was writing a significant part of other school activities. Aside from frequent "quasi-writing" activities—filling in blanks, circling the right answer on a worksheet, writing word or phrase answers to literal comprehension questions, or copying from the board—very little writing of any sort was done, except for composing sentences with spelling words. In fact, in only 5 out of 36 classrooms observed over the two-year period did we see any writing of texts longer than a sentence—this despite the representation of fifth, sixth, and seventh grade classrooms in our sample.

The most common sorts of writing assignments teachers reported giving were paragraphs and sentences. The *least* common types of assignments mentioned were book reports, essays, and journals. Not surprisingly, gains in the children's writing ability, both in length of passage produced and in holistic ratings of their quality, showed a clear relationship to the types of writing they practiced in school. Children whose teachers only mentioned assigning paragraphs or sentences showed little improvement across the two years of our study, while those children who had experience with reports, narratives, and other longer forms showed substantial gains. Similarly, children who did *written* homework, even short answers to questions about a textbook passage, for example, also made greater progress on our measures of writing ability than children who did homework limited to fill-in-the-blanks worksheets.

In our interviews with the children, we asked them how often they wrote at school; there was a significant correlation between the children's reported frequency of in-school writing and their writing production scores, confirming our hypothesis that opportunity to engage in writing in school has a major impact on children's writing ability.

Writing outside school. The everyday activities of the children in our sample provided them with relatively few opportunities to practice or to learn writing skills. We asked the mothers and the children themselves how often the children wrote letters, shopping lists, notes, stories, or other things "just for fun." Although many children engaged in what Fiering (1981) calls "unofficial writing" during the school day (for example, drawing and captioning cartoon strips, passing notes, composing love poems, recording pop song lyrics), these informal sorts of writing only occasionally took place outside school, rarely occurring when observers were present in the children's homes and mentioned infrequently in the diaries we had the children keep of one week's activities.

We suspect that the homes of many of the children were simply not places where written communication among family members or friends was customary or expected; within the often bleak but literate climate of the classroom, children expressed themselves in unofficial writing because writing was a sanctioned activity. Kevin Shea, a second grader with weak reading skills and a strong interest in fantasy, spent a phonics lesson surreptitiously drawing a picture of a superhero in a notebook and composing a detailed story to accompany his drawing. Although Kevin would have been punished by the teacher if he had been caught during this activity, his choice of writing was less likely to attract notice than the other sorts of play activities he might have engaged in. At home, where Kevin had a much freer choice of activities—television, active play outside with his younger brothers, Little League—and where no one around him engaged in writing regularly, he was less likely to write for fun.

Although almost 80 percent of the children were reported by their mothers to engage in some writing activity at home at least once a week, the most frequently reported activities were things like making up shopping lists and taking telephone messages, not writing letters or keeping diaries. While these writing activities might involve some challenge and some useful practice for the youngest children in the sample, they are not activities that contribute to text-level writing skills—maintaining cohesion, using revision, adhering to an organizational structure, or exploiting rhetorical devices. Thus, we were not surprised to find no relationship between this kind of informal writing practice and children's actual levels of writing skill.

The very low incidence of formal instruction in writing we saw taking place in school is disheartening. Only 3 of the 32 teachers in our study actually offered direct help with composing while observers were present. It seems, then, that the craft of writing descriptions, stories, explanations, and arguments is one which low-income Norwich children have little chance to learn, at least during their years at elementary school. It was precisely the craftsman's skills that were so notably missing in the writing samples we elicited from the children—knowledge of how to organize a paragraph, how to punctuate, how to read over a text and correct it. These are skills that do not just develop—they must be taught. Once taught, they must also be practiced.

Although the children could, and some did, provide their own opportunities for practice through in-school unofficial writing or by choosing out-of-school writing activities, they could not practice skills they had not acquired. Since neither the technical skills (such as punctuation and indentation) nor the skills of organization (revision and rhetoric) were being taught in Norwich, either by teachers in classrooms or by parents at home, children ended up differentiating themselves in writing tasks primarily by how much they had to say, and how confidently they approached the task of saying it. These variables were, in turn, affected by home factors that gave children self-confidence, the ability to plan, and the sense that their own thoughts were worth writing down.

The families that produced good writers were not different from those that produced poor writers in the value they placed on education, nor in the level of intellectual stimulation they offered. Rather, the major differences were in the degree of organization in the home and the degree to which the parent-child relationship was seen as affectively positive. Some families, those we have labeled "resilient," achieved both a high level of organization and positive affective relations within the family despite financial and psychological stress. Other families showed relatively low levels of organization and relatively negative interaction even in the absence of high levels of financial or social stress. It seems likely that the effect of the Resilient Family model on writing was especially strong in this community because writing was relatively neglected in Norwich schools.[7] Thus, the differences in children's abilities to perform created by their experiences in a resilient or a nonresilient family became large and important.

7. It should be noted that, after the completion of this study, the Norwich school system greatly increased attention to writing instruction in its classrooms. The system provided in-service training to teachers about writing instruction and put emphasis on writing as an outcome measure of importance in evaluating student progress. As a result, the quality of writing instruction and the amount of writing done in Norwich classrooms increased dramatically.

~ Chapter 6 ~

Parent-School Partnership

We have seen that cognitive factors in the home, idealized in the Family as Educator model, predict children's vocabulary and word recognition, whereas emotional factors, idealized in our Resilient Family model, relate to children's writing. Another hypothesis for the ways in which families can contribute to their children's academic achievement is that they form a partnership with the school. Research has consistently documented the importance for student achievement of family "involvement" (Epstein, 1983, 1986, 1988; Epstein and McPartland, 1979; Leichter, 1974; Lightfoot, 1978; Marjoribanks, 1979; McDill and Rigsby, 1973; Tangri and Moles, in press; Walberg, 1984). Parental involvement has been assumed to be an area where middle-class families have an advantage, in part because they are more aware of their rights and of the services (such as special educational help or enrichment programs) available to their children. In addition, they may be more effective advocates for the special help or changes they request because they are more skilled in writing letters, analyzing budgets, making arguments, marshaling support, or other such political and persuasive actions. Finally, middle-class parents may be more successful advocates for their children because of their greater credibility (in comparison to that of poorer parents) with the schools' gatekeepers and power brokers.

As children get older, they spend increasingly less time with their parents but a constant thirty hours a week in school. During the later elementary years, parental contributions to school achievement may be most efficiently mediated through parents' impact on the school as an institution, and their support at home of school-initiated learning activities, rather than, as may be the case for younger children, by direct parental teaching or modeling.

The Parent-School Partnership model attempts to test the notion that parents who take action to support the school's efforts are more successful in promoting their children's literacy achievement than those who do not. We identified the following variables as relevant to this model:

1. Formal parent-school involvement. Parental involvement with the school—by joining organizations such as the PTA, attending school concerts and other special programs, serving as volunteer classroom aide, or accompanying the class on trips and outings— reflects an attitude on the part of the parent that schools should be supported and improved. Whether or not such involvement is effective in actually changing schools, it may signal to the child that school achievement is important and worth working at. It may also affect teacher assessment of the family and teacher expectations for the child's performance.

2. Contacts with teachers. At the more micro-level of the child's classroom, frequency of contacts between parents and teachers may be a significant indicator of the parental partner role. Contacting teachers is a way of monitoring one's child's academic progress—being sure that all is going well, or finding out early if problems arise. Initiating contacts or responding promptly to teacher-initiated contacts may signal to teachers that parents are interested in their children's achievement, and may also enable teachers to recruit early and effective parental help for children.

3. Homework help. Parents who provide help with their children's homework exemplify the partnership model in two ways: they support the kind of learning that goes on at school and they inform themselves about the child's school experiences. Availability of help with homework also implies a sense of parental responsibility to see that homework is completed and turned in—a factor which, we will see later in this chapter, carries an important message to teachers.

4. Nature of parent-child interaction. Providing help with homework may not always make a positive contribution to children's school achievement, however. Parents can make homework an unpleasant or unproductive experience for children, by nag-

ging about it, failing to help constructively, or using homework as an occasion for recrimination. Other researchers' analyses of "homework scenes" have suggested that there can be much miscommunication and negative affect during parent-child interactions over homework (McDermott, Goldman, and Varenne, 1984). In order to assess the affect associated with homework help in our sample, we observed parent-child interaction during our homework-like task of filling in a diary.

5. School punctuality. One of the most basic contributions parents can make to the partnership is ensuring their children's attendance and punctuality. Most of the children in our study reported that they missed school only when sick or in unusual circumstances. Unlike attendance patterns, which showed little variation across children, there was a considerable range in how punctually the children in our sample arrived at school. Therefore we decided to use punctuality rather than attendance as a variable in the Parent-School Partnership model. Children who arrived late not only missed some instructional time, but may well have engendered lowered expectations and negative attitudes from their teachers.

Testing the Parent-School Partnership Model

The model was tested for its ability to explain variance on four measures of language and literacy: word recognition, vocabulary, writing production, and reading comprehension. We have seen that other models explain significant amounts of the variance on the first three of these. Of course this does not exclude the possibility that the Parent-School Partnership model might also have considerable explanatory force.

In fact, the model explained respectable amounts of variance on all four outcome measures: 21 percent of the variance on reading comprehension, 32 percent on both word recognition and writing, and 38 percent on vocabulary. These results suggest that parents who assume a partnership role with the school can simultaneously enhance several aspects of their children's literacy achievement across the board.

The single variable that showed up as significantly correlated with all four literacy outcome measures was formal parent-school

Table 6.1 Simple correlations between variables of the "Parent as Partner" model and literacy outcome measures

Variable	Word recognition	Reading comprehension	Vocabulary	Writing production
Parent-school involvement	.26	.32[a]	.33[a]	.30[a]
Contacts with teacher	−.32[a]	.03	.15	.03
Homework help	.15	−.09	.17	.00
Parent-child interaction	.19	.12	.19	.37[a]
School punctuality	.00	−.05	−.36[a]	.30[a]

a. $p < .05$

involvement (see Table 6.1). The widespread effect of parent-school involvement raises the important question of how parental involvement influences children's achievement. Perhaps parental involvement taught the parents something about the school environment so they could prepare their children more effectively for success. Seeing their parents' involvement with the schools may have convinced children that school was worth their own commitment. Or perhaps parental involvement enhanced children's chances in their teachers' eyes, thus making the children "good bets" for extra help, high standards, and raised expectations—beneficiaries of the well-known Pygmalion effect (Rosenthal and Jacobson, 1984). Whatever the explanation, all the aspects of literacy we tested were susceptible to the influence of parental involvement with schools (see Hewison and Tizard, 1980, for related findings).

Neither frequency of contact between parents and teachers nor frequency of parental help with children's homework was significantly related to children's achievement on any of our four literacy measures. However, we will see later in this chapter how both variables were associated with teachers' assessments of the contribution of the home to children's school success and with teachers' expectations for the children's future educational level, and how these two factors were, in turn, associated with children's gains in reading comprehension.

The nature of parent-child interaction over homework—how

affectively positive or negative it was—related only to children's scores on our measure of writing (as noted in the previous chapter). The effect of the parent-child interaction variable may have more to do with the emotional climate of the home than with parent-school partnership. Similarly, children's punctuality was positively related only to writing, indicating this variable may be less an index of instructional time than of parental attitude toward school or of organization in the home. Regularity of attendance, by contrast, was associated with gains in word recognition.

In addition to those variables which seemed most directly related to children's scores on our outcome measures, and which were therefore included in our formal model of the parent-school partnership, our study provides a wealth of other material which contributes to an understanding of these dynamics. We turn now to a broader discussion of points of contact between the parents in our study and the schools their children attended.

Formal Communications

School involvement. Traditionally, school involvement has been measured by parental attendance at parent-teacher associations, committee meetings, or school programs and assistance with field trips, class parties, or plays. About half of the mothers in our study reported going to PTA meetings, but only a third considered themselves actively involved in school-related activities. Only three mothers and one father were involved significantly in their children's school as volunteers; two were working parents, one a welfare recipient, and one a nonworking mother in a relatively well-off family. (Similarly, according to a 1984 study by Epstein, working mothers were as likely to be involved with evening school activities as mothers at home). All four of these parents had children who were above-average readers. The high achievement of the small number of children whose parents were involved directly in their classrooms suggests that this form of participation may foster growth in literacy. However, other more widespread forms of parent involvement may influence children's achievement as well.

Report cards. Another mechanism of formal contact between schools and parents is report cards, which Norwich schools send home four times a year. The children in our study received relatively good reports, but their grades did not always accurately reflect how the children were achieving, especially in reading.

During the first year of our study nearly three quarters of the children received A's and B's on their report cards in reading. Thus, despite the fact that about half our sample was reading below grade level, the reports sent home to parents conveyed that, for the most part, the children were doing above average work in reading. Needless to say, the grades given in reading showed a poor relationship to performance on our tests of reading achievement.

Teachers may give a high grade to encourage a child or to reward improvement or effort. But such grade inflation may not be a favor to the child, since it gives an inaccurate picture to parents about their child's reading achievement. Sixty-eight percent of mothers we interviewed thought their children were reading above grade level, 40 percent of them incorrectly. For example, the mother of one sixth grade girl who had received a B in reading, despite her most recent below-grade-level standardized test result, said she hadn't been to the school to talk with teachers that year because all her children were on the honor roll; a lower reading grade might have prompted this mother to meet with the teacher.

Informal Parent-Teacher Contacts

Focusing on formal occasions for parent participation may give a misleadingly low estimate of the level of involvement of working-class parents with their children's schools. As we began to analyze our data, it became clear that informal, one-to-one contact between parents and teachers was more prevalent than use of formal communication channels. (Similarly, in Epstein's 1986 study of more than 1,260 parents of first, third, and fifth graders, only 4 percent were active in all types of school involvement.) Moreover, individual contacts between parents and teachers were related both to children's achievement and to teachers' expectations. For the sake of clarity, we will differentiate between contacts that parents initiated with teachers and those that teachers initiated with parents, even though we recognize that this distinction may at times be an artificial one.

Parent-initiated contacts. Two-thirds of the families initiated some kind of contact with their children's classroom teachers in the first year of the study; fewer families did so in the second year, when teachers also made fewer contacts. In contrast to teachers, who most often used notes or the telephone in contacts they initiated, parents typically went to the school to talk face-to-face. Not surprisingly, parents who knew the teacher from other contexts— living in the same neighborhood or as a teacher for other family members—were more likely to initiate contacts. There were big differences, however, in the proportions of families who initiated contacts with teachers at the different schools in our study. All the families of focal children at one school, for example, contacted their child's teacher both years of the study; at another school, only 1 out of 7 families contacted the teacher the first year, and none the second year.

Dissatisfaction with the schools was an impetus for some parents. For instance, one mother in our study became active when her son was excluded from a college-track course, for reasons she thought had to do with race. Another mother began volunteering both because her child was placed in special education classes and because she was concerned about low academic standards and discipline problems at the school.

The mothers who contacted their children's teachers were not necessarily the ones for whom it was easiest to do so. Families in which the mother worked were more likely to telephone, visit, or send a note to the teacher than those in which the mother was at home. More mothers who said it was "not so easy" or "not easy at all" to get child care or time off from work actually visited the school than those who said it was "very easy." These findings replicate many reports that, while employed parents may say it is hard to attend events at their children's schools, they are at least as likely to do so as unemployed parents (Leitch and Tangri, 1988).

One might expect that the more literate mothers and the mothers who did more to provide literacy materials for their children would make more contacts than the less literate mothers or those who were rated lowest in provision of literacy materials for the children at home; such was not the case, however. Nor did parents with high educational aspirations for their children contact the school more than parents with more modest aspirations.

Teacher-initiated contacts. Many of the classroom teachers initiated one-to-one contacts with families. In the first year of the study, nearly two-thirds of the children's families were contacted by the teacher; in the second year, half the families were contacted. The average number of teacher-initiated contacts with each family was three per child in the first year of the study and two per child in the second year. The teachers reported that the family member with whom they communicated most frequently was the child's mother.

Only about a quarter of the focal children's teachers felt there were obstacles in communicating with particular families (these included language barriers, "parental indifference," and the parents' work schedules). Despite teachers' often-expressed concerns about working mothers, most of the mothers mentioned by teachers as difficult to contact did not work outside the home.

During both years of the study, teachers were more likely to make contact and had more frequent contact with families of children reading below grade level than with families of better readers. Parents of poorer readers, however, were no more likely to initiate contacts than were parents of better readers (perhaps because many of these poorer readers were receiving A's and B's in reading). Teachers were less likely to contact parents of black children, although black parents made as many or more contacts with teachers as white parents did. Lightfoot (1978), too, observed a bias by teachers against low-income and minority parents, contributing in Lightfoot's opinion to a misunderstanding between schools and families. In addition, in our study as in Epstein's (1986), teachers of older children contacted parents less often than did teachers of younger children. In parent-initiated contacts, however, we did not find grade-level variation.

Purpose of contacts. Parent-initiated contacts both years of the study were most frequently inspired by concern for the child's academic progress. Mothers who thought their children were having problems with schoolwork were most likely to initiate contacts with the teacher. Often parents who did not initiate contact either had children who were doing superior work or had inaccurate perceptions of their child's achievement (as we suggested above in discussing report cards).

The matters that led to teacher-initiated contact differed in the two years of the study. In the first year, teachers, like parents, were most likely to initiate contacts about the child's academic progress, while in the second year teachers were most likely to contact parents about behavior problems. Only half as many families were contacted by teachers about academic concerns the second as the first year. Both years teachers also contacted families about special education services, uncompleted homework, and excessive absences or tardiness.

The differences between the first and second years may be accounted for by the different group of teachers; they were no doubt enhanced by the fact that different concerns arise about children in higher grades. The purpose of teacher contacts shifted dramatically according to the children's grade level. Academic concerns were the subject of nearly all teachers' communications with the parents of second graders, but of only a fifth of the contacts with sixth graders' families, and none of the contacts with seventh graders'. Teachers contacted the families of older children in our study less and did so almost exclusively about discipline problems, although the older children were generally further below grade level in reading than were the younger children.

The purpose of teacher-initiated contacts also varied according to the race and sex of the child. Although there were no differences by race in the first year of the study, in the second year three-quarters of the contacts with black families were about behavior problems, compared to half of contacts with white families. During both years of the study, teachers had more contacts with families of boys about academic progress than with families of girls. These differences were not related to group differences in actual reading achievement since the boys and the blacks in our study scored no lower than the girls or the whites.

Consequences of contacts. Teacher-initiated contacts were associated with a number of positive factors for the child: a more positive teacher assessment of the family, more parent communication with the school, improved schoolwork, and gains on reading achievement tests. Children whose families were contacted by the teachers were much more likely to be moved up in reading group assignment than those who were not. Teachers were more likely to mention the home as a positive factor in a child's reading achievement when they had contacted the family over the course of the year. Families who had been contacted by the teacher were in turn more likely to initiate subsequent contacts themselves, especially when these teacher contacts had been about academic rather than behavior problems. Teachers generally felt that the contacts they initiated with families had positive consequences for the child's schoolwork. One teacher said, after repeated contacts with the family, "I started seeing changes [in the child's homework] about midyear; it turned itself around."

A strong relationship emerged between teacher contacts and children's gains in reading comprehension from the first to the second year of the study. Although the poorer readers as a group were less likely to gain a year in reading comprehension than the better readers, children whose families were contacted about academic concerns were more likely to gain substantially. Every one of the children whose families were contacted about academic concerns gained two years or more in measured reading comprehension ability during the second year of our study. Only half of those children whose families were contacted about behavior problems gained two years in reading level, and only a third of those whose families were never contacted gained as much. These results parallel those of a recent British study, which found a relationship between parent-teacher contacts about reading progress and eight-year-old children's reading achievement (Panton, 1986). They also confirm others' conclusions about the effects of home-school contacts. School-initiated contacts have been found to increase parents' and teachers' positive ratings of each other, reduce both truancy and behavior problems, and increase parents' under standing of what their children were being taught at school (Ayllon, Garber, and Pisor, 1975; Dougherty and Dougherty, 1977; Epstein, 1985; Sheats and Dunkleberger, 1979).

How are we to interpret these findings? The opportunity for speculation is almost limitless. We might posit, for example, that the most basic factor was ease of interaction between teacher and family—that the teachers tended to contact only those families they considered supportive of the school and its goals. Or we might start with teacher competence, and hypothesize that the best teachers also contacted their students' parents most often. If we take the family as the most important factor, we might hypothesize that teacher-initiated contacts tended to elicit family support and interest, which in turn led to higher reading-achievement scores.

Any of these explanations is in accord with the data, and all are probably true to some extent. In fact, this is a situation in which attempts to demonstrate that one factor or another is "the most important" are misguided; only an examination of the interactions among the multiple forces at work can do justice to the complexity of the real world of home and school, parent and teacher, expectation and achievement.

Whether teachers initiated contacts and what the contacts were about—factors powerfully associated with children's gains in reading comprehension—bore no relation to their gains in word recognition, vocabulary, or writing production. (See Chapter 7 for further discussion of this contrast between reading comprehension and the other literacy outcome variables.)

Parent-initiated contacts appear to have had several positive consequences for the child. Parents who initiated contacts were better able to judge whether their child was reading at grade level or not. In addition, teachers believed that parents who initiated contacts provided help with homework and contributed to the child's progress in school. Parent-initiated contacts seemed to modify teacher assessments of a child's abilities and prospects, perhaps by signaling to the teacher that someone valued the child's schooling and had high aspirations for the child's ultimate educational achievement.

Teachers were significantly more likely to expect children from families who initiated contacts to go on to a four-year college than the children of parents who initiated no contacts, although families of children experiencing academic difficulties were typically the ones who initiated contacts. Teachers' assessment of the family's contribution to the child's reading achievement and teachers' expectations as to the future educational level the child would achieve were, in turn, positively related to children's gains in reading comprehension. Thus we find the relationship between parent-teacher contacts and gains in achievement may well be mediated by the effects of contacts on teacher perceptions and expectations.

Homework

Another major link between home and school is homework. Parents in our study differed in the extent to which they thought homework actually made a difference in their children's skill development. A small number of parents saw their role vis-à-vis homework as an opportunity to provide direct teaching to their children, exemplifying the Family as Educator model. These parents emphasized the content of the homework as a source of learning. For instance, a mother of a below-average reader in the sixth grade described how she would review the reading with her daughter before her daughter began the homework: "When she reads ancient history, she doesn't know the words and it puts her head in a whirlwind. So I make her say what it means in her own words." Several parents said they asked teachers to give them materials to use with their children at home. One mother told us, "Ever since my oldest child's third grade teacher called up to say he'd forgotten his addition tables, I have worked with the kids during the summer so they don't forget." This mother was implicitly subscribing to the notion that homework extends the school day and thus extends a child's "time-on-task."

Rather than seeing homework as an opportunity for teaching, however, most parents in our study felt their responsibilities were limited to seeing that the homework got done. These parents felt their duty as concerned parents was to monitor homework completion; the child had the responsibility to see that it was completed correctly. All the parents understood that children who arrived at school with incomplete or no homework made a bad impression on the teacher. To avoid this, many parents felt they had to supervise their children, while a few actually did the homework themselves if they thought it was too difficult, too boring, or too long for their children. (See the Conlan case study, later in this chapter, for an example.)

Among teachers, too, there were various approaches to homework. A few, who saw it as an opportunity for children to learn something new, made reading and/or writing assignments. These teachers sometimes tried to get the parents involved in teaching their children. One second grade teacher, for example, assigned "getting parents to read aloud" or "getting help with a science project." Most teachers, however, assigned homework designed to reinforce skills already taught at school. The most prevalent form of homework was worksheets and workbook exercises that provided practice in word spelling and math computations. Many teachers contended that doing homework helped children develop good work habits and assume responsibility for completing a task. A number of teachers said they would like to give more homework, but they cited children's unwillingness to do more work and the lack of parental support as problems in doing so.

Some teachers used homework explicitly as a way of communicating to parents about what was happening at school and as a way of giving parents information about their children's progress. Some parents, too, appreciated homework as a source of information from the school or as an indication of the teacher's diligence or interest in their children's progress. The role of homework as a channel for communication between home and school may be as important as its direct pedagogical effects on the children (Paschal, Weinstein, and Walberg, 1984).

Two-thirds of the mothers and half of the fathers said they helped with homework, generally once a week or less.[1] But children whose parents helped with homework were no more likely to complete it or get it in on time than those whose parents rarely or never helped. The frequency with which children received help with homework was not related to achievement on any of our literacy measures. There was no relationship, furthermore, between turning in homework and *gain* on any of our literacy measures.

Teachers rated the family's contribution to school success much higher in families where children did homework consistently.

---

1. Some parents said they didn't feel confident about helping their children because of their own school experiences or because English was not their native language. One father commented, "The system is different from when I was growing up. The teacher advised not to try to help Joanne as it might confuse her." Some children, too, said of their parents' help: "They forgot how to do it"; or "It's hard homework and they can't do it." Naturally, some parents didn't help because their children figured out their problems by themselves and didn't ask for any help from their parents.

Siblings also helped with homework. Virtually all parents said that younger children in the family received help from their older siblings. One fourth grade girl told us that when she needed help with homework, her brother was usually the one available to help. Furthermore, older siblings were probably better informed in the procedures for completing the rather arcane worksheets and the "modern" math computation methods the children were learning. Occasionally, the help from siblings went well beyond what teachers might have hoped for. For example, one child said that she and her younger cousin "switch for each other, like she'll do my homework if I sweep the kitchen floor for her."

Teachers also tended to have higher expectations for these children's final educational outcomes. As pointed out above, the relationship between teachers' expectations for the child's ultimate educational attainment and the child's gain on reading comprehension was also positive and significant. Thus, while homework completion did not relate directly to literacy status or gains, there was an indirect relationship mediated by modified teacher expectations.

Attendance and Promptness at School

The fundamental way that parents can facilitate children's literacy development is to ensure that children attend school regularly. The more school days children are present, the more instruction and opportunities for engaging in literacy activities they are exposed to. Previous studies have shown that attendance predicts achievement, though the exact reasons for the connection are difficult to discern since experimental approaches to the question cannot be undertaken (Kean et al., 1979). The effects of better attendance are assumed to be similar to the well-documented effects of increased time-on-task.

Like other studies of low-income students (Kean et al., 1979; Rutter et al., 1979) we also found that attendance was related to literacy achievement. The children with higher levels of reading achievement missed school less often in the course of our study than the children with lower levels of achievement; students with better attendance records also showed greater *gains* over one year in word recognition. This result parallels those of time-on-task studies which find that the more mechanical areas of the curriculum show the greatest effect of increased instructional time (Evertsen et al., 1980; Wyne and Stuck, 1983).

In addition to ensuring greater access to literacy instruction, school attendance, like homework completion and contacts between parents and teachers, may have indirect effects on literacy development. A parent's efforts to ensure regular attendance may send a message to the child that school and the activities that occur there are important. A child's regular attendance may also signal to the teacher that the family is concerned about their child's progress in school.

Despite the common notion that low-income parents are indifferent to school attendance, we found that most of the families in our study took attendance seriously. On the average, the children in our study missed only ten days of school a year, considerably fewer than national samples of low-income children in urban schools. There were a couple of excessively truant children in the study, but even the father of one of these expressed concern about the effects of his son's absence from school.

Family resources may be more related to children's attendance patterns than parental attitudes are. Home observers' ratings of each family's emotional stability and structure (see Chapter 5 for definitions and measures) predicted children's attendance records, whereas parental statements about the importance of attendance did not. For example, one single parent with very high educational expectations for her children at times simply couldn't "get it together." Her part-time jobs and community college classes often wreaked havoc with the children's schedule as well as her own. As a result, her two children were often late to school or missed school entirely.

Parents may say they value education highly, but as far as the school is concerned actions speak louder than words. School absence is seen by many teachers as evidence of lack of parental interest in children's school achievement, or as a sign of extreme permissiveness or lack of discipline. One fourth grade teacher commented angrily, "Mrs. Conlan lets Jimmy stay home when there's one snowflake in the sky!" Teachers rated familial contribution to the child's school success much lower, and rated the family as less helpful and less facilitating, when the child had a poor attendance record. The impression given by repeated absences may also influence teachers' judgments of the children's abilities. Teachers in our study predicted significantly lower ultimate educational outcomes for students with more absences, independent of the students' actual current literacy achievement. The single mother described above showed an understanding of this effect when she sent a note to school explaining that it was her oversleeping that caused her son to be late to school. "Please don't blame Steven for my problem," she urged.

Tardiness was viewed by parents, children, and teachers as similar to absence from school. Two-thirds of the children said they were rarely or never late to school and parents agreed that promptness was important. Although tardiness failed to predict reading achievement, it influenced teacher judgments of the family's role as much as school absence did. Families whose children were often late to school were seen by teachers as less concerned and helpful. As with attendance, however, the families under stress were less able to ensure promptness: Children's lateness showed a strong relationship to observers' ratings of family stability.

Differences between First and Second Year Teachers

Second year teachers initiated fewer contacts with the families than first year teachers. As already noted, they were also more likely to contact parents about behavior problems, whereas first year teachers tended to contact parents about academic concerns. Contacts about behavior problems showed less relationship to gains in children's achievement than contacts initiated over academic concerns. Parents in turn were less likely to contact teachers in the second than in the first year of the study.

Second year teachers had generally lower estimates of the families' contributions to children's achievement than the first year teachers. Second year teachers were less likely to believe that parents helped with homework, in particular seeing the less-educated parents in the sample as less helpful (our own data, however, showed no relationship between maternal homework help and mother's level of education).

Second year teachers were less likely to see black families as supporting their children's achievement than the first year teachers had been (though it was evident from both parent and child interviews that black parents helped as much as white parents). Teachers in the second year of the study also had lower educational expectations for both black children and girls. Although our sample was carefully selected so that there were no race or gender differences in children's actual achievement, second year teachers, in contrast to the first year group, saw only white boys in the sample as headed for higher education. Teacher educational expectations were lower overall in the second year of the study, paralleling teachers' overall lower estimates of parental support and their less frequent contact with the families.

The differences we found between the two cohorts of teachers recall results reported by Becker and Epstein (1982) about teachers whose practice involved developing cooperation between schools and families. These teachers reported that all parents were helping their children with learning activities at home, while teachers who had not made efforts to contact parents said that parents with little education would not or could not help their children. The contrast between the first and second year teachers also highlights the interrelationships among amount of parent-teacher contact, teacher estimates of parental support, and teacher expectations for children's achievement. These interrelationships become particularly important in light of the connection we found between teacher expectations and gains in literacy achievement.

Before moving on to a discussion of our findings about the Parent-School Partnership model, let us look in more depth at two families that differ from each other primarily in terms of their relationship with and attitude toward their children's school. The Conlans and the St. Cyrs were both child-centered families in which the parents exerted themselves to educate their children and to have fun with them. Nonetheless, the two families provide a sharp contrast in most areas of the model discussed above: involvement with school organizations, contacts with teachers, and attitude toward homework and school attendance.

James Conlan, who showed no gain in reading comprehension during the fifth grade, lacked two of the factors found to be related to gain in this reading skill—contacts between his teacher and his family and positive assessment of the family by his teacher. Patti St. Cyr, by contrast, made gains in both word recognition and reading comprehension; her teacher contacted her family several times during the year and judged her family to have made a positive contribution to her reading achievement.

The St. Cyr Family

The St. Cyrs formed a structured, busy household. Mr. and Mrs. St. Cyr and their four children—Jacqueline, twenty-one, Jack (John, Jr.), twenty, Kenneth, nineteen, and Patti, twelve—lived in a third-floor apartment in West Norwich. The kitchen where the family often gathered had pictures, greeting cards, children's drawings, and knickknacks hung on the walls, along with a calendar filled with appointments and reminders. The St. Cyrs had lived in this apartment for seven years and before that had lived right next door for almost ten years. They loved the neighborhood because of its stability and familiarity. Also, they found it convenient to everything—there was a bus line just a block away, and they were close to shopping and to downtown Norwich. Since they went on many family outings, and the three older children commuted to school, the location was important to them.

Mr. and Mrs. St. Cyr monitored the children and their activities closely. Patti, called "the baby" by everyone in the family, was especially protected; everyone catered to her wishes. Mrs. St. Cyr expressed some disappointment with her youngest daughter's lack of independence and slight immaturity, yet she certainly seemed to do everything to keep Patti in that role. For example, she picked out Patti's clothes for her every morning; she and her husband (saying, "It keeps us young") took Patti everywhere with them, to visit with relatives and on outings to museums, concerts, and sports events.

Mrs. St. Cyr was one of the most involved parents in school activities. She was extremely active on school committees (in issues of school desegregation and racial balance, and in school evaluation), attended the PTA meetings every month, and worked as a Title 1 aide at Patti's elementary school. She was genuinely interested in what was going on at the schools and didn't want to miss anything, even though "sometimes I have to come home and take a Tylenol because at some of these meetings it's like knocking your head against a wall." Mrs. St. Cyr was also a troop leader for Patti's Girl Scout group (the oldest daughter, Jacqueline, said that the only reason Patti belonged to Girl Scouts was because her mother liked it so much!).

Mr. St. Cyr was not active in his children's schools—"I leave that to my wife"—but he had been very dedicated to youth baseball and hockey leagues in Norwich. He had risen from a mail clerk to salesman in the company for which he worked, and was doing quite well.

Mrs. St. Cyr became animated whenever she talked about the children, and spoke of all of them in highly positive terms. She was very "college-oriented" for her children. A good education for them was of great importance to her. She herself had finished high school, and her husband had completed ninth grade. Her ambitions were bearing fruit; Jacqueline was a senior at a state college, Jack had finished his second year at college, and Kenneth was a freshmen. Each of the older children lived at home to save money and worked part-time to help finance their schooling.

Patti's teachers saw her as college-bound, too, and thought her family contributed positively to her school achievements. Her fourth-grade teacher characterized the St. Cyrs as "vital, positive, school-oriented, and very interested in Patti's development." Teachers reported that Patti sometimes acted "silly" and was a bit sloppy in her independent work at school, but these behavior problems did not worry the teachers unduly, in light of their view of Patti as bright and highly motivated. Patti's fourth-grade teacher had taught the older St. Cyr children, and knew the family well, so she contacted Mrs. St. Cyr six or seven times in order to try to improve Patti's behavior in class. The St. Cyrs followed up on these contacts later.

Beneath Mrs. St. Cyr's competent and cheerful exterior was a woman who seemed somewhat frustrated with the limitations of her role as wife and mother. No doubt her interest in school improvement reflected a desire for an independent identity. Her efforts at home were well appreciated by the family. Patti chose to write about her mother as someone she admired, "because she is comforting and knows a lot and understands everything and knows how I feel and how I want to be and why I want to be that way and always takes me places and is always telling me right and wrong for my own good."

Mrs. St. Cyr was most vocal in her dislike of the family's television viewing habits, noting: "I don't think TV is a privilege, it's a nuisance. I'd rather for us to sit as a family and talk." Nonetheless, Patti could watch as much television as she wanted before her "firm bedtime." Until bedtime, Patti had control of the television set. "She gets to choose what she wants to watch since she has to go to bed at nine," agreed all family members. Although there were few time restrictions on Patti's TV viewing, she was not allowed to watch R-rated or horror movies.

Mrs. St. Cyr felt her husband watched too much TV. "When

he's watching TV the world could disappear and he wouldn't know. He tunes out." Mr. St. Cyr was the more lenient of the two of them regarding rules for the children, giving in if Patti wanted to do something or if she wanted him to watch a certain program with her. But both parents agreed that their approach to dealing with their children was one of reasoning and that the children never made unreasonable requests. They tended to "talk things over" even when it came to which TV program to watch.

Mr. St. Cyr wasn't an avid reader, but he made an effort to encourage Patti and sometimes he played Boggle or Scrabble with her. Mrs. St. Cyr's reading consisted of the daily newspapers, a neighborhood weekly, and *Family Circle*. She encouraged her children to read, since "I don't remember having a book in the house when I was growing up." She and Patti went to the library together, she helped Patti with homework ("I don't think they give them enough homework"), and talked with the teacher if she was concerned about Patti's work or about what was going on in class.

During our classroom observations Patti seemed interested in her lessons. She constantly had her hand up to volunteer in a vocabulary lesson even when she wasn't sure of the answer. During reading instruction she read aloud quite accurately but with considerable nervousness. She often finished her reading-based assignments earlier than other students were able to. Patti seemed most fully engaged doing games or chatting with other students.

The St. Cyr family had chosen collaboration with the schools and other institutions in their efforts to achieve success and advancement for their children. This strategy was clearly paying off for Patti; any problems she had in school were dismissed as minor by her teachers, who were impressed by her parents' role as "enthusiasts" in home-school collaboration.

The Conlan Family

James Conlan was an appealing eleven-year-old: slender, freckled, self-confidently polite, and pleasant. He and his equally attractive older sister, Michelle (age thirteen) lived in a rather cramped two-bedroom apartment with their parents. Michelle had her own bedroom, but James slept on a small bed in the apartment entryway. Their duplex was located on the outskirts of Norwich Corner, close to industrial terrain, in the neighborhood where many of Mrs. Conlan's relatives lived. Since Mrs. Conlan's mother lived next door, child care had never been a problem. The Conlans had lived for a time in a nearby town but disliked it because there were no parks and not enough activities for the children.

Mrs. Conlan worked as an insurance claims adjuster for the state: the position, as she pointed out, actually requires a bachelor's degree, but she had worked her way up to it through various office jobs. She could not attend college to become a pharmacist, as had been her plan, because of illness in her family and the consequent need for her to work to help support her younger brothers and sisters. She loved school as a child and still read a lot for pleasure. She was one of the few women in the study who spontaneously talked about the book she was reading, who recommended books by name, and who said she preferred reading to watching television. When she did watch TV, she chose movies rather than police dramas, soap operas, or sitcoms.

Mr. Conlan spent his leisure time after coming home from his job at the telephone company watching TV or playing with the Conlan's recently purchased ATARI. He was a warm, loving, involved father who participated in the active lifestyle the members of this family shared.

The many books in the Conlan household were usually hidden from view. When Mrs. Conlan sent Jimmy to bring out the book she'd just bought him, he extracted it from a kitchen drawer. There was no space for bookshelves in the tiny living room, though Michelle had some shelves in her bedroom. Mrs. Conlan had given a friend at work the book she had just finished. Mrs. Conlan mentioned that she still sometimes read aloud to the children, especially short stories.

Mrs. Conlan presented herself, not at all arrogantly but with self-confidence, as a sort of expert on producing children who read well. Without our asking, she offered us additional help with our study: "If you want kids for a study, we have them here." During our first visit she said, "I hope you find out why some kids like to read. Mine do because I read a lot and I always read to them a lot!"

Mrs. Conlan was very proud of her children. She showed us a poem Jimmy had written, a Mother's Day card he'd made, and a clipping of a story by Michelle that had been published. She also mentioned their many accomplishments, including Michelle's flute playing.

The children generally did some of their homework unsupervised in the afternoons before their parents got home, but Mrs. Conlan occasionally helped fill in the pages in Jimmy's worksheets if she thought he was too tired, or if "it's more work than should be expected of him." Both Mr. and Mrs. Conlan complained that their children got too much homework, because it interfered with family activities such as bowling, going out to eat one night a week, visiting with family and friends, Jimmy's catechism lessons, and Little League, and special excursions like going to see the tall ships and an aircraft carrier. The family also spent summer weekends at the beach, and the children shared in planning vacations.

A pleasant sense of mutual enjoyment and child-centeredness characterized this family, reflected in Jimmy's and Michelle's activities and comments about each other. They spent a lot of time together and seemed especially close and harmonious for siblings two years apart in age. This was one of the few families where the children were not described as constantly squabbling. This lack of sibling rivalry was even more remarkable in that Michelle was in many ways portrayed as the "favored" child in the family. She was a straight-A student, whereas Jimmy had his problems in school. Michelle's academic superiority was an open fact in the family; Jimmy walked in while we were asking his mother about differences between the children and answered before she could, "Michelle is smarter."

Although Jimmy was reading a year above grade level at the time, his third grade teacher gave him failing grades in math and near-failing grades in reading and referred him for special education services. When we observed Jimmy during fourth grade, he was generally quiet and seemed intermittently bored and frustrated by his schoolwork. In lessons which had a predictable routine he worked smoothly and confidently. Jimmy's fifth grade teacher was stern and quick to criticize. Jimmy frequently acted nervous in whole-group situations, tapping his pencil and jiggling his feet, while the teacher reprimanded other students. Jimmy never volunteered during math, reading, or social studies, although he generally worked quickly and competently during seatwork. At the end of the fourth grade, Jimmy was reading about two years above grade level but showed no improvement on reading comprehension tests a year later at the end of fifth grade.

In any discussion of Jimmy's school problems, Mrs. Conlan was clearly on the child's side, much more willing to assume that poor teaching or inappropriate assessment techniques were the cause rather than Jimmy's lack of competence. (It was the observers' view that his fifth grade classroom was characterized by a high level of negative affect and a low level of teaching quality and time-on-task in reading and writing.) As a result, Mrs. Conlan did not bother much with contacting the school or going to meetings, and she was more open and explicit in her criticisms of Jimmy's current and previous teachers than any other parent interviewed. Since Jimmy's third, fourth, and fifth grade teachers had not contacted the family either, their views of the Conlans were based on little data. Jimmy's fourth grade teacher characterized the family as "very encouraging and supportive," saying that Jimmy worked hard and was able to stay on task and complete assignments. She predicted he would complete four years of college. But his fifth grade teacher thought the parents let Jimmy miss school unnecessarily.

The Conlans felt relatively little sense of power to improve or influence the school. For instance, Mrs. Conlan said it was "a waste of time" to go to meetings on redistricting, since the school board would decide any way, and that, at PTA meetings she described as just "frosting," no substantive problems ever emerged.

The Conlans were quite willing to take the responsibility for their children's growth and education. They provided a home environment with characteristics of both the educating family and the resilient family. But they did not collaborate with the school to improve matters for the children. They therefore ran the risk that teachers thought badly of their children and of them. It was fortunate that Jimmy and Michelle read well and did generally good work in school, because it might have been hard for the Conlans to deal effectively with the schools if their children had started having serious problems.

The Significance of the Parent-School Partnership Model

The Conlans and the St. Cyrs represent extremes in our sample in terms of their styles of interaction with the schools. Mrs. St. Cyr's level of active participation was approached by only one or two other mothers in the sample, while Mrs. Conlan's open expression of disdain for teachers and her subversion of teacher authority in matters like homework were unique. Unfortunately, many of the parents in the sample who were supportive of the school and believed they could turn to the teachers for help made no more contact than the Conlans, although they felt differently. If no personal contact existed between home and school, the teachers tended to assume the worst about parental willingness and ability to contribute to their children's education. Under these circumstances, the responsibility to make the rectifying contact clearly lies with the school. As Epstein (1988) points out, "teachers' practices, not the education, marital status, or work place of the parents . . . made the difference in whether parents were productive partners with schools in their children's education" (p. 58).

We found parents in our low-income sample were generally concerned about their children's educational achievement and motivated to cooperate with the schools to promote it. But in this low-income sample, as has been reported for middle-income groups, the parents who were active participants were a minority. Toomey (1986) warns that attempting to improve academic achievement by involving parents as volunteers helps only the minority of children whose parents are "enthusiasts" (like the St. Cyrs). The parents to whom he refers as the "silent majority" (interested but not involved) cannot be distinguished by school personnel from the truly disinterested or disaffected (like the Conlans). As a result, the children of the silent majority are not likely to show any positive impact of most programs to increase parent-school involvement. Toomey recommends instead programs that include teacher-initiated contacts and planned home visits—programs that ensure contacts even with those parents who won't come to school or call the teacher. Epstein (1985, 1986) takes a very different approach. She says that although only a minority of parents are active at the school, these parents convey a message to teachers that parents are interested, and as a result teachers may be more willing to ask all parents to conduct learning activities with their children at home. Epstein would probably concur with Toomey's conclusion, however, since she says that teachers who are leaders in involving parents in learning activities at home can positively affect the reading achievement of all students. In another study (1983) she found that although 70 percent of parents of elementary school children had never helped the teacher in the classroom or on field trips, over 85 percent spent at least a quarter-hour helping their children at home when requested by the teacher and were willing to spend even more time if asked.

The willingness of parents in our study to be involved in their children's education was better reflected in their initiation of and response to one-on-one contacts with teachers than in their participation in PTA, classroom volunteering, or formal school programs. In her study of parent-teacher contacts, Hauser-Cram (1983) found that parents initiated more contacts than teachers, and that low-income parents were as likely to initiate contacts as middle-income parents. These findings by Hauser-Cram, like ours, point up again the incorrectness of the "sociological myth" (Hargreaves, 1974) that low-income parents are ineffective and disinterested in furthering their children's educational achievement. M. Snow (1982) also found that low-income parents wanted to cooperate with teachers and had as positive attitudes toward talks with teachers as did parents with higher incomes. Most parents in our study were interested in their children's schooling but were often prevented from collaborating effectively with the teachers in improving their children's performance by a frustrating cycle of miscommunication. Parents want to know if their children are having trouble with school work (Gotts, 1984) and what they can do to help (McAfee, 1987). Parents in our study, too, expected to be contacted when academic problems arose, but they received report cards full of A's and B's and little information indicating problems even when their children's academic performance was poor. Teachers, especially in the second year of the study, often thought parents were not interested in their children's performance and so contacted parents primarily about behavior problems. When parents did contact teachers, teacher opinions of parental interest and contributions rose, and children's achievement improved as well. These changes in teacher attitudes may have been paralleled by changes in parental understanding; Epstein (1985) found that parents whose children's teachers were leaders in parent involvement gained in comprehension about what their child was being taught in school and rated the teacher higher in interpersonal skill and teaching ability.

Unfortunately, although low-income children's academic problems tend to become more severe as they go further in school, the frequency of potentially rectifying parent-teacher contacts decreases. This finding, in our study and in many others (such as Stevenson and Baker, 1987), suggests that attempts to influence the contacts between schools and parents should focus on the later elementary, junior high, and high school years. Indeed, parental involvement in the education of high school children is generally reported to be very low, despite sustained parental belief that involvement is appropriate (Dornbusch and Ritter, 1988; Prescott, Pelton, and Dornbusch, 1986). As Dornbusch and Ritter (1988) point out, "it is obvious that a reservoir of parental energy and commitment exists that has not been tapped by American high schools." (See Chapter 9 for a discussion of our families' contributions to their high school children's education.)

Children who completed their homework, got to school on time, and attended school more regularly were, in general, somewhat better readers than those who did not. The families within which homework completion and school attendance were most regular were also, not surprisingly, the families that rated high on the variables discussed in Chapter 5 as related to the resilient family. Clearly, a family that is too severely stressed to achieve domestic order and interpersonal harmony is also unlikely to have the resources to enter into an active partnership with the school, with the additional demands on time and energy which that imposes.

There were important indirect effects of these family variables as well, since parent-teacher contacts, regardless of who initiated them, were positively correlated with teacher perceptions of the home's contributions to the child's learning, with teacher expectations for the child's ultimate educational achievement, and with children's gains in reading comprehension. These findings confirm others' conclusions about the effects of home-school contacts (Ayllon, Garber, and Pisor, 1975; Dougherty and Dougherty,

1977; Sheats and Dunkleberger, 1979). The findings by Hauser-Cram (1983) and by Epstein (in press) that parent-teacher contacts affect achievement in reading and language but not in math suggest a possible mechanism of action for the effects of parent-teacher contact. It is widely recognized that children's performance in reading comprehension is influenced by the collaboration of the teacher in instructional contexts. Teachers ask more challenging questions during reading instruction of students they think of as better; they ask inferential rather than literal comprehension questions, probe more deeply for answers, and pose more questions asking for interpretation and elaboration of the material read (Allington, 1980; Collins, 1986; Eder, 1981; Gumperz, 1970; Lawrence, 1969; McDermott, 1978; Moll, Estrada, Diaz, and Lopes, 1982). Teachers who expect more of students may unwittingly collaborate with the students to demonstrate the students' greater competence; in the process they may also unintentionally engage in instructional practices best designed to elicit maximum gains. Our own classroom observations confirmed the picture derived from Allington (1980), Eder (1981), and others that reading instruction in the better reading groups focused on comprehension, inference, and analysis, whereas instruction in the poorer groups was limited to the difficulties of word recognition and comprehension of detail. Thus, the children who were perceived initially as better readers also experienced instructional contexts that could help them make bigger gains in reading comprehension.

The Parent-School Partnership model is unique among the three models we have discussed in that it explains a respectable amount of the variance in all four of the literacy outcome measures we considered, though it is not the best single model for any of the four. The Resilient Family and Family as Educator models explained 43 to 60 percent of the variance in writing, vocabulary, and word recognition, but none of the models we have considered thus far has accounted for more than 28 percent of the variance in reading comprehension. This is a disconcerting finding, since reading comprehension is the measure of reading most critically related to success in the middle and high school years.

Chapter 7

Reading Comprehension and the Relation of Home to School Factors

Factors Influencing Reading Comprehension

In considering the home influences on each of our literacy outcomes we had little difficulty in identifying the "best model" for explaining word recognition, vocabulary, and writing. In each of those cases, one model for family influences stood out as better than any other. Reading comprehension as an outcome variable showed a less tractable relationship to our models of home influence. Each of the models we tested explained a significant portion of the variance of reading comprehension, but none was better than any other, and all explained only moderate amounts of variance. The power of all three models reflects the wide variety of predictor variables that showed sizable simple correlations with reading comprehension: literacy environment of the home, .30; TV rules, .24; mother's educational expectations, .19; outings with adults, .24; per capita income, .18; and parent-school involvement, .32. Reading comprehension seems to be sensitive to parental behaviors that encourage literacy practice, to increased opportunities for contacts with adults, to parental expectations, and to variables reflecting lack of stress and a high degree of organization in the home. None of the other literacy outcomes showed such a range of significant influences.

The classroom factors that related to gains in reading comprehension were also quite diverse. Three types of variables related strongly to growth in reading comprehension for our sample: practice with structured materials (such as workbook homework); direct teaching (the amount of time allocated for reading instruction, the quality of instruction ratings, the presence of explicit teaching of comprehension strategies); and wide exposure to literacy materials (visits to the library, use of varied materials in reading instruction, use of more difficult texts).

The question arises why reading comprehension is so much more multiply influenced than the other literacy outcome variables we have considered. We can only speculate about this question briefly here. Reading comprehension may be a more complex outcome variable than word recognition or vocabulary. If so, that might mean it is a skill that can be achieved through a wider variety of pathways than word recognition or vocabulary. Alternately, it may mean that successful progress in reading comprehension depends on access to a wider variety of learning experiences—structured materials, direct teaching, and varied, challenging literacy experiences as well—than progress in other literacy areas. The greater complexity of reading comprehension as a skill may also mean that parents cannot intervene so effectively as they can with other domains of school success. Whatever the reason, it is clear that reading comprehension—perhaps the most important single literacy outcome variable we have looked at—is also the most complexly determined and widely influenced by both school and home variables.

Because reading comprehension is so multiply determined, it is an intriguing domain in which to consider the relationship between home and school influences. There are a number of possible models for the relationship between home and school; two which can be contrasted are the "complementation" and the "compensation" models. The complementation model suggests that home and school each has a distinct responsibility in preparing a child for literacy and that these responsibilities are complementary. The compensation model, by contrast, suggests that home and school produce roughly the same opportunities for learning; thus, if one fails its responsibilities the other can compensate (at least temporarily) to support progress in literacy. These models are really end points on a continuum. We do not mean to suggest that some aspects of compensation cannot coexist with some aspects of complementation. But in order to conceptualize the relationship between home and school factors, it is perhaps useful to consider extreme versions of the two models.

We have thus chosen two children from our sample as examples of what can happen when either home or school provides an absolute minimum of the kinds of experiences we have identified above as important in the development of literacy. Charles Baxter, a fourth grader, came from the home that scored the lowest within the sample on measures of emotional support and organization, very low on measures of enrichment, literacy and access to adults, and extremely low on indicators of cooperation between home and school as well; he did, however, have the good fortune to spend one year of the study in a classroom where the quality of teaching and the degree of responsiveness of the teacher to his needs were exceptionally high. Charles contrasts sharply with Christina Khouri, a fourth grader who came from a pleasant, organized, emotionally supportive home that scored near the top of the sample in terms of the enrichment it provided; Christina spent both years of the study in classrooms that scored relatively low on the factors that we found were important to literacy gains—focused instruction, practice, and variety of materials and activities.

Charles Baxter

At home. When visiting Charles Baxter's home, it was hard to think that improving his reading should in any sense be a priority for him. One would be inclined first to wash his face and find him some clean clothes, perhaps fix him a decent meal and then take him to see a doctor about his asthma. Twelve-year-old Charles seemed to be pretty much ignored at home. He spent a lot of time watching television or "hanging out" in the neighborhood with a group of kids described by his older sister Louise, fourteen, as "bad." Charles was not an unappealing child, however. Although rather shy, undersized, and grubby looking, he was cooperative and pleasant to talk to.

Charles Baxter's parents were socially isolated and dependent upon each other. Mrs. Baxter had no family, except for her father in a nursing home, whom she never saw. Although she had spent her whole life living on the same street, she said that since her only girl friend moved away a few years ago she had had no interactions with the neighbors. Mr. Baxter's mother, brother, and sister-in-law lived several streets away and helped out by being the back-up phone contact for Mr. Baxter's emergency road service business; yet Mrs. Baxter had never been inside her mother-in-law's home. The family's daily schedule was tied to the uncertainties of Mr. Baxter's work, with Mrs. Baxter and Charles frequently accompanying Mr. Baxter on road calls. During one of our visits to the Baxter household, Charles was home from school because of a cold; yet he rushed out the door with his father in response to a phone call for road service. Mrs. Baxter would probably have gone along, too, had we not been there.

Despite this sense of togetherness, Mr. and Mrs. Baxter were often only vaguely aware of their children's comings and goings. Charles had not returned home until 10 P.M. one night during the period when we were interviewing the family; Mr. and Mrs. Baxter accepted his excuse that he'd been fishing. School officials frequently complained to the Baxters about Charles's truancy, but they seemed unable or unwilling to make sure their son got to school. Few rules governed the Baxter household, and unlike most families in the study, there was no requirement that Charles or his sister do chores. There was an atmosphere of aimlessness in the family: their lives revolved around unpredictable phone calls; their record in keeping appointments with the research staff or with school personnel was very poor; and they reported no regularly scheduled activity nor any leisure activities other than "driving around" and watching television. The house was deserted much of the time. There were frequent arguments between the parents over which TV shows to watch; "If my father is watching sports, we don't dare turn it or else he yells his head off at us."

Mr. Baxter had his own business as an automobile mechanic in addition to his emergency road service operation. The family's income was among the highest in our study, and the Baxters were able to own their own home with a small yard on a quiet street. Despite their relative prosperity, the house they lived in was in bad repair. It contained little usable furniture and showed signs of infrequent cleaning. There was no place for a child simply to sit quietly; the living room sofa, for example, was covered with dismantled parts from Mr. Baxter's motorcycle. The kitchen counters were covered with rows of empty beer and soda bottles. No literacy materials of any kind were evident when observers were present except for a notepad in the kitchen for recording telephone messages and one old textbook amid the clutter on the dining room table. Mrs. Baxter, like her house, was in need of attention. She was extremely underweight, had rashes on her hands, and reported other health problems. Both Mr. and Mrs. Baxter described themselves as people who had hated school and had been poor students; both had quit school before receiving high school diplomas. Mr. Baxter read only the sports page of a newspaper. Mrs. Baxter said she read Harlequin romances but couldn't recall the titles or authors of any she had read recently.

Mrs. Baxter often behaved with her son as if he were much younger than his twelve years. She had her arms around Charles during much of the time we met with the family and got down on the floor to play with him and his toy cars. In addition, Charles was the only fourth grader in our study whose mother did his diary writing task for him. Teachers also reported that he submitted homework in her handwriting. Although Mrs. Baxter's characterizations of her son were affectionate, her interaction with him during the diary task was rated as quite negative, and she described his difficulties in school with little evident concern.

In the Baxter household the children had few resources and no apparent reason to succeed at school. One teacher actually characterized Mr. and Mrs. Baxter's contribution to Charles's reading achievement as "none—they impede progress." Mrs. Baxter was one of only a handful of parents in our study who conceded that her child might not go as far in school as she would hope. Mrs. Baxter thought this might be the case for Charles not because of outside adversity (a situation other parents suggested) but because "he just doesn't have it in him to go to college."

At school. Little in Charles's early experience of schooling broke the grim pattern of his family life. Charles did not attend nursery school or kindergarten; his schooling began at the neighborhood school in first grade. School records show that he failed to learn to read in first grade and was therefore held back. He started missing school regularly during the second year he spent in first grade. He was diagnosed as having learning disabilities and began receiving pull-out remedial help in reading and emotional-behavioral counseling several times a week. Although Charles was absent as much as a third of the time in each of the next years, he typically received grades of "good" or "satisfactory" and was promoted.

By fourth grade, Charles was seriously behind his classmates in literacy development. His reading comprehension scores were a year and a half below grade level, and spelling and vocabulary two years below grade level. Despite continued remedial help he struggled with a lower-level third grade reader, getting through only part of it in the course of his fourth grade year. Charles's asthma became a problem; the school nurse threatened the Baxters with an official neglect order after they ignored repeated requests to provide Charles with treatment. Other contacts between the school and the Baxters were minimal; the fourth grade teacher sent one note home and made one telephone call, both to investigate excessive absences. Charles received failing grades in fourth grade—for the first time in his school career!

During our observations of his fourth grade class, Charles daydreamed, played with toys under the cover of his desk, and talked or roughhoused with other children during lessons. His teacher rarely intervened, seeming content if Charles was not openly disruptive. Classroom lessons consisted of individual seatwork or of class recitation from standard texts that were difficult for Charles and rarely lively enough to capture his interest. Charles sat in the back of the room, avoided making eye contact with adults, and answered the few questions directed to him in soft monosyllables.

School life changed dramatically for Charles in his fifth grade year when he was assigned to Ms. Pasquale's room. This teacher gave Charles a sense of adult concern and interest and provided exceptional opportunities for literacy development. Ms. Pasquale saw the use of "real" books as an important part of a school reading program and thus assembled a classroom library of over six hundred titles. She also provided masses of comics, magazines, and newspapers. Ms. Pasquale included conventional texts and skills workbooks in her lessons, and we saw Charles using these, but her classroom provided the opportunity to use a wide variety of other literacy materials as well. (See Chapter 2 for a longer description of Ms. Pasquale's classroom.)

Ms. Pasquale told us that the types of reading Charles had done in school in the past had failed to engage him. Her main goal for Charles was "getting him to just sit and read quietly for thirty minutes." In addition to small group work with phonics and comprehension workbooks (and the continuing special pull-out lessons), Charles and his classmates spent three half-hour periods a week simply reading. In the weeks we were present, Charles chose a children's biography of Bobby Orr, an Encyclopedia Brown mystery story, and a National Geographic wildlife book. Every other Thursday Ms. Pasquale also walked her class to a well-stocked branch library, where students selected books to read at home.

Before fifth grade, Charles had relatively little opportunity for vocabulary and concept development, partly because he was out of school so much and partly because the classrooms he was in did not emphasize these skills. Activities in his fourth grade class had often seemed pitched to the level of somewhat younger children; for example, several periods were taken up with coloring a calendar page for that month. Little time was devoted to social studies or science, which teach concepts and vocabulary as well as content.

Ms. Pasquale's room was different. Science and math were emphasized. Microscopes, simple physics kits, commercial posters of the planets and of animals, Cuisenaire rods, brightly colored abacuses, protractors, magnets, pocket compasses, and commercial math kits were all available in the classroom and used by the children. In a math lesson we observed, Ms. Pasquale quizzed children on the definitions of "geometry," "pentagon," "rectangle," and "quadrilateral." Charles managed the assignment for this lesson which involved following directions for connecting end points and labeling different line segments.

During our observations of his fourth grade year, we saw Charles and his teacher evolve techniques of mutual avoidance. Here, too, Ms. Pasquale broke with previous practices. As she said in an interview, "Charles needs direction in getting started [on classroom activities] and will not seek help. I have to monitor his facial expressions and body language to tell when he needs help."

During reading seatwork we saw Ms. Pasquale stop by Charles's desk and ask, "Can you read me the directions?" She followed up on this by asking him to work through a sample exercise and then explain how he'd done the problem ("So you put an 'X' under this character's name because . . . "). Ms. Pasquale made a point of calling on Charles by name during a composition class ("Charles, do you remember any of our steps?") and during a math lesson ("What did we learn about lines yesterday, Charles?"). Her monitoring extended to sending another student to fetch Charles from the bathroom ("Tell him I said he's taking too long"), a contrast with the previous year when Charles would disappear for whole lessons.

These forms of attention were needed if Charles was to stay "on track." They probably also gave him a sense of adult concern and interest in his progress. These factors, together with the excellent literacy instruction Charles received in the fifth grade, may explain the considerable gains Charles made during the year. His WISC-R vocabulary score rose the equivalent of 40 IQ points; his reading comprehension score increased by 2.2 years. These gains are even more impressive weighed against his continuing problems: frequent absences, illnesses, tardiness, familial dysfunction, and lack of warm clothing, all of which were sources of deep concern for his teacher.

Ms. Pasquale contacted Mrs. Baxter about these problems "close to 15 times," finally abandoning this approach when Charles reported he was physically punished when his teacher called home. Ms. Pasquale commented that "little has changed for Charles as a result of these [contacts]. Promises are made but usually not kept." She said Mrs. Baxter was "willing to come [to school for conferences] but had her own agenda of unrelated needs concerning herself."

Charles was fortunate to be assigned to Ms. Pasquale for a second fifth grade year after she contested plans for yet another social promotion. Despite the progress he had made, Ms. Pasquale realistically assessed Charles's chance of finishing high school as "doubtful," given his overwhelming handicaps.

Christina Khouri

At home. The Khouri household exemplified a very low-income, immigrant family that provided a rich learning environment and emotional support for the children. In this family a high value was placed on academic achievement; the importance of reading was almost taken for granted, and all the children were successful in school.

An interest in reading was nurtured by both Mr. and Mrs. Khouri, who read to all their children when they were younger.

Mr. Khouri also made up stories and acted out plays with the children. Classic children's books like *Island of the Blue Dolphin, The Secret Garden,* and *Little House on the Prairie* were in the bookcase in the room the girls shared; back issues of *Family Circle* and *Women's Day* were neatly stacked next to the living room table. We saw word games like Scrabble and Boggle in a cabinet in the dining room.

Christina, eleven, was the most avid reader in the family. According to her parents, she was always interested in books, pretending to read and memorizing stories before she entered school. She reported that reading was her favorite activity, and she usually spent at least an hour a day reading books from the public library or school, completing several each week.

Mr. and Mrs. Khouri spoke of Christina's academic work in glowing terms. They indicated that she was doing well in school, much better than other children her age, and that she was getting A's in all her subjects. Said her father, "She does great work!" They felt she had fewer problems getting used to school and learning to read than her age-mates. The Khouris generally tried to encourage her in subjects that weren't her real interest, like math. Mrs. Khouri said, "I hug and kiss her when she brings home her report card."

Both parents had high educational expectations for Christina as well as for their other children, Paul (fourteen), John (twelve), and Lydia (nine). They hoped and expected that Christina would earn at least a master's degree. They agreed that she would make a good teacher, although Mrs. Khouri wanted her to become a doctor.

The family lived in an ethnically mixed neighborhood where most of the residents were blue-collar workers or students. The children's school was two blocks away. The Khouri's small duplex with a fenced-in yard was owned by Mr. Khouri's father. Inside, the five rooms shared by the six family members seemed extremely cramped but not disorganized. During one of our home visits we were not surprised to hear one child say to another, "I want my privacy"—something hard to come by in this household.

There were few frills in the Khouri household except for a computer—last year's Christmas gift to the children, for which they had also saved and contributed money. Rather than buying a video game system, Mr. Khouri thought it was wiser to spend a little more money for a programmable computer, which he described as "a tool for learning." All the children knew how to operate the computer and enjoyed doing so, but the boys were encouraged much more than the girls to use it; it was hooked up to an old TV screen in the boys' bedroom. During several of our home visits much of the activity of the boys and their friends centered around the computer.

Organized after-school activities were encouraged by the parents: Christina, for example, took music and cooking lessons. The children were expected to do chores. Christina's daily task was setting the table for meals, and Mrs. Khouri commented that Christina was especially competent at straightening up the house.

The Khouri children spent a lot of time together, although they had varied interests and separate friends. Like many siblings close in age, they fought a lot, to the consternation of their mother. Christina and her siblings watched several hours of television a day, despite their parents' attempts at restricting their viewing. The children were expected to finish their homework before watching TV and were not supposed to watch violent programs, but these rules were frequently broken and were the source of some bickering in the family. At the same time, there was an unself-conscious sharing of responsibility and pleasure in the family. During our observation of the homework-like task, Lydia and Mrs. Khouri offered suggestions to Christina while Mrs. Khouri baby-sat for a neighbor's infant, and the girls took turns holding the baby. Observers rated the parent-child interaction during this task as being one of the most positive in our sample.

Both Mr. and Mrs. Khouri were born in Lebanon. Whereas Mr. Khouri attended high school and technical college in the United States, Mrs. Khouri did not come to this country until after she was twenty, having completed the eleventh grade in Lebanon. Mrs. Khouri's family still lived in Lebanon, while most of Mr. Khouri's family lived nearby and visited frequently. The parents spoke Arabic to each other and occasionally to the children, but the children spoke English exclusively.

Mrs. Khouri devoted all her time to her husband and four children and had not worked outside the home. Because she was not a native speaker of English, she lacked confidence about helping her children with their schoolwork. She did not see herself as a resource for helping the children with homework once they got older, and urged Christina to go to her father or older brother for help. She worried about protecting her children from some of the negative features of American society—for example, drugs and "the way some kids talk."

Mr. Khouri had been retired on a disability pension for several years, a situation that brought some stress to the household. He spent a great deal of time with his children and commented to us, "No matter what else is going on, the children are my joy." He regularly took them to museums and also accompanied them to the library. He was himself a reader, reporting that he enjoyed technical books, electronics magazines, Lebanese newspapers, and the *Wall Street Journal.*

In contrast to most of the fathers in our study, Mr. Khouri was as knowledgeable and involved with his children's school progress as his wife. He had always been the family's school liaison and recently became involved with the PTA and the Community School Committee.

The Khouris provided a strong literacy environment for their children and placed a great deal of emphasis on the importance of learning, managing to provide well for their family with minimal economic resources.

At school. Christina's school records confirm the picture given by her parents of her early school experience. She attended school regularly, received good grades, and made a strong early start in reading. At the end of first grade she scored two years above grade level on standardized reading tests; in subsequent years she maintained this two-year advantage. At the end of fifth grade her reading comprehension score was at an eighth grade level, and her word recognition score was at a ninth grade level.

When we first observed Christina in fourth grade, she and her classmates were having a difficult year. Their originally assigned teacher, who was reputed to be an inspired instructor, was promoted to a central office job partway into the first term. Following her departure, Christina's class had a series of short-term substitutes until Mrs. Sosa, a provisional teacher for whom this was her first full-time assignment, arrived in February. The children by all accounts had run wild for months when Mrs. Sosa took over. She described her priorities as restoring physical order in the room—collecting full sets of texts, repairing wall displays and equipment—and establishing routines and discipline standards for the children. Mrs. Sosa quickly learned from others in the school that the administration had assigned all the "problem" fourth graders to her class, ostensibly because of her predecessor's superior teaching ability. Mrs. Sosa, like her predecessor, was one of only two Hispanic teachers in the school outside the separate bilingual program. She felt she was working under the eyes of an unsympathetic principal and staff who were holding her accountable for shaping up the behavior of this group of problem children, many of whom were also Hispanic.

Activities and lessons in Mrs. Sosa's class seemed designed more to keep the students occupied and out of the kind of noisy trouble that could bring a critical principal to her room than to stimulate their interest or expand their horizons. A typical language arts lesson began with a dictated list of one hundred spelling words and was followed by an assignment to copy a page from a grammar text, adding correct paragraph indentation.

Mrs. Sosa closely followed teachers' guide "scripts" in conducting a reading lesson for Christina's top group. After students took turns at reading the passage orally, teacher questions and student responses followed.

Mrs. Sosa What's the main topic of the story you've just read?
Freddy The Pacific Ocean.
Mrs. Sosa No, look back over the story.
Christina It's about thousands of fish in the Pacific Ocean.
Mrs. Sosa So, it's about . . . fish.

Christina adopted this strategy for use on her own. During a seatwork lesson we observed, she quickly read a story from her basal reader about the Arctic Sea and then flipped back through the text to find answers to comprehension question.

The teacher originally assigned to the class had assembled a classroom library, but many of the books had disappeared during the period when various substitutes were in charge. Mrs. Sosa occasionally used this collection. For example, she announced one afternoon that children could either do their homework for fifteen minutes or do free reading. Christina chose to do homework. While some of her classmates were observed reading joke books, comic books, young teen novels, and non-fiction trade books during seatwork, Christina worked on her assignments. She was frequently asked to serve as class monitor, checking off the names of children who completed seatwork, helping others with their assignments, and keeping lists of students who misbehaved when the teacher was out of the room. Mrs. Sosa liked Christina, describing her to us as a "beautiful student, really hard-working." She expected her to go as far as graduate school and some kind of professional career.

Christina was assigned to Ms. Peña's room for her fifth grade year. In contrast to Mrs. Sosa, who was soft-spoken and friendly to the children, Ms. Peña was usually harsh and critical. As a consequence Christina's behavior became noticeably different from what we had observed the previous year. Although she was virtually the only child whom Ms. Peña did not criticize during our observation sessions, Christina seemed very nervous during exchanges with the fifth grade teacher, biting her nails and breathing heavily when it was her turn to recite or when Ms. Peña scolded other children ("I don't believe how stupid you people can be.") Christina was extremely quiet, once again this year usually finishing her work ahead of most other children. During a social studies lesson on outlining, Christina quickly copied all the titles and subtitles out of the book as requested, stopping only to offer help to a classmate. We also saw her complete a large part of her math homework during the time set aside for social studies seatwork.

In our visits to Ms. Peña's room we observed endless drills and testing—long divisions at the blackboard, spelling tests, and multiple-choice questions on short, timed reading comprehension passages. Ms. Peña's running commentary during these lessons made for a rather grim classroom: "The next one won't be so easy. Do you think I'll sit here and let you get them all right? No, the point of my coming here is for you to get them all wrong so I can yell." The students checked their answers after a reading comprehension exercise but never discussed why an answer was correct or incorrect ("This stuff is a foreign language to you; you're just playing a guessing game.") Compositions were written very infrequently. When we visited Christina's classroom in February, Halloween compositions were still hanging on one bulletin board and two-year-old papers about Martin Luther King on another.

Unlike Charles Baxter's teacher, who used a wide variety of reading materials, Ms. Peña depended almost entirely upon textbooks and accompanying workbooks for her reading lessons. Ms. Peña said the reading skills she emphasized in her classroom were literal comprehension, vocabulary, and study skills. Reading groups met irregularly because large chunks of class time were taken up with whole-class work in math, spelling and social studies. Ms. Peña, like Mrs. Sosa, complained to us of pressure from the administration to move the class through the prescribed curriculum as found in the textbooks for each subject. When the reading groups did meet, the primary activity was reading aloud (a practice not recommended in most fifth grade basal reading programs) and emphasis was put on getting the proper expression and intonation ("Now I want you to go back and read the paragraph again. You act like you've never seen these words before. It's ridiculous. Read it and read it right this time."). The children were quizzed about word meanings, which they looked up in the glossary. But there was no discussion that might help the children draw connections between the unfamiliar words and their personal experiences or general knowledge.

During this year with Ms. Peña, Christina made gains that kept her reading scores well above grade level. However, she showed only minimal progress in vocabulary, and no progress in writing, weaknesses that reflect deficiencies in the classroom where she spent her fifth grade year.

Contrasting Christina and Charles

Christina Khouri and Charles Baxter represent extremes of both home and school variables, though neither Christina's home experience nor her school experience was as atypical as Charles's. At least for the years of the study, we can argue that if these children made progress in literacy, the Khouris can be given most of the credit for Christina's gains, and Ms. Pasquale for Charles's.

Let us compare the children's achievement directly. Our testing showed that Charles made considerable progress in literacy from grade 4 to 5, particularly in those areas that Ms. Pasquale emphasized in her teaching (vocabulary and comprehension). But he was still slightly below the expected scores for his school grade by the end of the fifth grade, and given the likelihood that he will continue to be frequently ill, frequently truant, and totally unsupported in school achievement by the activities he engages in at home, he probably will not catch up fully with his classmates, let alone his age-mates, during his second year in her classroom. And of course, when Charles leaves Ms. Pasquale's fifth grade classroom, he will be lucky if he is assigned to a sixth grade teacher who lives up to Ms. Pasquale's standards for quality of instruction, sensitivity to Charles's needs, and willingness to invest energy in him. A year of excellent teaching made a big difference for Charles—but being a successful student requires continuing to make gains year after year. The chances that Charles will be able to, without any sustained support from home, are small. In contrast, Christina's progress during two years of poor teaching may be attributed to the pleasant, emotionally supportive home provided by her parents, and to their values that support learning, literacy, and educational achievement. These home influences have so far been enough to keep her at or above grade level in the various literacy skills, and even to enable her to improve her literacy skills during her year with Ms. Peña, whose classroom provided few challenging literacy experiences for a child of Christina's level. Christina's vocabulary and writing scores showed little progress, however—an indication that, as she gets older and these literacy areas are increasingly emphasized, her family's influences may become increasingly insufficient. In Christina's case in particular, since her parents are not native English speakers, exposure to more challenging vocabulary in school is essential. If the school contribution remains weak in this area, Christina may experience problems despite her parents' considerable support.

The cases of Christina and Charles help illustrate our general findings: both home and school have significant, and separable, impact on children's literacy development. The home and school relationship can be compensatory, one providing what the other fails to provide, such that deficiencies of either home or school need have no disastrous consequences for the child's literacy development. However, neither Charles nor Christina was achieving at grade level in all literacy areas by the end of fifth grade, suggesting that deficits in either the home or school contribution cannot be completely compensated for by strengths in the other.

The Whole Sample

We have seen, through the cases of Charles and Christina, that literacy can be acquired under less than ideal conditions. But what of the children whose home and school situations are less extreme than Charles's and Christina's? Does their progress in reading achievement tell us anything about the relative importance of home and school factors in promoting literacy? Let us first review what we found to be the ideal conditions in the classroom and home; these are presented in Tables 7.1 and 7.2.

The ratings for each child's classrooms for the two years of the study on quality of instruction, emotional climate, and literacy environment were combined, yielding possible scores from 6 to 18 points. Five children in our sample were in classrooms that received high composite ratings two years in a row (scores of 16 or above), and all made the expected gains (at least one grade level per year) in reading comprehension. Eight children were in classrooms that received low composite ratings both years (scores of 7 or below); only 3 of these made the expected gains. Fifteen children with mixed classroom experiences over the two years of the study (between 8 and 15 points)[1] showed more variable patterns; 9 made appropriate gains, and 6 fell behind.

Of the 15 children whose families received high composite ratings on our five scales (18 points or above out of a maximum of 23 points), 13 showed the expected gains in reading comprehension, and 2 did not. Of the 13 children whose families scored lower than 18 points, only 4 gained as much or more than expected in reading comprehension over two years, and 9 did not. We see, then, that the results for the whole sample confirm what the cases of Charles and Christina suggested: either home or school seems to be able to support reading gains, but risk of failure increases if either home or school provides a less than optimal environment for learning to read.

We would expect that the children who made the strongest gains and the steadiest progress were those whose home *and* school

1. Scores between 8 and 15 points reflected the school experiences of children who spent one year in a high-rated classroom and one year in a low-rated classroom, who spent two years in a medium-rated classroom, or who spent one year in a medium-rated and one year in a low-rated classroom.

Table 7.1 Classroom environment ratings by observers

Rating	Description
Instruction	
1. Negative	Chaotic and/or rigid. Heavy emphasis on discipline (not always effective). Little or boring instruction.
2. Neutral	Some direct instruction. Children lack stimulating constructive activity. Some routines in classroom.
3. Positive	Direct instruction, children have routines, classroom is orderly in a positive manner. May include open classroom or traditional format. Most children seem challenged and involved.
Emotional climate	
1. Negative	Lots of reprimands. Inconsistent teacher signals, evidence of anxiety among children. Ridicule of individual children by teacher in front of whole class.
2. Neutral	Calm, not much teacher-student exchange.
3. Positive	Supportive, friendly, encouraging. A lot of constructive teacher-student exchange.
Literacy environment	
1. Impoverished	Lack of variety of reading materials. Infrequent library visits. Teacher does not carry out reading activities appropriate to child's reading level. Physical environment bleak and lacking displays of student work.
2. Average	Standard instruction, following a basal text. Some variety in reading materials. Some library visits.
3. Enriched	Variety of reading materials (trade books and basal readers). Frequent library visits. Stimulating activities, e.g., doing word meaning exercises, vocabulary, writing (creative and expository). Teacher asks many inferential questions of students. Physical environment includes displays of student work.

Table 7.2 Home-family environment ratings by interviewers and observers

Mother's literacy and father's literacy
1. Non-reader
2. Minimal reader
3. Reader (reads newspapers or magazines)
4. Print-worm (reads books)

Provision of literacy for child
1. No provision of formal or informal materials/experiences
2. Responds positively to literacy desires of child
3. Provides rich literacy experiences
4. Seeks out opportunities to provide literacy experiences

Organization: family structure
1. No rules or rules not taken seriously, absence of predictable schedule, no expectation for focal child's activities
2. Few expectations for focal child, little sense of predictable schedule
3. Some rules, but they are easily transgressed, focal child might miss school, schedules unpredictable, some expectations for focal child
4. Rules and expectations are clear, but no need for highly rigid expectations about the focal child; some flexibility in schedules
5. Very high expectations for the focal child, much reliance on the child; fairly predictable schedules for meals, bedtime, homework

Organization: physical environment
1. Chaotic, dirty
2. Disorganized, dirty
3. Generally clean, somewhat disorganized or inconsistent in organization
4. Clean, pleasant, organized
5. "House proud," very neat, always organized

Family emotional stability
1. Environment seems emotionally unstable, conflictual, perhaps even bizarre
2. Family has some emotional hazards, some difficulties that affect healthy emotional environment
3. Family has some problems, but they are not serious
4. Environment generally stable
5. Family appears to provide a stable, sound, healthy emotional environment for the focal child

Table 7.3 Percentages of children making expected gains in reading comprehension

Ratings of classrooms (over two years)	Ratings of homes	
	High	Low
High	100% (3/3)	100% (2/2)
Mixed	100% (7/7)	25% (2/8)
Low	60% (3/5)	0% (0/3)

experiences were optimal, and that those with neither high-rated homes nor high-rated classrooms would be at the greatest risk for failure. Does this prediction hold true? Table 7.3 presents the answer (Goodman and Hemphill, 1982; Hemphill and Goodman, 1982). Fortunately, only 3 children in our sample experienced *both* low-rated classrooms and low-rated homes; none made adequate progress in reading comprehension. Adequate progress was made by all the children from high-rated homes except for those who experienced two successive years of low-rated classrooms. The difference between a high- and a low-rated home was especially striking for children in the classrooms rated intermediate, from which all the children from high-rated homes made expected reading gains, but only 25 percent of children from low-rated homes did. The 2 children from low-rated homes who spent two years in high-rated classrooms made adequate reading gains. These findings suggest then, that *excellent* classrooms can compensate for less than ideal home conditions, but that ideal home conditions (at least within the range sampled in this study) cannot always compensate for very poor classrooms. However, for the majority of children in intermediate classrooms, home and school appear to have a complementary relationship—home experiences seem adequately to provide what schools cannot. In the absence of excellence in the classroom, the role of the home becomes much more important.

In our sample, the complementarity may have been enhanced by the relative similarity of beliefs and practices maintained by the parents and teachers. These parents and teachers were, to a large extent, members of the same community. A large proportion of the teachers in our study grew up in blue-collar Norwich families, attended Norwich public schools, and, in many cases, still lived in the working-class neighborhoods served by the schools in which they taught. Although the teachers lived in the more prosperous sections of these neighborhoods, they often shared ethnicity, church affiliation, membership in clubs and local civic groups, and a multiplicity of personal ties with the students' families. Not surprisingly then, parents and teachers in our study gave similar answers to questions such as, "How would you describe a good student?" The answers "Trying your best" and "Doing what is expected of you" figure in both groups' descriptions of a good learner.

The instructional ideologies of parents and teachers in our sample were relatively similar. Our observations of the parents helping the children at home with a homework-like task (see Chandler et al., 1986) confirm that the parents took a role similar to that of the teachers: structuring the physical environment to make the task more salient (by finding pencils, turning off the TV, clearing off the work space); motivating the child by providing reassurance, issuing praise, and minimizing the importance of errors; guiding the child in using the form (especially with spelling help, but also with tips for handwriting and placing items in the right boxes); and directing the content (by asking structuring questions, breaking the task down into component parts, and suggesting shortcuts). Specific parental behaviors that were exact replications of behaviors we saw teachers carry out in classrooms included checking that children had read the instructions, checking that they knew the meanings of words used in the assignment, pointing out careless spelling errors, and suggesting that the children proofread their work.

A last point of correspondence between school and family supports for literacy was the similar nature of the environments they provided for learning. The strongest family environments for fostering literacy had features in common with those of the best classrooms: generous provision of books and other reading material, conversations between adults and children about the content of books and articles or actual shared experiences, a predictable and secure atmosphere, and high standards for children's achievement coupled with emotional support. Given all these parallels, it is not surprising that parents at home could provide much of what the elementary school did to foster success at literacy tasks.

~ *Chapter 8* ~

Implications for Practice
and Research

Current census figures tell us that elementary school enrollments will continue to increase throughout the 1990s. The proportion of low-income children will grow at an even faster pace, with over 25 percent of infants and children in the United States projected to live in homes below the poverty level. Furthermore, few of these children will live in two-parent families, with the extra resources of time, money, and psychological support provided by the presence of two parents. Clearly, in terms of many of the factors this and other studies have identified as important in promoting literacy, a growing proportion of school-age children will be at some risk of failure.

These elementary school children may not encounter a similar profusion of well-trained teachers. Teaching is currently not an attractive profession, especially to the brightest college under-graduates. We can no longer rely on the hidden subsidy of sex discrimination to provide adequate numbers of dedicated women to staff schools, as women are now more likely to go into more highly respected and remunerative professions, leaving class-rooms staffed with teachers of lower academic achievement and less experience than ever before. Whereas in 1963 50 percent of female undergraduates in American universities were education majors, in 1985 fewer than 15 percent were (Carnegie Foundation, 1986). Who will teach the children of the 1990s?[1]

1. It is increasingly the case that the reservoir of future teachers is provided not by new university graduates but by former teachers returning to the teaching profession, and by adults switching from other professions to teaching in mid-career (see, for example, Murnane, Singer, and Willett, 1988). Although these trends may suggest that the shortage of teachers projected by the Carnegie report

In such times especially, looking for a quick-fix method for ensuring the literacy achievement of low-income children is a chimera. Having a significant effect on literacy achievement will require operating in several domains: effecting changes in homes and schools, encouraging communication between parents and teachers, working to reform curriculum and school management, and enlisting community, state, and federal support for education. While the goal of making changes in all these areas may seem idealistic and unreachable, we can take heart from our findings, which suggest that improved conditions either at home or at school should produce improvements in children's literacy outcomes.

School Policy and Practice

Varied and enriching materials and activities. We did not expect to find a simple recipe for improving school practice with low-income children, and we did not succeed in doing so. Many different aspects of school practice had an effect on the literacy achievement of the children in this study, and different school practices affected different literacy outcomes as well. However, classrooms that produced solid gains in vocabulary and reading comprehension were those in which a wide variety of materials and activities were used for literacy instruction.

Our findings suggest that classrooms should, as standard equipment, be provided with substantial libraries of trade books, magazines, newspapers, encyclopedias, almanacs, and other reference books. These are as crucial as basal readers and content textbooks to adequate literacy training. We found that exposure to materials on a variety of subjects and at a wide range of difficulty was especially important in ensuring gains in reading comprehension and vocabulary, both areas in which low-income children are at risk for lack of achievement. These materials also contributed to the children's knowledge about the varied uses of literacy—a

---

is exaggerated, they do not give us much hope for addressing the needs of the growing numbers of minority and non–English speaking children in American schools, since these children need teachers from their own ethnic and language backgrounds, to serve as role models or to teach in bilingual programs.

lesson particularly important to children from literacy-poor homes who might otherwise have little chance to learn that literacy skills involve anything beyond reading basals and filling in workbooks. There should be a wide variety of children's literature in the classroom, so that any child can find books interesting enough to be worth struggling with syntax a little more complex and vocabulary a little less familiar than that presented in the basal reader or in other textbooks. Another means of enrichment is hearing even more difficult texts read aloud by the teacher, to give poorer readers access to language and ideas not found in their own reading.

Challenge is a theme that recurs throughout the school experiences we found to be most effective in facilitating many aspects of literacy in the middle grades. Even in using basals and content area textbooks, it is crucial that these not be below the child's own "easy-reading level" if they are to contribute to literacy achievement.

In addition to being exposed to varied, interesting, and challenging reading materials, children need to be asked to think about those materials in ways that go beyond deciding which blank to fill in on a workbook page. Discussing what has been read, posing inference as well as literal comprehension questions, and asking students to produce book reports or other sorts of book projects constitute effective teacher practices that were too infrequent in many of the classrooms we visited.

Oral discussions can also be used by teachers to expand children's vocabularies and world knowledge, if teachers are aware of the possibilities inherent in discussions to introduce new concepts and new words. Field trips provide a source of shared experiences that are obvious topics for such discussions. Scheduling regular sessions in which children must report on a magazine or newspaper article read at home provides another basis for broadening classroom discussions. The exact nature of the classroom techniques used to stretch and enrich the child's store of world knowledge and of less frequent lexical items is not so important; there are many ways of teaching vocabulary effectively by presenting novel words in diverse contexts that make their meaning clear. Unfortunately, the techniques most widely relied upon for vocabulary training—looking up word meanings in dictionaries and preteaching vocabulary in basal reading passages—actually showed a negative relationship to vocabulary growth in our study. Whatever method is used, it is crucial that teachers recognize the centrality of vocabulary knowledge to literacy and school achievement, and recognize their responsibility for providing classroom activities that stimulate vocabulary learning. Restricting classroom reading instruction to easy reading, to the use of basals and workbooks, to round-robin oral reading, and to literal comprehension checks is inadequate to provide continuing gains in reading comprehension and vocabulary knowledge for low-income children.

Field trips and visits to museums should be part of the school curriculum because they enhance children's background knowledge, thus contributing to children's growth in vocabulary and reading comprehension. As already noted, the value of these educational experiences is greatly enhanced if they are used as a basis for oral discussion; but they can also be used to stimulate supplementary reading and writing activities in the classroom. Since it is harder for low-income families to take their children on outings, it is especially important that the school provide them and exploit them as opportunities for teaching literacy skills.

Similarly, broad exposure to content area instruction in mathematics, social studies, and science can contribute to children's world knowledge and thus to their growth in vocabulary and reading comprehension. Low-income children, in particular, may lack exposure to these domains outside school as a consequence of their parents' and peers' limited educational background and restricted resources. Activities and instructional approaches that view these content areas as important for vocabulary and concept development can compensate for otherwise limited exposure to these domains.

Literacy instruction in the primary grades typically includes goal-specified, teacher-led lessons in which basal readers and workbooks are utilized, word attack strategies are explicitly taught, both literal and inference comprehension questions are posed, and ample opportunities for practice are provided. Approaches like these focus children's attention closely on the text and may help children formulate generalizations about the reading process.

The ability to acquire new knowledge from reading a text requires that the child be sufficiently fluent and skillful at reading to free his or her attention to process the novel information. Otherwise, the child's cognitive system is overloaded by the need to perform two difficult tasks, reading and learning, at the same time. Fluency in reading requires practice; it seems from our findings that the Norwich children were receiving considerable practice in some reading skills—the phonics and word recognition skills drilled during workbook exercises—but rather little practice in reading longer texts. Most Norwich children had learned to recognize and sound out words well by the second and third grades. Many were not fluent readers, however, suggesting that they did not spend sufficient time reading connected texts. The presence of trade books in the classroom stimulates practice because the books are more interesting and varied than basals. If directed to books at appropriate reading levels and about topics of interest to them, children willingly engage in periods of sustained silent reading that provide the practice they need. Another procedure for ensuring some sustained reading practice that a few teachers in our study employed was to assign reading as homework, that is, to assign a half-hour of reading at home or of reading aloud to a parent or sibling. This procedure has shown success in stimulating reading achievement among low-income children particularly (Hewison and Tizard, 1980). However achieved, children need practice in reading; getting this practice should be considered a central part of their reading instruction (Applebee et al., 1988; National Assessment of Educational Progress, 1985).

Attention to writing. Our findings strongly support the notion that writing instruction should begin in the primary grades and should not be postponed until after children read well or have received instruction in grammar, punctuation, and other mechanical skills. As important as these skills are, teaching them does not constitute teaching writing. We found that children who were required to write texts of at least paragraph length were better writers; quasi-writing such as filling in blanks, copying poems from the board or definitions from dictionaries, and doing worksheets did not relate to children's writing skills. Importantly, children who were given practice writing longer passages also showed greater gains in reading comprehension.

Much has been written about the advantages and disadvantages of various methods of teaching writing; since so little writing instruction occurred in the Norwich elementary schools we observed, we cannot speak to this issue directly. However, the strong relationship we found between emotional factors in the children's homes and their production on a writing task suggests that instructional techniques that rely heavily on teacher corrections, that stress producing mechanically perfect texts, and that fail to provide an appreciative audience for even the poorest writers' efforts, may be especially frustrating to children who confront the writing task with little confidence in their ability to say something of interest to others. As good teachers have long recognized, they must be sensitive to the child's feelings and avoid threats to the child's self-confidence. Writing is an activity of self-disclosure and therefore makes children especially vulnerable to critical reactions.

More instructional time needs to be devoted to writing. If children are not taught how to write nor given the opportunity to practice writing, they remain unable to express their ideas—which are often lively and varied. Some of the problems children have with writing, such as organizing a text and taking the needs of the audience into account, can be approached during practice with oral language skills such as show and tell or oral reports to the class. Although training in spelling and punctuation should eventually be incorporated into a writing curriculum, such training should not come at the expense of children's enjoyment of writing. Children's use of writing to communicate their own ideas should be the core of any writing curriculum; this means that many "writing exercises" (filling in blanks, completing sentences, rewriting paragraphs with corrections, and so on) do not constitute training in writing at all. Children need the experience of composing their own essays, stories, letters, and reports if they are to become competent and motivated writers.

Literacy and the content areas. Particularly in the middle elementary grades, literacy and language skills are presupposed by and involved in almost every kind of school learning that occurs. We were struck, therefore, that teachers in general made little use of the opportunities available during social studies and science instruction to continue or reinforce their teaching of reading, writing, and vocabulary. Techniques for extending literacy and vocabulary training into all the hours of the school day should be developed, and their use encouraged by all teachers, particularly those dealing with children in fourth grade and beyond.

Links between Home and School

Report cards. We found that many of the parents in our study had an incomplete or incorrect idea about their children's status in the classroom, as readers and as learners. Many parents thought their children were achieving much better than they actually were. A major source of the parents' misinformation came from the teachers themselves, who typically put relatively high grades on children's report cards. The low-income families in our study had, in general, high expectations and high aspirations for their children's educational achievement, but their understanding of what level of achievement their children's grades reflected often differed from the teachers'. As a result, parents interpreted grades of B's and C's as reflecting adequate progress, whereas teachers often gave these grades to children in academic trouble. Since parents whose children received B's and C's felt their children were making adequate progress, they undertook no special action to ensure better performance in the future. Teachers, feeling they had informed parents of their children's inadequate progress, often interpreted lack of parental reaction as lack of interest. As a result, children could slip below grade level gradually but disastrously without the benefit of either parental or school-based intervention.

We recommend that schools examine the system of grading and reporting to parents. While it is common in some schools to assign grades based on progress in relation to estimated aptitude, parents should also be informed about where their children stand in relation to district and national norms. In addition, they should be told what levels of performance must be achieved if the children are to be successfully promoted to the next grade, selected for special academic enrichment programs, admitted to the academic track in high school, and qualified to compete for vocational training programs or college admission. Middle-class parents participate actively in guiding their children's academic decisions, advising them for example to take college preparatory courses in high school (Baker and Stevenson, 1986). Parents who themselves have had fewer years of schooling may be insufficiently informed about the bases on which decisions about tracking, participation in special programs, and admission to further training are made; they are, thus, less able to help their own children meet the goals that children and parents may share.

Teachers' contacts with parents. One of our most robust findings was the improved performance of children whose teachers were in contact with their parents, facilitating transmittal of information in both directions. The teacher can explain grades and initiate discussion of a child's academic strengths and weaknesses; parents have the opportunity to reveal their true level of interest and concern about their children's achievement. Such contacts provide opportunities for a child's deteriorating performance to be discussed and acted upon before it becomes serious.

The parents in our study tended to expect teachers to contact them if their children were experiencing academic difficulties; teachers, meanwhile, expected the parents to make contacts about children who received poor grades. Especially concerning older children and in the second year of the study there was considerable miscommunication. Since most teacher-initiated contacts concerned discipline, even parents who were contacted thought their children had no academic problems. And since parents rarely contacted teachers about academic issues, teachers concluded that parents had little interest in their children's academic achievement.

When the contact between parents and teachers improved children's performance, this may well have resulted from a change in teachers' estimates of the helpfulness of the home environment. Stereotypes about low-income parents, which affect teachers as much as other members of society, suggest that low-income parents do not care about their children's schooling, are not competent to help with homework, and do not encourage achievement. Few of the low-income parents in our study fit this stereotype. Yet, the degree to which they violated it became clear to us only after we had talked to them, visited them in their homes, and gotten to know them. Teachers may have been able to abandon their stereotypes only as a result of similar experiences.

Contacts appear to have had beneficial effects that were separable from good teaching practices. Parent-initiated contacts were as powerful as teacher-initiated contacts in stimulating children's

progress. Thus, increased achievement was not simply a consequence of better teachers making more contacts. It was striking,
though, that many teachers and many parents never met in the
course of an entire school year, and that contacts were more likely
to occur as the result of individual parent or teacher initiative than
through institutionalized events such as PTA meetings. In light of
our findings about the power of teacher-parent contacts in improving children's achievement, it seems clear that school personnel must assume more responsibility for initiating contacts with
parents.

Homework. Homework is often, in middle-class homes, an opportunity for parents to help children and talk about what they are
doing at school. Yet for many low-income parents, who may not
have the time to help their children or who may not be conversant
with the lessons their children receive in the middle and upper
elementary grades, homework may not automatically serve this
function. It is possible for teachers to promote parent involvement
in children's schoolwork, and in the process increase the time children are spending alone with parents, by assigning homework
activities that require parental cooperation. We found that children were more likely to turn to older siblings than to parents for
help on traditional, worksheet homework—presumably because
the older siblings had themselves learned the tricks of the workbook trade. A few innovative teachers assigned other kinds of
homework, designed to involve parents: reading aloud to them,
being read aloud to by them, interviewing adult family members
about various topics, or discussing an article from the newspaper
with an adult as preparation for an oral report to a class on current
events. Our findings suggest that ten or twenty minutes a day
alone with an adult is more than most children have access to, but
that even so little time can make a difference in children's vocabularies and in their reading comprehension skills.

Family Policy

In developing policies that affect low-income families, some
thought should be given to the role these families play in the
educational achievement of their children. Policies that seek a
long-term solution to the problem of poverty in this society must

be assessed in terms of their effects on the family's capacity to contribute to its children's academic achievement, if we hope to avoid the intergenerational transmission of poverty and illiteracy.

Stress. Even within the only moderately stressed group of families included in this study, we found that indicators of stress and disorganization in the family system related negatively to the children's literacy performance. Welfare payments, food stamps, housing subsidies, unemployment compensation, and other such programs are of course designed to ameliorate financial sources of stress for families (though they often introduce other kinds of stress in the process—when, for example, they require that the presence of a man in the household be concealed).

For many low-income families, psychological stress is as serious a problem as financial stress, and one for which fewer governmental or community forms of assistance are provided. Interpersonal conflict among family members, loss of employment, death or illness of a family member, having to move, the personal dangers of living in many low-income neighborhoods, drug or alcohol dependency in a family member, parents who feel powerless or hopeless, and many other circumstances constitute stress on the family system and can have consequences for the academic achievement of the children. Our findings support the expansion of mental health and other services directed at these problems in low-income communities. Greater support for child care facilities, after-school programs, and short-term in-home help during family crises could significantly reduce the consequences of psychological stress factors.

Provision of literacy. We have seen that "provision of literacy" to children by their parents promotes the children's acquisition of reading skill. The provision of literacy by parents can take many forms and is of greatest effect if its form changes as children get older. In the earlier grades, reading to children, encouraging them to read aloud, and taking them to libraries are all important. Not just reading, but also *re*reading books can be an important route for children to the kind of fluency in reading that becomes increasingly important to academic success as children get older.

In light of these findings, it is worth considering a role for schools in promoting parental literacy, in informing parents about what their children should be reading, and in making trade books available to children to take home for long periods. Short-term borrowing from libraries is valuable but should be supplemented by programs that allow children to own some favorite books and thus read them again and again. Giving children trade books should be as normal a school practice as providing them with free textbooks. In addition, adult literacy training should be available to those parents whose involvement in their children's literacy achievement is hampered by their own inadequate literacy skills. Indeed, the desire to help one's children with schoolwork often provides a powerful motive for illiterate adults to seek literacy training. Finally, practices which encourage direct parental help, such as asking children to read aloud regularly to a parent, should be more widely adopted.

Time with adults. Our findings from home observations and interviews indicate that children who spend some time with adults have an advantage over children who spend all their time with siblings and/or peers. This was particularly noticeable in the results of our vocabulary and reading comprehension measures. Such a finding is not surprising since dialogue with an adult is likely to be more challenging linguistically and more informative about the world than dialogue with another child. Parents are not the only adult resource who can provide this kind of experience—extended family members, neighbors, and adults in the community all can be seen as resources for children.

Our society has many opportunities for providing the interactions with adults needed by these children—in adult supervised after-school centers, story hours in libraries, big brother/big sister programs, adopt-a-grandparent programs, organized vacation activities, and lessons and programs organized in community centers. The growth in language and literacy of the children affected would more than pay the salaries of the adults and teenagers who staff such programs.

Contacts between parents and the school. Parents must be made to feel that they have the right to visit their children's school and to talk to the principal and the teachers. It should not be necessary to go to PTA meetings or use the official parent-teacher conferences in order to meet teachers; parents should feel welcome in their children's classrooms at regular lessons and should have opportunities to meet with principals and special teachers as well.

Schools which do not make parents feel welcome to visit the classroom or to speak to teachers and administrators are not doing their best to ensure educational progress for all children.

One way to make schools more accessible to parents is to involve the parents in classroom activities more directly, by inviting them to demonstrate special skills, to join the audience at special class presentations, to accompany the class on field trips, to talk about their jobs or their childhoods, or to volunteer as classroom aides. Our own small sample included a number of parents who regularly volunteered in their children's classrooms. Outreach to low-income parents could increase the numbers who participate directly. Parents who have assumed a teaching role at school are more likely to do so at home with their children as well.

In a broader context, schools must recognize that they are responsible for satisfying parents' educational goals for their children. Parents who think their children's schools are not good enough have three options: they can supplement school learning by taking partial responsibility for educating their children themselves; they can take an activist role, attempting to improve the school through the parent organizations, through education-action committees, or through the Board of Education; or they can, as a last resort, consider switching their children to different classrooms within the school or to a different school altogether. Low-income parents are less likely than more affluent and better educated parents to be aware that all these options are open to them. Although it may seem to go beyond the role of the school to educate parents about their rights of protest, the strong evidence indicating how important parental involvement is in producing good schools suggests that such an effort might well be to the school's advantage.

Research Directions

A study like this one, which has a somewhat exploratory nature, and which is being reported several years after it was first planned, must be judged in part on whether it generates indicators for further research and in part on how it fits with conclusions from other, similar research efforts. In this section, we discuss what we see as major emergent issues in research on literacy among low-income children, both to assess how our study contributes to these issues, and to sketch out what we see as the next research tasks in each case.

Emergent literacy. In the last ten years or so a major shift has occurred in research in the field traditionally called "reading." An emblem of this shift, of which our own research constitutes a part, is the adoption of the term "literacy" to refer to the phenomenon under study. The term "literacy" signals a recognition of the complex relationships among reading, writing, ways of talking, ways of learning, and ways of knowing. Literacy is not just a cognitive achievement on the part of the child; it is also participation in culturally defined structures of knowledge and communication.

If becoming literate means achieving membership in a culture (whereas "reading" means successfully mastering a curriculum), then it is clear that much literacy acquisition occurs outside school and a considerable amount might occur before school entry. The notion "emergent literacy" (see, for example, Scollon and Scollon, 1981; Teale and Sulzby, 1986) refers to the literate ways of behaving displayed by very young children, such as pretend storybook reading, pretend writing, oral storytelling that shows literate traits, beliefs about literacy, production of certain oral language forms, and recognition of letters, logos, labels, and frequently encountered words. Since these emergent literacy behaviors are not directly print-related, or if print-related are "rote" rather than analytic, their relation to literacy has often gone unrecognized.

There has been considerable speculation that a major source of failure in school derives from the lack of participation in this literate culture by children from some ethnic backgrounds. Obviously if some children arrive at school much more advanced than others in these emergent literacy skills, they will build upon these skills and make progress in literacy more easily than other children who are not "emergently literate." Indeed, some successful interventions with children at risk of failure in school have involved introducing gradual transitions from relevant preschool skills to "school literacy." Examples include the reading curriculum of the Kamehameha School, which builds on native Hawaiian children's experience with collaborative rather than monologue-style storytelling (Au and Jordan, 1981), and Don Holdaway's Literacy Centers, which introduce school reading as a choral recitation, building on children's experiences singing songs or reading nursery rhymes at home (Holdaway, 1984).

Although the children in our study were beyond the stage of emergent literacy, we were still interested in the hypotheses generated by this line of thought about sources of school achievement. Accordingly, we collected retrospective information from the parents in our study about their children's early literacy experiences. We also informally observed parents with our focal children's younger siblings and considered the degree to which these families could be considered to be excluded from mainstream American literate culture.

The parents in our study were quite diverse in their own uses of literacy, and in the degree to which they had provided literacy experiences to their children. However, all were participants in mainstream literate culture, in that, commonly, children owned at least a few storybooks, "Sesame Street" was watched by preschoolers, newspapers were checked for specials at the local supermarket, family members wrote messages and notes to one another, calendars were ubiquitous, bills were paid by writing and sending checks, and choices of television programs were made by consulting *TV Guide*. Furthermore, the parents in our study all reported their children knew the alphabet before entering kindergarten, had used pencils, pens, and crayons at home, and liked being read to. Although a few of the children in our study had been held back in first grade, all succeeded in acquiring the phoneme-grapheme mapping skills that are taught in first grade, and even the poorest second graders in the study were not seriously below grade level. Accordingly, we feel there is little evidence that, for this group of children, lack of emergent literacy skills caused difficulty in access to school-based notions about literacy. For these children problems emerged with the literacy demands of the *middle* grades—acquiring new knowledge, critically assessing what one reads, expressing one's own ideas, organizing one's own knowledge, and learning the vocabulary and syntax used for literate purposes.

Underestimating children's literacy. Related to the emergent literacy view is a body of work designed to provide more extensive information about the uses of literacy by children seen as school failures. Much of this work falls within the tradition identified as the "ethnography of literacy" (Bloome, 1980, 1981; Gilmore and Smith, 1982; see also the chapters in Schieffelin and Gilmore,

1986). A major conclusion from these various studies is that many children identified in school as "nonliterate" in fact engage in considerable literacy-based behavior. Since their ways of using literacy differ from the ways prescribed by school practice, however, the literacy skills such children possess are ignored or devalued.

Examples of literacy displayed by school failures include reading the menu at Burger King (Bloome, 1980), studying and learning the words to chants that form the background to elaborate stepping routines (Gilmore, 1983), and using literacy in nonsanctioned games such as Dungeons and Dragons (Gilmore, 1986). The behaviors displayed in these uses of literacy often deviate from the rules that govern school literacy; for example, literacy is often a group activity, in which several children collaborate to decipher the menu or the words to the chant. Since school reading is an autonomous activity, the skills that children can display in their collaborative reading activities never surface in the classroom.

Needless to say we also observed considerable child-generated literacy activities during our classroom observations, much of it from children who were not considered good readers or writers by their teachers. While the existence of these nonsanctioned literacy activities is in itself interesting, we were not at all surprised to observe them, since as we discuss above the children in our study were not outsiders to the mainstream literate culture. The problem with ascribing too much importance to the literacy skills used in these activities is that, in fact, they were typically neither highly developed nor relevant to school success. Children encountered problems with literacy tasks that required dealing with long connected texts, understanding novel information from reading, and writing paragraphs or stories; such school-set literacy tasks are quite different from those children undertook for their own purposes. The child-generated literacy activities were, in some cases, more creative and more challenging than the workbook exercises that constituted literacy in some of the classrooms we observed, but they still represented a very limited array of uses for (or challenges to) children's literacy skills.

High school failures. Much attention in the early 1980s was directed to academic failure in the high school (Boyer, 1983; Lightfoot, 1983; Sizer, 1984). Recent proposals for solving the American educational crisis have, likewise, mostly pertained to high school curricula and management (Grant, 1988; Powell, Farrar, and Cohen, 1985). The comparison of academic standards in American and European high schools is, indeed, cause for alarm, as is the low level of literacy skills of a significant proportion of American high school graduates.

We believe, though, that impugning high schools may divert attention from a problem not entirely of their making—that many of the children entering high school are not adequately prepared to do the sort of academic work that should be expected of them. We believe that the seeds of poor academic achievement in high school may be sown in the middle elementary years, when the literacy skills that are the basis for successful high school academic work must be acquired. Weaknesses in vocabulary, reading comprehension, and writing that start in the middle elementary years may accumulate in later grades and expand into more and more content areas as instruction in all academic areas becomes increasingly dependent on literacy skills. Attention must be redirected to literacy achievement in the elementary school if we are to solve the problems of high school dropout and low academic achievement of graduates. Similarly, adult illiteracy is not a problem that starts in adulthood; most adult illiterates in the United States today spent many years in school. To prevent the next generation of high school failures and adult illiterates, we must change what is happening inside elementary classrooms today.

Some of the recent national data on school achievement are encouraging—they indicate that the gap between black and white children is decreasing, for example, and that schools with a sense of mission, an emphasis on rigorous academic standards, and a positive climate can minimize the achievement differences between rich and poor children (Levine and Stark, 1981). Much, however, remains depressing. Low-income minority twelfth graders (seventeen-year-olds) score at levels attained by more affluent thirteen-year-olds. Urban schools produce much poorer results than suburban schools. The problem of educational equity *can* be solved, but it has not been. We are justified in holding high expectations for the educational achievement of American children from all social classes, but the evidence suggests those expectations are not yet being fulfilled.

~ Chapter 9 ~
Epilogue:
Four Years Later

At the end of the original study we had relatively high expectations for the literacy achievement of low-income children. At least within our sample, many children were scoring at or above grade level. Furthermore, parents in our sample, like those described in other studies of low-income families, were involved with their children's school despite limited resources, and they supported literacy achievement in diverse ways outside school. Although we certainly found deficiencies in many of the home and school environments we observed, we discovered that a compensatory relationship existed between home and school. Shortcomings in one could be offset by strengths in the other, ensuring that children would continue to make progress in their literacy achievement.

Information from studies of low-income students' experiences in secondary school suggests, however, that our expectations might have been too high. Several recent national studies show that large numbers of low-income students fall behind their more affluent peers, failing to achieve levels of literacy defined as adequate by national norms (Applebee, Langer, and Mullis, 1988; National Assessment of Educational Progress, 1985). In fact, among disadvantaged urban youth, an alarming 13 percent of thirteen-year-olds do not have basic level reading skills (estimated by Carroll, 1987, to be the level necessary to understand grade 3 basal readers), and 34 percent of seventeen-year-olds have not achieved an intermediate level of reading proficiency (according to Carroll, the level required for reading simple popular magazines).

Low levels of literacy have been found to have a variety of negative consequences for older low-income students. Poor literacy skills cause increasing problems at successive transition points in school, resulting in high dropout rates and thus impeding entry into the workforce. Transition to high school is a difficult process even for relatively privileged children achieving at grade level (Blyth, Simmons, and Carlton-Ford, 1983), and is often accompanied by severe difficulties for low-achieving students (Hill, 1983). It is very likely that these difficulties contribute to the high dropout rate among low-income, disadvantaged, and minority urban youth (Bachman, Green, and Wirtanen, 1971; Boston Public Schools, 1986; Ekstrom et al., 1986). Furthermore, the potentially remediating effect of home-school partnership is typically unavailable, as parental contact with teachers and involvement in school governance declines through junior high and high school (Epstein, 1984; Henderson, Marburger, and Ooms, 1986; Johnson and Ransom, 1983).

Although there is heightened awareness that both schools and families play a role in educating children, the focus of the recent spate of high school studies has been on what is wrong with the school (see, for example, Clark, 1983; Lightfoot, 1983; Powell et al., 1985; Rutter et al., 1979; Sizer, 1984). Studies that have addressed the experiences of low-income students in high school have not looked at both home and school factors as sources of adolescents' successes or failures. Although they add to the information we have about the school side of the equation, they do not help answer the question of whether a compensatory relationship between home and school continues to exist for high school students.

Because of the relative lack of information about the experiences of low-income students in high school, we were curious to examine the continuing relationship between home and school for our sample. In light of the depressing national picture of literacy achievement for urban disadvantaged youth, we wished to assess the accomplishments of our sample of children, many of whom had been doing fairly well in elementary school, as they progressed through secondary school. Thus, in the winter of 1986 several members of the research team discussed informally the possibility of following up on the students who had participated in our research in the years 1980–1982.[1] This follow-up was much

1. The follow-up study of the sample was initiated by Irene Goodman, who took the lead in locating the families and reestablishing contact with them. Goodman, Barnes, Chandler, and Hemphill all participated in follow-up interviews and testing and were primarily responsible for writing this chapter.

smaller in scale than the original study and did not include classroom observations or teacher interviews; nonetheless, we were
able to spend time with the adolescents and their families (at home
and in their neighborhoods) and to test the students' reading and
writing skills.

The students were at the time of our follow-up in seventh,
ninth, and eleventh grades. We sought to examine whether they
were experiencing continued academic growth, whether their literacy achievement would reflect the declines predicted for this
population, whether the connection between family and school
had become weaker, whether adapting to high school had been
problematic, and whether the compensatory relationship between
home and school that had existed during their elementary school
years was still in effect.

First, we had to make sure we could locate enough of the original families to warrant a systematic study. Many of the families
were not listed in the phone directory, and many had changed
phone numbers or moved. But after substantial detective work, we
were able to locate 29 of the original 31 families. Of the remaining
families, 1 had moved out of the state, and 1 child, who had left
both the original and subsequent school districts, could not be
traced. Another student whose family we did locate could not
participate in the follow-up because he had dropped out of ninth
grade in 1986 and run away from home, according to his mother.

During our first follow-up phone calls, the families volunteered
much information about their lives and the children's educational
experiences in the four years since our last official contact. These
preliminary conversations with the parents and with the students
themselves indicated that new issues had emerged for the families
as our subjects moved into and through adolescence. For instance,
many students and some of their siblings reported academic problems in adjusting to high school. These calls also indicated that we
continued to have the families' trust. All of the 28 students we
located agreed to participate in follow-up testing sessions and interviews. We conducted interviews with them and administered a
battery of nine achievement tests. There were 15 females and 13
males in the follow-up group, 8 from the youngest cohort (in sixth
and seventh grades at the time of the follow-up), 11 from the
middle cohort (in ninth grade at follow-up) and 9 in the oldest
cohort (eleventh grade). We contacted, tested, and interviewed

them once again in the spring of 1987, when they were in the eighth, tenth, and twelfth grades.

Family Changes

The 28 adolescents we located lived in 27 families, 1 of which included the 2 focal children who are siblings. The household composition had changed for several of the children. Half now lived in two-parent households and half in mother-headed households (in contrast to the original study, when only a third of the children lived in single-parent households). Three fathers had died during the interim period. In 2 other families the parents had divorced and the father had moved out of the household. Two mothers who were previously divorced had remarried.

For Lisa Palmieri and Derek Pagliucca, changed family circumstances seemed to offer hope for the children. Lisa's family, discussed in Chapter 5, was one of the least resilient families in our original study. Although there was attention given to the children, it was colored with decidedly negative affect and punitive actions. Lisa also did not receive academic support from her family. In the interim between original study and follow-up the family environment improved, according to both family members and observers. The family moved from one relative's house to another and, although the surroundings were more cramped, there was less tension than before. Lisa's parents were still together, despite earlier conflict and talk of separation. The father had a stable job now, and the mother had received steady raises in her job.

Like several of her peers from the original second grade cohort, Lisa was held back in school. Her older sister had flunked several high school courses, and cousins were held back in school as well, continuing a familial pattern of academic failure (neither parent had finished high school). Yet Lisa, despite her mostly below-average scores on tests, was determined to graduate from high school. She continued to bring home better report cards than her older sister and had become a spirited, self-directed, flexible child from a somewhat chaotic family. Lisa's forte was social involvement; she spoke animatedly about her class activities and her eighth grade graduation party as well as a big party she was giving for her classmates. She knew high school would be difficult but was looking forward to a new school environment.

Derek Pagliucca, first introduced in Chapter 4, was succeeding better than we would have expected, given his earlier academic and home environments. Four years earlier, he had scored very low on all the factors that were associated with achievement in vocabulary and word recognition. His home literacy environment was quite meager, and his mother offered little encouragement, possibly because of her own school phobia as well as her laissez-faire attitude about Derek's learning. In second grade Derek was inattentive and not achieving at grade level, but in third grade an active and concerned teacher helped him improve his reading skills dramatically. Nonetheless, his overall achievement was still quite uneven.

When we revisited Derek four years later, the family had moved into a newer, more spacious apartment. His mother was working part-time to augment the public assistance the family was receiving. Because she was at work when the boys got home from school, she was counting on Derek and his siblings to take on more responsibility. We saw several notes she had left, with detailed instructions about chores and other things to do before she returned home.

Derek was now a strapping thirteen-year-old with a great interest in dirt bikes and sports figures. Derek's father, who had remarried and had a young child by his current wife, was more accessible to Derek at the time of our follow-up. Derek had acquired step-siblings and a broader family network. He talked about wanting to go to college, a desire he shared with his best friend, but said he didn't think his mother had any idea that that was what he wanted. Derek's test scores were, on the whole, quite good.

Several of the households experienced a change in composition; in 5 cases, a grandparent or aunt now lived with the family. Some of these changes followed the loss of a parent through death or divorce. Straitened financial situations and the need for additional emotional support seemed to play a role in these families' decisions to have an extended family member reside with them.

The number of siblings living at home had changed marginally. In 8 families, older siblings had moved out of the household since our last contact, in 2 cases to live at college, and in the remaining cases to get married or just to be on their own. Only 1 family had a new baby in the interim.

Nearly half of the families moved at some point between our original study and the follow-up. Although this seems like a high proportion, most stayed within their own neighborhoods, and only

2 families moved as far as the next school district. Three families moved to nicer housing because of improved family financial circumstances, whereas 2 families moved to more modest housing. Four families moved into new buildings at the same location as a result of public housing renovations in Norwich.

One of the more dramatic changes in our sample was that 2 of the girls in the oldest group had become mothers themselves. One had a two-month-old son, a fact that did not surprise us. She had already dropped out of school and was sexually active as a younger teen. She continued to live with her family, who helped take care of her baby. When we asked about her plans, she could not think ahead about life with her child in two or five years; rather, she was concerned about the day-to-day responsibilities, just "getting up in the morning when Shauna is crying." Getting a Graduation Equivalency Diploma was not in her plans in the near future.

The other young mother's situation was more surprising because she was one of the highest achievers in our original study. Robin Henderson had been a very bright sixth grader from a strict family that had high expectations and concern abut the quality of the children's education. There was real pressure for achievement in her family, an emphasis on manners and good behavior, and generous provision of literacy materials. Yet, there was a certain coldness in the family, with Robin talking about her mother being "picky . . . not very nice, and impossible to please." Robin's mother took care of the baby for a few months while Robin continued school, but then Robin moved to her own apartment with her baby and boyfriend.

In contrast to her parents' expectations, Robin's teachers' early expectations for her were low, and thus her teachers did not encourage her academically. Robin showed no academic growth after sixth grade, according to her test scores. She dropped out of school temporarily to go have her baby in another city, returning to a high school program for teenage mothers. She still had unrealistic career expectations, mentioning her desire to be a pop star or a model. Robin was a young woman for whom our expectations based on her early academic achievement were decreasingly likely to be fulfilled.

School Changes

At the time of our 1986 follow-up study, 82 percent of the children were in the expected grade. Three children—all in the youngest group in our study—had repeated a grade in the interim and were a year behind. All 11 of the original fourth graders had progressed without retentions. Two children—both in the oldest group—had dropped out of school in the ninth grade; both were students whose mothers and teachers had predicted five years earlier that they would not finish high school.

A year later, in 1987, those 6 of the oldest group who were still in school graduated from high school. One of the 11 students in the middle group dropped out on his sixteenth birthday. All in the youngest group advanced to the next grade.

As other studies (such as Blyth et al., 1983) would predict, the transition from elementary/junior high school to high school was problematic even for previously high achievers. Several of the students, along with some of their siblings, reported academic problems, a dramatic drop in their grades, and general difficulty adjusting to high school. Both parents and adolescents spoke of the striking changes the students faced upon entering high school— changes for which they had not been in any way prepared. Not only did the reading demands increase, but the demands for studying and organizing did also, as most students had at least six different courses, often rotating schedules, and much more homework. As one mother said of her daughter, "She had trouble adjusting to high school. It's much bigger and much easier to cut classes there."

Often, freshman students said that their best year in school had been the previous year, when they were the "big kids" in the elementary school. One boy told us, "My teachers say 'you may hate school now, but later you'll learn to like it.' I can't believe that will happen."

At the time of our follow-up, the youngest group of students were still in elementary/middle school where their courses were decided for them and they were not yet "tracked" into different courses of study. The older students were in high school, where they were either in the "general track" which includes some college preparatory courses, or in vocational or remedial tracks. Of the 17 students still in school in the older two groups, 3 (2 males and 1 female) were taking either advanced or honors courses in high school, while 6 were in general academic courses and 6 were in the basic program, which is geared toward remediation. Two of the students were in vocational programs to study a trade.

Although the majority of students indicated their desire to attend college, very few were taking the courses necessary for college entrance. Only 6 of the 17 high school students in our follow-up—all in the middle age group—were taking a foreign language, either French or Spanish. None of the oldest group had taken a foreign language. Slightly more students (8) were taking a laboratory science course, either basic biology or chemistry. Most of the students in the two older groups were taking an algebra course, but only 4 were planning to take a third or fourth year high school math course.

With only one exception, all the students in the two older groups who had been reading above grade level in elementary school were in general academic classes in high school. Moreover, all of those originally reading below grade level were now in basic or remedial classes.

We found that some of the students who did well academically and socially in elementary school had lost their motivation to achieve in high school. They were bored in their classes, not sufficiently challenged by their courses, often lacked respect for their teachers, and felt that teachers, in turn, did not respect them. Those who initially had done poorly in elementary school were falling even further behind in high school, often slipping into truancy because they were not receiving enough guidance about how they might improve. For a few, the experience of academic failure and the perception that school personnel cared little about their staying, compounded by lack of family support for remaining in school, resulted in their dropping out.

Patti St. Cyr and Charles Baxter were two children from the same grade level who ended up on opposite ends of the spectrum in terms of academic success in high school. Patti, introduced in Chapter 6, came from a family that marshaled its limited resources to help their children succeed (and in some cases, excel) in school and be "college oriented." Mrs. St. Cyr and, to a lesser extent, Mr. St. Cyr were involved in the PTA, school committees, and neighborhood committees, feeling that collaboration with the school was important for their children's progress. Patti's teachers were impressed with her family's interest and felt Patti would do well throughout school.

Four years later, Patti was enrolled in a small parochial high school, which her parents had chosen because its academic standards were higher than the large public high school's. Although she originally had difficulty adjusting to the demands of high school, she had managed to adapt. She continued to do well on achievement tests, scoring well above grade level on vocabulary, reading comprehension, and word recognition; she also wrote exceptionally good essays.

Patti had more realistic ideas about her future and how to pursue what she wanted than did most of the other high school students in our follow-up study. This was in good part because she had been working during the summers in a program for low-income youth initiated by the city council, systematically trying out various career fields. For instance, because she was initially interested in health research, she took a job one summer as a lab assistant, but when she realized that she preferred to work with people, she tried out another job that would give her "people experience." This sense of purpose and control over her future was fostered by her family's practical approach to life and by their high aspirations for Patti.

In contrast to Patti, Charles Baxter, first described in Chapter 7, was having a troubled adolescence. For Charles, the compensatory effect of his excellent fifth grade teacher did not balance the detrimental effects of his home life. His truancy had escalated, and he had turned to petty crime. He had "gotten in trouble with the law," was on probation, and wanted to drop out of school. One of the days we went to visit, he had just been back in court; his mother told us she expected him to stay in school no longer than the judge ordered him to.

Charles had gone even further downhill in his academic achievement than when we last assessed him in 1982. He was substantially below average on writing, vocabulary, and word recognition, and in ninth grade was reading at a third grade level, even lower than his fifth grade scores. Charles's older sister, who had been fairly successful academically, had recently dropped out of school and run off with a twenty-five-year-old biker. The Baxter household was as chaotic and socially isolated as when we first visited. The family's dynamics continued to encourage Charles's truancy; for instance, he still went on repair calls with his father during school hours and missed school more often than he attended. Despite Charles's tough behavior, his mother continued to arrange his activities (he was the only adolescent whose parent scheduled a time for him to meet with us), do his homework for him on the few occasions he bothered to go to school, and protect him in other ways.

Changing Supports at Home and at School

As younger children, our subjects had spent quite a bit of time with their parents and siblings. As they moved into adolescence, they reported spending less time with parents and other adult family members and more time with friends and close-age siblings, replicating the patterns of American adolescents in general (Csikszentmihalyi and Larson, 1984). They also reported spending more time listening to music and talking on the phone to friends, and generally spending more time alone than they did when younger. Their activities fit into traditional sex role patterns, boys participating in sports, girls socializing with friends. Boys tended to admire sports figures, while girls tended to look up to family members—either an older sibling or parent.

Christina Khouri came from a nurturing and emotionally supportive environment that compensated for her experience of two years of poor teaching during our original observation period. Her family and her classroom experience were first described in Chapter 7. In fifth grade, her vocabulary and writing scores showed little progress, although her reading comprehension and word recognition scores were well above average, and she was one of the highest achievers in our sample.

Between our original study and the follow-up interviews, Christina's father had died suddenly. His death was a shock to the close-knit family, causing both financial and emotional stress. Mr. Khouri had had an active partnership with the school and had been interested in his children's academic enterprises. Despite losing their father, the children retained achievement goals, which helped them continue to do well in high school. All the children took on small paying jobs to help out, in addition to studying and going to school regularly.

As with other adolescents, Christina's social network had changed. Whereas earlier she had spent most of her time with her parents and oldest sibling (who all had helped her with homework), now her contacts were with friends and her slightly older brothers. Her mother didn't feel she knew what was going on in Christina's life as the girl moved into adolescence and was "sometimes a world away." Spending a lot of time on the phone with her friends and going to the mall distanced Christina from other family members, but she felt she needed her "privacy . . . and that's hard with so many people in the house."

Christina continued to be a high achiever when she got to high school. She did not like the fact that her friends were in different classes (she was in the general track, taking honors courses, and they were in remedial classes). Yet she knew that to go to college she would need to make some sacrifices. Her older siblings, particularly one older brother, were her role models for doing well in school, serving also to provide moral support. Christina told us that "my brother is more than a brother. He's also a friend and a confidant. If I have a problem it becomes his problem." In this respect, Christina was functioning in a way typical of low-income adolescents, turning to slightly older siblings and friends for social and practical support (Eckert, 1988). In contrast, middle-income adolescents typically rely on adults (parents and teachers) to serve as academic and occupational role models and as sources of advice and sponsorship.

Most of the high school students in our study reported being disappointed with their relationships with teachers, although when asked whether they could name one or more teachers who had been helpful to them, most of the students said there had been at least one helpful teacher in school, and four students mentioned three or more teachers. Several of these teachers, however, were from the elementary or middle schools.

Students looked to teachers for social as well as academic support, but few found it. In contrast to a seventh grader who talked about how her teacher "sticks up for me when the kids bother me," many high school students were more likely to give answers such as, "If somebody's bothering you, the teachers don't do anything." Several students spoke of not respecting their high school teachers. "He lectures you. He's boring and doesn't know what he's talking about."

In contrast were some senior high students who had very positive things to say about one or more teachers. They mentioned that particularly helpful or admirable teachers let students speak their minds, were understanding, encouraged students to confide in them, or made it fun to learn. One student said she liked a teacher because he would "explain things really carefully, explain what you did wrong. Most tell you what to do and don't explain after."

Only a handful of students mentioned talking with a guidance counselor about appropriate coursework, college or training, and future job plans. One of the students who was managing to do well in school recognized the value of contact with a counselor: "I was doing badly a couple weeks ago. [The guidance counselor] talked about how I could change if I want or take the course as a challenge. He recommends courses and teachers to me to plan for the future." Unfortunately the high schools attended by these adolescents typically had too few counselors to serve all the students effectively; college-bound students in the honors track were more likely to seek and obtain help from counselors.

When we again asked students to write essays about a special person they admired, we noticed striking differences between the essays by adolescents who were substantially above average in their literacy achievement and those by students who were substantially below average. Nearly all of the adolescents who were doing well in school conveyed in their essays that they had supportive figures at home or at school—individuals who understood them, helped them with their problems, and often broadened their perspective on the world.

It is worth noting that in only a few of the essays, even those by the high achievers, was a teacher selected as the object of admiration (see Csikszentmihalyi and McCormack, 1986, for a discussion of the untapped potential of relationships with teachers in adolescent development). One ninth grade boy wrote about his admiration for his basketball coach: "He believes in us and we believe in him and in ourselves . . . If you are down or not doing well he will help." A seventh grade boy admired a teacher who had been especially supportive following the death of his father: "He understands problems . . . He told me he felt the same way sometimes but you had to go on and try to hold up." Although a few students found support at school, many more described support at home. An adolescent wrote: "My mother listens when we have problems and tries to work them out with us . . . My father helps with school work or future decisions and also with current affairs . . . He knows what's going on in the world." An eleventh grader said she admired her mother: "My mother encourages us and tells us to set our goals . . . She seems to know what to do or say when we have a problem." A seventh grade girl described an admired figure outside her family, Bill Cosby: "I look up to Bill Cosby because he is funny, kind and understands children a lot. Bill Cosby is very serious about his career . . . He's not lecturing to kids all the time and he is his own person and I admire that. He encourages kids to do good and be what you want to be."

In contrast, the adolescents scoring substantially below average typically expressed admiration for a family member who provided for only their basic needs for food and clothes, rather than academic or psychological needs. For example, a ninth grader wrote: "I admire my mother and father because they feed me and give me a roof over my head." Another low-achieving student, in the eleventh grade, wrote that she admired her brother because "if I ask him for money he gives it to me," and her mother because "she buys me clothes when I need them."

The reasons the students gave for *why* people were admired were even more telling than *who* the people were. One seventh grade student admired a wrestler because "being a wrestler you get to see parts of the world." Contrast this reason with that given by a ninth grade boy who admired the body builder Arnold Schwartzenegger: "He keeps himself in good shape . . . He did something with his body and got respect from people."

There were at least four adolescents who wrote in their essays that they did not admire anyone. One self-absorbed eleventh grade girl wrote, "I don't admire anyone. I envy some people but I hate them. I can't think of anyone I admire. Everyone's a pain. There's no one I want to be like." A younger adolescent boy inquired whether he could make someone up because there was no one he looked up to or admired.

Parent-School Contacts

Parents were not as involved with teachers at the high school as they had been with teachers at the elementary school. In the original study, contacts between parents and teachers were fairly widespread and showed a relationship to growth in literacy. But the picture changed as the students moved into adolescence and into a different school environment. Although students still looked to their parents for emotional support, they did not typically receive much help from them on academic matters. During the follow-up interviews, some parents spoke with resignation about their children's decline in achievement and their feelings of powerlessness in communicating with the high school.

Parents of the younger subjects in our study spoke more knowledgeably about school and teachers and "going up to the school." Only three parents of students in the older two groups mentioned having had contact with someone at the high school regarding their child's progress. Parents generally practiced a policy of non-interference. For instance, one parent explained that her son was finding high school "real hard. English is very hard for him. I get progress reports which say he might fail. I tell him he might have to take it over." However, she—like some other parents—said, "I don't want to push him," and made no contact with the school.

Another parent said her son needed help in grammar school and got it, "but in high school you don't get the same kind of help." The adolescents' growing independence was reflected in these parents' comments: "If it's okay with him, it's okay with me." The parent of an eleventh grade girl told us, "She's doing well. She doesn't complain . . . if she does, she doesn't tell me." This same attitude was evident in the parents' expectations for their children's future education: go ahead and do what you want, I'll support your choice.

Many parents seemed to feel either that their continued involvement with their children's academic progress was not sought after or that they lacked the resources to be advocates for their children. Like parents of high school students in general (see Leitch and Tangri, 1988), they mentioned many barriers to their involvement, such as being intimidated by the size and structure of the high school, ignorance of the high school curriculum, their own past academic failures at the high school level, and logistical problems including distance from the school and difficulty getting to school meetings. A major theme in the parents' comments was their own lack of competence in the subject areas their children were studying at high school. The children were not able to turn to parents for help with homework, as they might have done a few years earlier, because the parents did not (or felt they did not) understand the content of the high school courses.

It appears that those students who were able to seek out and consult with nurturing teachers or guidance counselors showed somewhat better adjustment to high school than those who were unable to find helpful adults. But most students received little, if any, guidance about possibilities or choices available to them. There were not enough guidance counselors to serve the many hundreds of students, and guidance typically had not been promoted in the first years of high school, when students were making consequential decisions about what courses to take. Many students expressed the opinion that it wasn't worth the effort to do well in high school because they couldn't afford to go to college anyway. Others knew that they had to "do well" to be admitted to college or get a good job, but were uninformed about what courses they should be taking, or the availability of academic support services, let alone procedures for applying to college or to technical training programs.

Beth Gallagher, one of our promising students in the oldest group, suffered in high school, partly because she had neither academic role models nor guidance. Beth's family, described in Chapter 5, lived in straitened circumstances, even before her father's illness and resultant job layoff. Four of the five teenage children in the family worked to help support the family. When we revisited the Gallaghers during the follow-up, a strong positive, stable emotional force still existed in the family. Sadly, though, her family's emotional support was not sufficient to keep Beth succeeding as well as she might have in school. She was graduating from high school but had no plans for work or college and had absolutely no idea how to obtain information to help plan her future. Beth was an average student who could have gone on to college had she received effective guidance from someone in her family or in school.

Ironically, early on in Beth's schooling everyone had high aspirations for her. Her teachers thought she was competent and eager, and her parents were proud of her achievements. Knowing she was doing well and "on the honor roll," her parents didn't feel the need to visit the school or her teachers. A negative cycle had started by late elementary school, with Beth's teachers feeling the girl's family was insufficiently supportive and expressing no expectations that Beth would go on to college. The Gallaghers' non-involvement continued when Beth was in high school. With Beth and her siblings on their way to graduating from high school, her parents told us, "They're doing well. They turned out nicely." Yet, Beth's parents were mystified about what went on in high school; her mother remarked, "The children have a lot of homework and things like term papers with outlines . . . it's hard to do and I wouldn't know how to help." Family problems kept the Gallagher parents preoccupied during Beth's last years of high school, when they might otherwise have been available to help her make future plans.

Educational Expectations

In the original study, parents' expectations as well as their aspirations for their children's education were relatively high, ranging from high school to college graduation. Four years later, expectations for half had changed somewhat. In 48 percent of the families, mothers had the same educational expectations for their children as they expressed at the time of the original study: 9 expected their children to complete a college education, 2 expected their children to obtain some college education, and 2 expected their children to graduate from high school. In 44 percent of the families, parents' expectations seemed to change in light of their children's academic performance: 7 parents lowered and 5 raised their expectations. For instance, the parents of a high achiever had originally thought their daughter would graduate from college, but her interest in school had waned, and four years later they thought that high school graduation was realistic. In contrast, a mother who initially thought her daughter would be lucky to get through high school upgraded her expectations as her daughter's academic performance improved.

In 70 percent of the families, adolescent and parental expectations for the adolescent's educational achievement were congruent at the time of the follow-up. In 12 families, both adolescent and mother expected the adolescent to graduate from college, while in 3 families both expected the adolescent to attend a two-year college or technical school. Several of the students for whom there was a "press for college" were worried about getting the money to go. An exception was the girl who said, "my mom has saved up money from the day in the hospital I was born. She'd pay for my dorm and food and everything. I only need the grades."

In the families where expectations did not match, 2 boys in the youngest group expected to complete more school than their mothers expected them to. A seventh grade boy commented, "I want to go to college, but I don't think I can get a scholarship for football and baseball. I don't know if [mother] knows I want to go to college . . . Right now I don't even know if I'll drop out of high school." In contrast, 2 mothers expected their daughters to graduate from college, whereas the girls felt they might get through only two years of "something after high school." In 2 other cases, the parent and child disagreed as to whether the adolescent would finish high school.

In only a quarter of the families were all children expected by both parents and the adolescents themselves to attend college. For instance, an eleventh grader said her parents expected "everyone [all four siblings] to go through college and get a good job." Another eleventh grader said he would go "real far because you have to have an education. You can't drop out and expect to get ahead. Definitely college. I don't know about grad school. Mom always said I was the smartest one in the house; she expects me to go real far. [My siblings will] go just as far as me, but I'll probably stand out." This boy's family was representative of many in our sample that selected particular siblings to be the "achievers." In some families, however, only the achiever was expected by everyone in the family to go on to college; the other siblings were not seen by parents as college material. For example, an eleventh grade girl with no current plans for college indicated that her brother would "go on, because he's got the brains."

Another of our subjects, James Conlan, told us that his parents expected his sister to graduate from college, while they expected him to go no further than high school. Earlier, his parents had been sure he would go to college, even though he was not the academic "star" his sister was. The Conlan family, introduced in Chapter 6, represented an extreme lack of parental involvement with the school. In fifth grade, Jimmy showed no gains in reading comprehension, lacking two of the factors found to be related to gain in this reading skill—contacts between his teacher and his family and positive assessment of the family by his teacher. The family's lack of involvement continued right through the middle grades and into high school. The sibling differentiation regarding academics continued as well; Jimmy's older sister was graduating from high school with honors and getting a scholarship to college, whereas Jimmy's grades had slipped even more, and he was still having difficulty in high school.

Mrs. Conlan continued to sing her children's praises, saying that Jimmy would be terrific at whatever he chose to do. He excelled in non-academic subjects and had selected the vocational track at the high school. Despite Jimmy's academic difficulties, the Conlans continued to eschew contact with the school. Mrs. Conlan was just as willing to blame Jimmy's academic problems on the school as she had been when he was in elementary school. But she was unable to help him as she had earlier; she could not, for instance, do his high school homework for him anymore.

The family togetherness that we saw initially was still present. A real sense of mutual respect and enjoyment was evident. Family outings continued to be important, even if it meant Jimmy would not do all of his homework. That seemed less important to his parents than the emotional well-being fostered by their shared activities.

In almost a quarter of the families, older siblings had either dropped out or were seriously contemplating not finishing high school, and this had had some influence on the adolescents' plans. In some of the families with younger children it was still too early to tell whether they would actually go on to college. Some of them had not discussed future plans with their parents. As one seventh grader explained, "Mom probably thinks I'll go to college, but I've never talked to her about it."

Job Plans and Preparation

The adolescents' occupational expectations ranged from semi-skilled to professional work. Two of the oldest students, both girls, planned to be beauticians. Four others planned to do skilled work: two wanted to be electricians, and two wanted to go into law enforcement. Three girls wanted to work in an office. Three students planned to capitalize on their artistic talents and become commercial artists. Five students—three girls and two boys—said they wanted to be either doctors or lawyers. Other occupational goals included work in electronics or computers and radio broadcasting.

Renee Grant, introduced in the second chapter, was a below-average student in elementary school and a below-average student in high school. Her weak academic skills and casual attitude toward school and homework were not helped by the lax standards for academic achievement set by her family. However, unlike some of her peers who dropped out or were held back, Renee graduated from high school (and proudly showed us her high school diploma on one of our visits). Why did Renee manage to succeed despite the decided lack of a "press for achievement"? Her academic failings were compensated by very strong social skills and a stable family environment. Her sunny personality was infectious, a trait that made her popular with her peers and her teachers. Furthermore, the Grant family had provided Renee with a wide array of financially and emotionally independent female role models. For example, she often mentioned her aunt (and wrote about her in an essay for us) who "went all the way through school." This aunt had graduated from high school and made a real impression on Renee, perhaps because she was the only one in the family ever to have done so. In addition, Renee's grandmother, who headed the household in which she grew up, was working full-time, taking care of family members, foster children, and pursuing adult literacy classes.

Renee had worked at several jobs through high school and her practical experience enabled her to make a realistic assessment of her job opportunities. For the time being, she was working with young children, but she wanted to attend community college and get a degree so that she could do some work in counseling or some other "people kind of job." It is interesting that one of Renee's friends in sixth grade chose to write about Renee for her essay on someone she admired; she wrote "she has a lot of ideas that make sense." This assessment held true five years later.

The adolescents' job plans were somewhat more realistic than their earlier aspirations, which had been strongly influenced by their television viewing. As one high school student commented, "Everyone wants to be an actress or model, but then you move into reality." But six students said they had "no idea" what they would like to do after finishing high school, adding "before, I wanted to be a [lawyer] [lab technician] [teacher], but I'm not sure now."

Although their job plans had become more realistic since elementary school, even most of the students who seemed thoughtful about the kind of job they wanted lacked realistic orientation to the future and understanding about how to plan for "what's out there" after high school. Those who did have a career idea were misinformed about the training or degree necessary to pursue that career. For instance, those students who mentioned their desires to be doctors or lawyers were ignorant of the educational prerequisites for either of these professions. Those who talked about going to work in fashion design, the police, or with computers were similarly uninformed.

In interviews with the students in the older group, when most had completed twelfth grade, half described themselves as neither working nor planning to attend college in the near future. They reported feeling confused about how to get a job they would be interested in. Their lack of preparation or entry-level skills made it difficult for them to find meaningful work. One girl admitted "feeling the pressure about what you're going to do with your life."

Academic Achievement

We designed a battery of tests to access the students' achievement in the same areas of literacy we had tested in 1981–82. Once again, we assessed student progress in word recognition, vocabulary, writing, and reading comprehension. Of the 28 students we were able to make contact with, 26 took this battery of tests in 1986. Thus we were able to compare the achievement of our subjects when they were in grades 3, 5, and 7 with their achievement in grades 7, 9, and 11, to see how much progress they had made in literacy skills in the intervening four years.

Word recognition. In the spring of 1986 we administered the Word Recognition subtest of the Wide Range Achievement Test (WRAT), Level 2, to the 26 students available for follow-up study. We then compared their grade equivalent score on the WRAT from 1986 with the same students' score on the Roswell-Chall Word Recognition elementary level subtest administered in the spring of 1982. We expected students to gain 4.0 years between

1982 and 1986, but the average gain in word recognition for the 26 students was only 1.4 years over the four-year period. Only 3 students made the expected gain, and these were all from our youngest group—the seventh graders. None of the eleventh graders showed even a full-year gain across the four years between testings.

Only a fifth of our students scored at or above grade level in word recognition in 1986, although over three-quarters of these students had done so in 1982. All but one of the students scoring at or above grade level in 1986 were in our youngest group (seventh graders). On the average, our students scored 1.6 years below national norms on the WRAT Word Recognition subtest. Our oldest group (eleventh graders) were 4 years behind their age-mates nationally, on the average. A typical eleventh grader in our group could not correctly read aloud words like "municipal," "decisive," and "scald."

Vocabulary. In 1986 we used two different assessments of our students' knowledge of vocabulary: the Weschler Intelligence Scale for Children–Revised (WISC-R) Vocabulary subtest and the Peabody Picture Vocabulary Test–Revised. Comparing the performance on the WISC-R Vocabulary subtest from the same students in 1986 and 1982, the average gain for this four-year period was 3.3 years. Approximately two-fifths of the students gained at least 4 years on this test; 2 students actually scored lower than before.

The Peabody Picture Vocabulary Test–Revised provides better comparisons with national norms for students aged twelve through sixteen than does the WISC. On the average, our students' vocabulary scores were 1.8 years below their age-mates nationally. Just under a third of our students scored at or above national norms on the Peabody. Even one of our higher-scoring eleventh graders could not recognize the meaning of words such as "constellation," "ascending," "exterior," and "fatigued" when presented with a choice of pictures illustrating the meaning. An average seventh grader in our group did not know the meaning of "citrus," "pedestrian," and "link."

Writing. As in the original study, we collected narrative and expository writing samples from each subject. In the spring of 1986 students again wrote a narrative in response to the picture of an old woman holding tomatoes and an expository essay on the topic "Who Do You Admire?" (see Figures 9.1–9.3). These essays were

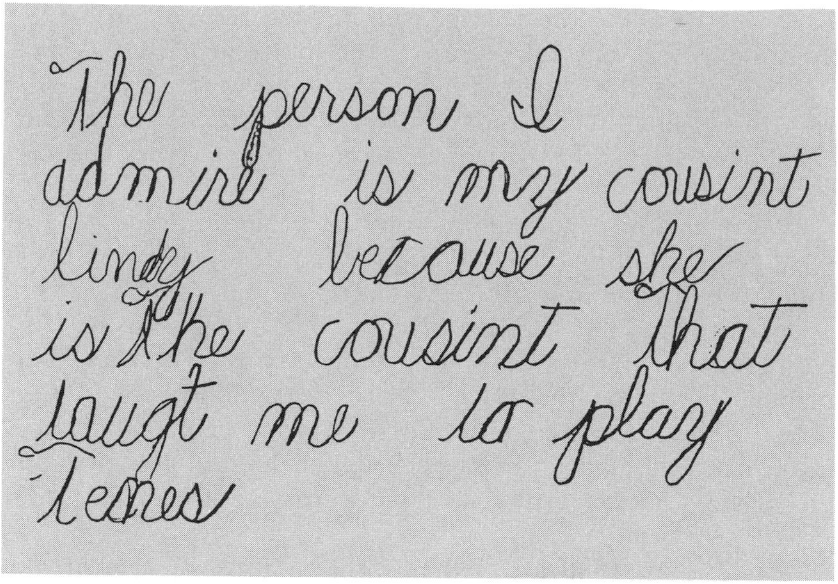

The person I
admire is my cousint
lindy because she
is the cousint that
laugt me to play
Tenes

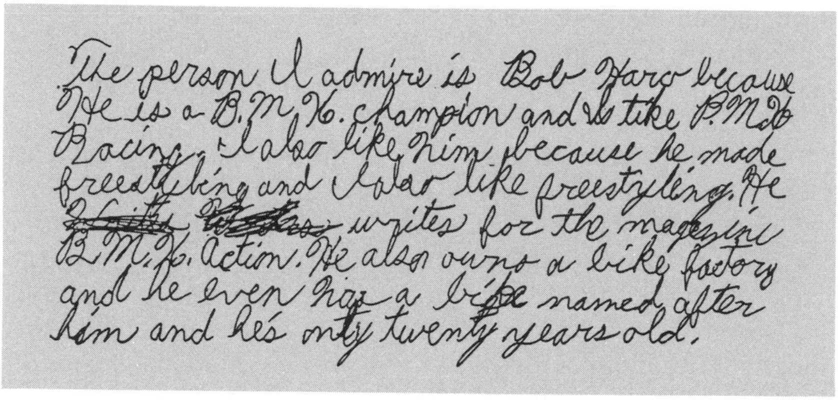

The person I admire is Bob Haro becaue
He is a B.M.X. champion and I like B.M.X.
Racing, I also like him because he made
freestyleing and I also like freestyleing. He
~~B.M.X. action~~ writes for the magazine
B.M.X. Action. He also owns a bike factory
and he even has a bike named after
him and he's only twenty years old.

Figure 9.1 Excerpts from third grader's original and follow-up
essays. In this and the next two figures, writing
samples from a third, fifth, and seventh grader in the
original sample are juxtaposed to samples written by
the same children four years later. Whereas the
third and fifth graders' essays show considerable
improvement in length and quality over the four-year
interval, the seventh grader produced an essay in
eleventh grade that was at about the same level of
sophistication as her original essay.

My mother and father because they buy me close and toys. an my friend to drawer my friend plays with me. and he tells me jokes.

I admire My teacher Mr. Daniel Raymond I admire him as the coach of our basketball team, I admire him because our team had been in the league for three years now, he did not coach us in the first season, 1983-1984 but he did coach our second and third season in 1983-1984 we won 3 games and lost 11 games. When Mr. Raymond came to coach us in 1984-1985 we won 2 games and lost 12, but in the season of 1985-1986 we improved to an even 7 wins 7 losses and we made the playoffs. The moral of this story is that Mr. Raymond never gave up on the team he believes in us and we believe in him and ourselves, he is returning with us next season and we will be the champions of our league

Figure 9.2   Excerpts from fifth grader's original and follow-up essays.

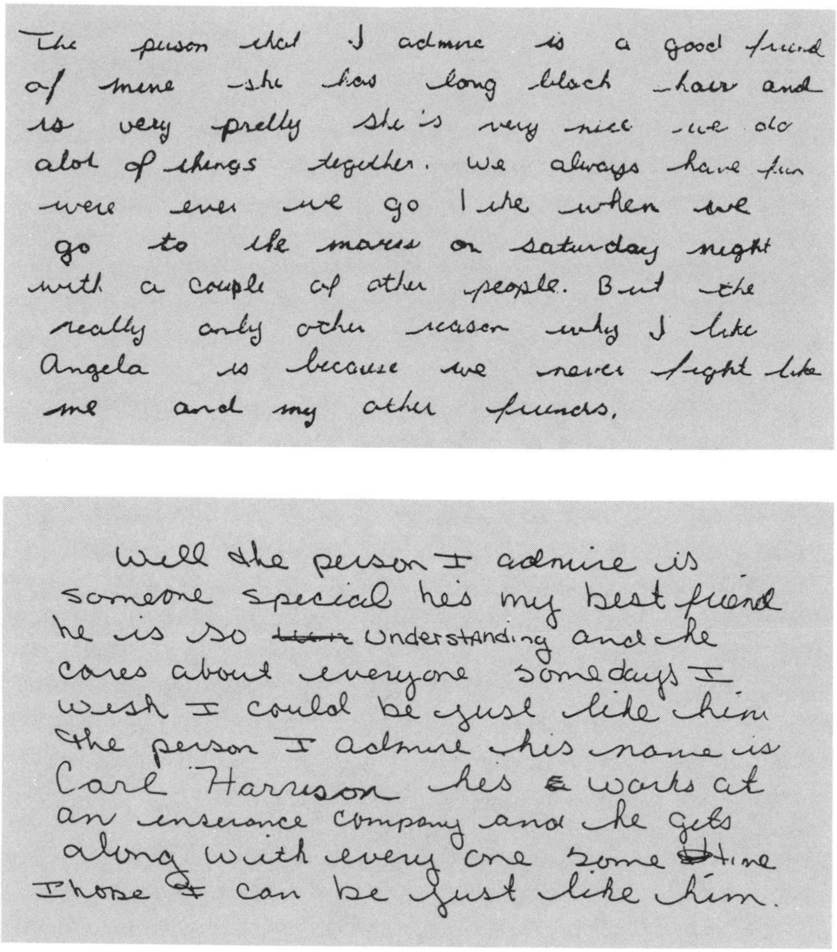

The person that I admire is a good friend of mine she has long black hair and is very pretty she's very nice we do alot of things together. We always have fun were ever we go like when we go to the movies on saturday night with a couple of other people. But the really only other reason why I like Angela is because we never fight like me and my other friends.

Well the person I admire is someone special he's my best friend he is so ~~than~~ understanding and he cares about everyone some days I wish I could be just like him the person I admire his name is Carl Harrison he's ~~a~~ works at an insurance company and he gets along with every one some ~~time~~ I hope I can be just like him.

Figure 9.3 Excerpts from seventh grader's original and follow-up essays.

combined with ones collected from the same children in 1981 and in 1982 and were holistically rated by three independent raters (Fowles, 1978).[2] On a 9-point scale, the average gain between 1981

2. Since essays that are holistically rated are scored relative to each other, it is important in measuring improvement to have all the essays in the same rating pool. Thus we needed to re-rate the essays from 1981 and 1982 along with the new ones collected in 1986. Since this rating pool contained essays from second

samples and 1982 samples was three-quarters of a point. If students continued to improve in their writing ability at the same rate over the next four years, we would expect a gain of 3 points between 1982 and 1986. However, the average gain in narrative ratings in this period was less than 2 points—only a little more than half of what we might expect. Just under a third of the students made the expected gain between 1982 and 1986. Fifteen percent of the students' narratives were given the same or lower ratings in 1986 as in 1982.

The expository essays from 1981, 1982, and 1986 were combined and holistically rated on a 6-point scale. The average gain in ratings of expository writing between 1981 and 1982 was half a point. Projecting similar gains in expository ratings over the next four years, one would expect an average gain of 2.2. However, our students' average gain on ratings of their expository essays between 1982 and 1986 was only 1.2—again only about half of what might be expected. Only 15 percent of our students showed the expected improvement between 1982 and 1986, and another 15 percent received ratings that were the same or worse.

Since holistic scores can be interpreted only relative to other scores given at the same rating session, our students' writing cannot be compared with national norms.

Reading comprehension. Students' reading comprehension ability in 1986 was assessed through the Metropolitan Survey Battery Reading subtest. To calculate gains, we then compared the grade-equivalent score to the same student's score on the Roswell-Chall Silent Reading subtest taken in 1982. The average gain in this four-year period was 3.3 years, with nearly half of the students achieving more than the expected gain of 4.0 years and only 2 students scoring lower than before.

The pattern of individual student gains in reading comprehension is very similar to their gain in word meaning. All 10 of the students who showed the expected gain in word meaning also did so

---

graders through eleventh graders, the range of quality was quite large. We wanted to use a scale with enough points on it to reflect fully the distinctions we could reliably make among the essays. There was a wider range of quality in the narrative essays than in the expository ones; therefore, in rating the former, we used a 9-point scale, while a 6-point scale was used for the latter.

in reading comprehension, and the 2 students who scored lower than before also did so on both the word meaning and reading comprehension tests.

In contrast to the other literacy areas, our students' achievement in reading comprehension in 1986 was relatively high. More than half (14 of 26) scored at or above national norms on the Metropolitan Survey Battery Reading subtest. The group as a whole averaged about half a year below grade level in reading comprehension.

Overall Assessment of Literacy Gains

If students had been progressing steadily since the end of our project in 1982, we would expect a 4-year gain on average by the time they were retested in 1986. In the literacy areas of vocabulary and reading comprehension our students came closest to meeting this expectation, showing an average gain of 3.3 years. However, in writing (holistically scored narrative and expository samples), students gained only about half of what was expected. In word recognition, the picture was even bleaker: the average gain was a mere 1.4 years over the four-year period. Although gains in vocabulary and reading comprehension were better than in the other literacy areas measured, by junior and senior high school age our students were still not keeping pace with the levels of achievement one would have predicted for them from their performance in elementary school.

We were also concerned about our students' achievement levels as compared to national norms for their grade levels. Reading comprehension was the area where our students came closest to achieving national standards, scoring on average about half a year below grade level. In the other areas for which we had national comparisons, by contrast, our students scored close to 2 years below grade level—an average of 1.6 years behind in word recognition and 1.8 in vocabulary.

What these two subtests (word recognition and vocabulary) have in common is that both require familiarity with more challenging words from literary or technical domains in order to pronounce or define them correctly. The vocabulary that junior and senior high school students are expected to know include such literary words as "consuming," "wrath," and "arrogant," and words from content areas like "perpendicular," "peninsula," and "barricade." For students to have learned the meanings of words at this level, they must have encountered them through wide reading or have been exposed to them in conversation at home or school or in content area instruction. If low-income students are not taking sufficiently challenging courses in English, math, history, and science, and they are not reading difficult material on their own, they are not likely to achieve at grade level on tests of word meaning. We know from our follow-up interviews that few of our students were taking college preparatory courses and that their leisure reading was essentially limited to comic books and Harlequin romances.

Our students' problems with word recognition have similar sources. They typically could not pronounce words like "predatory," "decisive," and "bibliography." Unlike such words as "chin," "block," and "cliff," knowledge of simple phonic principles is not sufficient for correctly pronouncing these more difficult words. Our students, for example, tended to put the accent on the wrong syllable in these multisyllabic words. To pronounce these words correctly, one has to have heard them either in lectures at school or in conversation outside school. We know from follow-up interviews that many of our students were disaffected with school at this age and often tuned out the lectures they heard in school. In addition, most of these adolescents spent little time with adults outside school, and their family members themselves generally had not had enough exposure to these words to use them confidently in conversation.

It might seem surprising that, given their broad deficits in word knowledge, our students scored as close to national norms as they did in reading comprehension. Unlike the other literacy areas, which assessed students' knowledge of words presented in isolation, reading comprehension was assessed by having students read connected text and select answers to multiple-choice questions. Students can be unfamiliar with many of the individual words in passages like those used in reading comprehension assessments and still use the supporting context to choose the correct answer. Our students were able to achieve scores close to grade level by selecting the correct answer when the information was presented in the same words in the question and in the passage. However, when a question required rearranging or synthesizing information from the passage, not just locating it in the same form, most of our students had difficulty. In addition, students generally had problems interpreting the motives of characters in fictional passages and identifying the purpose of expository passages, and they missed most questions about figurative uses of language.

Although the picture that emerged from examining the academic achievement of our group of students in 1986 was fairly gloomy, there was considerable variability in individuals' performance. For example, in reading comprehension, students in our follow-up group ranged from 5 years above grade level to 8 years below grade level.

Original Family Variables and Student Achievement

We were curious to see how strong an association there would be between our original family variables and students' achievement five years later as junior and senior high school students. To determine whether any relation existed, we computed correlations between the outcome variables from 1986 and the family variables that were strongly related to earlier achievement measures. Two variables in particular were significantly related to all or nearly all of our 1986 outcome measures. The family's provision of literacy in 1981 was the most powerful predictor variable; it was related at impressive levels of significance to student achievement four years later in word recognition, vocabulary, and reading comprehension and showed a lower correlation with writing production.[3] The provision of literacy, it will be recalled, was an observer rating of the degree to which parents provided literacy experiences for their children (buying books, reading to them, taking them to the library, and discussing books, magazines, and newspaper articles with them). This may indicate that the types of parents who were successfully providing a rich variety of literacy experiences for their children in the early and middle elementary grades continued to support their children's academic achievement. Alternatively, it may indicate that the good start in literacy some children had gotten helped them throughout school, even without continued parental efforts to provide literacy experiences.

3. Writing production was used in this analysis because our holistic ratings were inappropriate for correlational analyses.

The second most powerful predictor variable was maternal expectations for children's education. When interviewed in 1981, 56 percent of the mothers expected their children to finish college or professional school (8 percent expected some college) whereas just over a third expected only high school graduation. These original expectations were significantly related to three of our outcome measures four years later—vocabulary, reading comprehension, and writing production. (Interestingly, early teacher expectations for students' further education were even more strongly related than mothers' to vocabulary, reading comprehension, and writing production outcomes.)

In addition to these two major predictors, a number of other family variables from 1981 showed relationships to particular areas of student achievement in 1986. For example, maternal education showed a relationship to word recognition. Observer ratings of family structure as well as the presence of rules governing television use, observer ratings of emotional stability, and observer ratings of the cleanliness and orderliness of the physical environment of the home were all related to students' vocabulary scores four years later. The variety of activities the elementary school children had engaged in after school was related only to writing production in 1986, bearing the same relationship it had shown in 1982. Interestingly, the quality of parent-child interaction during a homework-like task in 1981 was not related to any outcome variable in 1986, although it had been associated with writing achievement in 1982. Our 1981 rating of parent-child interaction reflected the child's particular style and skill at doing homework at that time as well as the parent's style of responding. It is, then, perhaps not surprising that it failed to predict our measures of academic achievement four or five years later.

It is striking that so many and such strong relationships exist between characteristics of a child's early home environment and achievement five years later. Of course many of the predictor variables mark enduring characteristics of families that may continue to have influence through the high school years. The possibility must be considered, however, that some effect of these variables derived from the head start they gave children in literacy achievement. Indeed this theory is supported by the fact that we found similar patterns of relationships with outcome variables in 1982.

Table 9.1 Intercorrelations among the outcome measures

	PPVT	Reading comprehension	Word recognition
Reading comprehension	.82		
Word recognition	.61	.68	
WISC	.80	.86	.68

Note: All reported correlations were significant at $p < .001$.

Although the various outcome measures are all fairly highly intercorrelated (see Table 9.1), they show distinctive relationships to the predictor variables (see Table 9.2). For example, provision of literacy and maternal educational expectations were highly correlated with all the outcome variables, whereas measures of the emotional and organizational aspects of family life (emotional stability, physical environment, family structure, and TV rules) were significantly related only to vocabulary, and maternal education related only to word recognition scores.

Later Environmental Variables and Student Achievement

In addition to relating our original family variables to students' achievement as junior and senior high school students, we also sought to relate key aspects of the students' experiences as secondary students to their 1986 achievement. Parents' provision of literacy materials for the students when they were in elementary school showed strong relationships with literacy achievement. Once students are in secondary school, however, the parents' role in providing access to out-of-school literacy experiences becomes less important. Because of their increasing independence, students can now arrange their own library visits, buy their own books, and organize their free time to include reading for pleasure, or do none of these things. Thus we conceptualize the provision of out-of-school literacy for adolescents as a variable that reflects students' own behavior rather than that of their parents.

In interviews with the adolescents we probed different aspects of their reading habits. Reading books was not a leisure-time activity frequently selected by these adolescents. Asked how many books they had read for fun in the last month, just over half said none, while a third indicated they had read one or two books during the past month. A common response was, "I read school books all the time, so I can't read for fun." One disaffected boy said, "I never did read [a book] for fun," while a sixteen-year-old girl thought for a minute and then said, "Sometimes I read, get into a book, but usually something comes up and I don't finish it. I try to read at night but fall asleep." Some of these young people indicated that they read comics and magazines or "just stories," but would read books only if they were required to do so for their school work.

Table 9.2 Relations between early predictors and later outcome measures

Predictors			Outcome measures		
	PPVT	WISC	Reading comprehension	Word recognition	Writing production
Provision of literacy	.66[c]	.52[b]	.62[c]	.49[b]	.38
Maternal ed. expectations	.41[a]	.49[b]	.46[a]	.32	.42[a]
Teacher ed. expectations	.28	.57[b]	.55[b]	.29	.57[b]
Maternal education	.24	.24	.27	.42[a]	.07
Family structure	.20	.38[a]	.30	.30	.13
TV rules	.33	.45[a]	.38	.22	.15
Emotional stability	.24	.40[a]	.36	.07	.24
Physical environment	.29	.38[a]	.33	.27	.09
Children's activities	.25	.27	.27	−.01	.54[b]
Parent-child interaction	.04	.16	.27	.14	.29

a. $p < .05$
b. $p < .01$
c. $p < .001$

Only one of our students was an avid reader: "I knock out two Harlequin romances in a day."

One question that we included was who, if anyone, students considered to be their favorite author. We found in our original interviews with students' mothers that this was an excellent indicator of the breadth and seriousness of mothers' involvement with reading (see also Chomsky, 1972). When we asked this question of the adolescents, only about a third named one favorite author, and only 15 percent could name more than one. Their responses showed a significant association with achievement in one of the literacy areas assessed, vocabulary. Of those students naming one or more favorite authors half (both boys and girls) mentioned Judy Blume. Otherwise, authors were nonentities to them. As one student explained, "I don't look for books by authors."

Another area important for students' achievement as elementary school students was the degree to which their parents forged cooperative relationships with teachers. As discussed above, by junior and senior high school parents were much less involved in the students' school lives, in part because of the change from smaller neighborhood schools to large citywide schools, and in part because of the greater number of teachers involved with secondary (as opposed to elementary) school students. Some of our students were able to seek out teachers in high school as advisors, mentors, and boosters, but many others were not. Those who successfully built these relationships were in a position similar to elementary students whose parents formed collaborations on their child's behalf with the classroom teacher. We therefore related a measure of students' success in establishing productive relationships with teachers with our 1986 achievement outcomes. Our index of students' achievement in building relations with teachers was the number of "helpful teachers" adolescents named in interviews. This measure showed a very strong association with students' word production in writing but only modest associations with other literacy areas.

Mothers' original educational expectations for the children in our study showed powerful relationships with achievement, both in elementary and secondary school. We conceptualize this effect as the result of maternal encouragement, goal setting, and active intervention on the child's behalf, for example, advocating that the child get remedial help or transferring the child to a better school. By adolescence, although students may have shown the cumulative benefits of these earlier efforts, most of our working-class parents had withdrawn from such active involvement. In our 1986 interviews, parents reported seeing school-related planning and goal setting as their adolescent children's own responsibility. Activities such as studying for PSATs, filling out college applications, selecting courses, and completing homework were left up to the students' own initiative (whereas middle-class parents tend to be rather heavily involved in these activities with their adolescent children; Baker and Stevenson, 1986). Because students' initiative had become more important, we broadened our original conception of family educational expectations to include the students' own, as well as their mothers' educational expectations. We thus related two measures of expectations to 1986 achievement levels: the students' expectations for themselves, and their report of their mothers' expectations, both from our 1986 interviews. Students' own educational expectations showed significant associations with three out of our four literacy outcomes: reading comprehension most strongly, and vocabulary and word recognition, at the .05 level. Mothers' educational expectations as reported by their children, by contrast, showed no significant relations with outcome measures.

These results parallel in many ways our findings from the original study. Provision of out-of-school literacy experiences, whether by adolescents for themselves or by parents for younger children, continued to be strongly related to growth in vocabulary. The benefits of this for other areas of literacy appeared to diminish as students progress into junior and senior high school. Wide reading, the factor measured by our "favorite author" question, seems not to relate to the reading comprehension abilities of older students the way "liking to read" had when these students were younger. As we argued above in interpreting the relatively poor performance of our group on most 1986 literacy measures, literacy skills show the increasing influence of explicit instruction in and exposure to content areas as students advance into secondary school. Out-of-school reading, particularly of the undemanding kind engaged in by even the brightest of our subjects, cannot make up for the lack of exposure to higher level reading tasks and various content areas in school.

Our finding that students' mention of helpful teachers related to writing production parallels our earlier finding that children with positive family relationships wrote longer essays. Writing for an adult audience involves self-disclosure; students who enjoy relatively positive relations with parents and teachers are likely to reveal more of themselves in their writing and to do so at greater length. Students with less positive relations more typically see the audience for their writing as an unfriendly critical adult, what Britton et al. (1975) have called the "teacher as examiner." Thus they write less, producing less of what might be harshly judged.

Relations with helpful teachers showed no broader associations with achievement. In part, this may reflect the diffuse nature of instruction in secondary schools. A friendly math or gym teacher cannot be a major source of educational advantage the way an exceptionally interested elementary school teacher in a self-contained classroom can be. Supportive teachers may have given a boost in their own subject area, but generally they could not influence literacy achievement across the board. It is not surprising, then, that the influence of helpful teachers seems restricted to the more affective domain of writing production.

We found that adolescents' own expectations for their educational achievement was associated with test scores in nearly all areas of literacy, while reports of their mothers' expectations in 1986 (unlike maternal expectations in 1981) showed less clear associations. In part, this reflects the greater realism of the adolescents themselves. One of our typical subjects said, "My mother still wants me to go to four year college, but I'm going to settle for beautician's school." Parents, at least in their children's eyes, held fast to their dreams of high achievement, while the adolescents were scaling down their own aspirations. But what had changed most in the years since the students were in elementary school was the parents' ability to act on their relatively high expectations. The mother cited in the quotation above had not made it through high school herself. She was intimidated by the array of principals, department chairpersons, guidance counselors, assistant principals, and homeroom teachers at her daughter's high school, and hence had no contacts with school personnel once her daughter left junior high. At the neighborhood elementary school this parent had been a familiar figure, active in school affairs, well spoken of by teachers and the principal, who knew her well and respected her high standards for her children. Although her expectations showed no decline, her ability to support and advance her daughter's academic career was considerably lessened in secondary school.

The prospects for the children we interviewed and tested in 1980–81 and 1981–82 seemed quite bright. Only a few of them were in serious academic trouble then, and even those scoring the lowest on our tests showed the capacity to make great gains under the influence of excellent teachers. Our expectations for these children matched, and often exceeded, those of their own parents. Most of them seemed likely to finish high school, and many seemed like good college prospects.

The follow-up interviews and testing revealed to us how idealistic our expectations had been. Few of the students in the study had continued to make gains in literacy consonant with their abilities. Only a small minority were taking courses that would qualify them for entry to college. Several were high school dropouts, and very few planned to go on to training of any sort after high school. This small group of adolescents is, unfortunately, typical of children from low-income families across the United States. Their own expectations of emerging into prosperity, financial stability, and middle-class lives through schooling have not, in general, been met; their parents', their teachers', and society's expectations for them have also been disappointed. Yet, none of those expectations was ill-founded or unrealistic, and most of them could, under other circumstances, have been fulfilled.

We can only hope that society will not, in response to this discrepancy between early expectations and ultimate achievement, choose to lower its expectations for low-income American children. Academic goals such as high school graduation, access to academic or vocational training, a level of proficiency in reading that exposes students to books and newspapers as sources of information and to literature as a source of entertainment, a level of skill in writing that makes both applying for jobs and expressing one's innermost thoughts possible—none of these should be out of the reach of children from low-income families. Their parents' and their own expectations that they will meet such goals should not be unrealistic. American society is faced with making the choices to ensure that goals like these can be fulfilled for all children.

Appendixes

References

Acknowledgments

Index

Appendix 1. Number of subjects for which various categories of data are available

	Mother interview	Father interview	Child interview	Diary I	Diary II	Diary observations
Complete	26	11	32	15	20	27
Partial	5	7	0	5	0	—
Refused	1	5	0	1	8	5
Not available	0	9	0	11	4	—

Family SYMLOG	Teacher questionnaire		Classroom observations		School biography	School test scores	School SYMLOGS
	80–81	81–82	80–81	81–82			
24	32	21	30	26	31	18	20
0	0	8	—	—	—	2	—
8	—	—	—	2	—	—	10
0	0	3	2	4	1	12	2

Appendix 2. Diary and checklists

Name _____   Day _____

Morning

	What were you doing?	Where were you?	Who were you with? (Mother, father, brother or sister, friend, adult friend, relative, or by yourself)
6:00			
6:15			
6:30			
6:45			
7:00			
7:15			
7:30			
7:45			
8:00			
8:15			
8:30			
8:45			
9:00			
9:15			
9:30			
9:45			

Continuous through 11:00 P.M.

Name _____   Day _____

Please put a check in the box next to anything you did at school today.

☐ Have reading group

☐ Do math

☐ Have social studies

☐ Have language arts

☐ Have science

☐ Do spelling

☐ Eat lunch

☐ Have recess

☐ Go on field trip

☐ See a movie

☐ Have assembly

☐ Play an outdoor game

☐ Write a story or play

☐ Write a composition

☐ Draw pictures

☐ Act out a part in a play

☐ Give a report

☐ Have show and tell

☐ Do a puzzle or word game

☐ Write a letter

☐ Have music

☐ Have physical education

☐ Have art

☐ Have health

☐ Visit the school library

☐ Read to yourself for fun

☐ Listen to the teacher read

☐ Fill in blanks in a workbook or on a worksheet

☐ Practice handwriting

☐ Copy things over

☐ Read out loud in a group

☐ Take a test

☐ Do homework

☐ Play an instrument

☐ Go to resource room

☐ Be tutored

Name ——————————————— Day ——————————

Please put a check in the box next to anything you did today.

At Home

☐ Make things

☐ Play games

☐ Do chores

☐ Babysit

☐ Play with dolls, stuffed animals, or puppets

☐ Play with toys

☐ Play dressup

☐ Cook

☐ Play school

☐ Play store

☐ Practice an instrument

☐ Draw

☐ Write

☐ Take a nap/rest

☐ Watch T.V.

☐ Read

☐ Take care or play with pet

☐ Take a bath/shower

☐ Talk on the telephone

☐ Do homework

☐ Have a friend over

☐ Have a talk with mother

☐ Have a talk with father

☐ Play games like tag, jumprope, or superheroes

☐ Play with a pet

☐ Go to playground

☐ Go to visit relatives

☐ Go to a friend's house

☐ Go downtown

☐ Go to the corner store

☐ Go out to do errands

☐ Go shopping

☐ Go out to eat

☐ Go to a museum

☐ Go to lessons

☐ Go swimming

☐ Go to a movie

☐ Go to watch a game, sports event

☐ Go to play soccer, football or other game

☐ Go to doctor

☐ Go to the Y, Youth Center, Rec Center

☐ Go to church/Sunday school

☐ Go to work with mom or dad

☐ Go to babysitter's

☐ Have a talk with brother

☐ Have a talk with sister

☐ Play ball

☐ Ride a bike

☐ Rollerskate, iceskate

☐ Stay at school for after-school program

☐ Go in the car

☐ Go on a bus

☐ Go on excursion

Appendix 3. Correlations between school variables and three literacy outcome variables

School variable	Word recognition gain	Reading comprehension gain	Vocabulary gain
Reading lesson observations			
Exclusive use of basal or workbook	.26	.10	−.48[b]
Substantial oral reading	.14	−.03	−.14
Explicit word attack instruction	−.25	−.12	.34
Explicit comprehension instruction	−.06	.39[a]	.14
Explicit vocabulary instruction	−.13	.09	−.09
Use of materials beyond basals or workbooks	−.26	−.10	.48[b]
Inference questioning	−.27	.14	.25
Relating reading to content areas	−.23	−.10	.15
Observer ratings			
Quality of instruction	−.31	.28	.27
Literacy environment	−.33[a]	.22	.36[a]
Teacher reports			
Emphasis on critical thinking	−.33[a]	−.01	.19
Emphasis on comprehension	−.15	−.16	.26
Emphasis on vocabulary	−.11	.01	−.07
Library visits	−.04	.39[a]	.16

School variable	Word recognition gain	Reading comprehension gain	Vocabulary gain
Reading and writing homework	−.32[a]	−.39[a]	−.14
Trade books	−.18	−.14	.23
Types of materials	−.03	.40[a]	.26
Book reports	.06	−.13	−.11
Creative writing	−.40[a]	−.13	.21
Writing frequency	−.35[a]	−.06	.06
Teacher-directed lessons	−.10	−.23	.09
Workbook homework	.32[a]	.39[a]	.14
Difficulty level of reading text	.17	.28	−.56[a]
Text completion	−.11	−.08	.15
Allocated time for reading instruction	−.03	.41[a]	−.09
Single skills emphasis	−.23	−.02	.22
Student attendance	.32[a]	.13	−.10
Field trips	−.05	−.26	−.04

a. $p < .05$
b. $p < .01$

Appendix 4. Correlations between home factors and literacy measures

Home factor	Word recognition				Reading comprehension				Vocabulary				Word production			
	2d	4th	6th	Total	2d	4th	6th	Total	2d	4th	6th	Total	2d	4th	6th	Total
Family income (1=low)	.56a	.51a	.63a	.48b	.31	.53a	-.12	.36b	-.02	.27	-.28	.10	-.15	-.25	-.05	.02
Income per capita	-.05	-.30	.43	-.00	.16	-.04	.24	-.18	.26	-.06	.13	.14	-.42	-.45	.42	-.10
Rating of mother's literacy (1=nonreader)	.28	.41	.38	.32b	.11	.26	.63b	.31b	.21	.39	.33	.27a	-.37	.32	.70b	.17
Number of mother's favorite authors	.77	—	—	.69b	.70	—	—	.05	.77	—	—	.31	.18	—	—	-.20
Number of magazines read regularly	.56	-.82b	—	-.12	.17	-.59	—	-.11	-.22	-.27	—	-.29	-.22	-.02	—	.05
Level of newspaper read regularly (1=local, 5=national)	.53	.11	.87a	.40a	.33	-.23	.97b	.21	.75	.47	.97b	.56b	-.77a	.42	.80	.17
Number of favorite books as a child that mother remembers	.15	.53	.00	.36	-.21	.95	.46	.33	.50	.99b	-1.00c	.26	.95a	.88	.40	.24
Number of favorite authors as child	—	—	—	.81b	—	—	—	-.12	—	—	—	.24	—	—	—	.45
Rating of provision of literacy for child	-.17	.12	.52a	.18	.05	-.47a	.20	-.03	-.26	.24	.34	.14	.46a	.59b	.47	.36b
Number of books child owns	-.14	-.07	.17	-.03	.04	.04	.35	.31b	-.06	.09	.08	.05	-.33	-.03	.28	.29b
Frequency mother writes notes to child (1=infrequent)	.24	.06	-.70b	-.16	.81b	-.45	-.03	-.02	.50	-.13	-.33	-.21	-.74b	-.06	.08	.24
Mother's report: Age child learned to read (1=early)	-.75c	-.75c	-.40	-.58c	-.72b	-.59b	-.47	-.50c	-.25	-.59b	-.39	-.44c	.43	-.03	-.17	.02
Child's report: Age child learned to read (1=early)	.45	-.11	.39	.17	.18	-.20	.21	.05	.37	-.53b	.35	-.04	-.51b	-.02	.11	.06
Mother's report: Number of problems in first grade (1=fewer)	-.28	-.66b	-.36	-.29a	.35	.16	-.32	.24	.43	-.32	-.05	.15	.21	-.29	-.32	-.03

Mother's report: Number of problems learning to read (1=fewer)	.40	-.47[a]	-.31	-.28[a]	.26	.00	-.32	.02	.49[a]	-.68[c]	-.10	-.27[a]	.34	-.78[c]	-.66[b]	-.37[b]	
Mother's report: Child's reading group in first grade (1=high)	-.21	.58[b]	.27	.26	-.28	-.18	.61[a]	-.06	-.44	.26	.45	-.04	-.09	.40	.05	-.20	
Mother's report: Child had favorite books as a young child (1=no)	-.01	-.63[a]	.93	.01	.60	-.65[b]	.97[a]	-.22	.28	-.35	-.87	-.21	-.51	-.08	-.36	.06	
Mother's report: Number of books read/month	.22	.03	.11	.03	.57[b]	.50[a]	.20	.44[c]	.26	-.05	-.24	.01	-.18	.10	-.20	.20	
Mother's report: Hours/week read for pleasure	.31	.56	.47	.47[c]	.36	-.11	.47	.33[a]	.29	.41	.19	.34[b]	-.05	.46	.48	.39[b]	
Mother's report: Hours/week read for assignment	.62	-.20	.49	.19	.00	.28	.05	.09	.19	.22	-.03	.06	.71	-.28	.19	.14	
Mother's report: Reading group now (1=bottom)	.02	-.50[a]	-.38	-.32	-.03	-.44	-.58	-.34[b]	.32	-.31	-.34	-.08	-.27	-.00	-.36	-.10	
Child likes to read (1=little)	-.23	.37	.07	.01	.03	.55[b]	.14	.31[b]	-.15	.07	.00	.01	.10	.39	.09	.13	
How well child thinks s/he reads (1=not well)	.04	.36	-.01	.20	-.01	.14	-.31	-.04	-.37	.25	-.12	.03	.35	-.23	-.66[b]	-.26	
How fast child says s/he reads (1=slow)	-.44[a]	.04	.52[a]	.11	.17	.38	.55[a]	.40[c]	.31	.58[b]	.46	.50[c]	.35	-.09	.44	.08	
How important is reading (1=not important)	.21	.57[b]	.38	.37[b]	.24	.70[c]	.25	.44[c]	.01	.33	.18	.19	-.09	-.23	-.07	.05	
Number of books read for fun	-.49[a]	.34	-.27	-.20	-.50[a]	.64[b]	.55[a]	.45[c]	-.17	.25	.23	.07	.52[b]	-.36	.17	.29[a]	
Frequency to library (1=rarely)	.14	.21	-.59[a]	-.08	.43	.72[c]	.18	.51[c]	.12	.27	.19	.19	.12	-.43	.57[a]	.00	
Frequency child writes in school (child report)	-.51[a]	-.03	.08	-.28[a]	.18	.04	-.34	.04	.06	-.33	-.17	-.12	.16	-.49[a]	-.59[b]	.12	
Residential status in U.S. (1=long-term residents)	-.28	-.07	-.01	-.10	-.18	-.37	.53	.06	-.57[b]	-.24	.25	-.20	.31	.68[c]	.21	.41[c]	
Number of adults in household (1=one parent)	-.16	.07	.33	.08	-.33	-.06	-.27	-.15	-.55[b]	-.37	-.37	-.35[b]	.25	.19	-.19	-.05	
Number of children in household	.38	.18	.02	.10	.57[b]	.04	-.12	.12	.54[b]	-.16	-.28	-.06	-.40	.48	.33	.40[c]	

Appendix 4. (*Continued*)

Home factor	Word recognition				Reading comprehension				Vocabulary				Word production			
	2d	4th	6th	Total	2d	4th	6th	Total	2d	4th	6th	Total	2d	4th	6th	Total
Number of children in household younger than focal child	-.02	-.05	-.05	-.03	-.41	-.03	.19	.12	.09	-.14	-.12	-.03	.25	.39	.05	.35b
Birth order of child	.07	.37	.04	.10	.77c	.14	-.19	.12	.36	-.00	-.16	.00	-.50a	.30	.23	.26
Mother's education	.16	-.21	.87c	.45c	.03	-.66b	.12	-.05	.18	-.08	.36	.21	-.60b	.03	.21	-.13
Mother liked school as a child (1=little)	.05	.09	-.30	-.02	.39	-.24	-.50	-.15	-.05	.17	-.54	.03	.01	.15	-.91b	-.23
Mother's satisfaction with job	-.36	.28	-.42	-.08	-.48a	.20	-.10	.16	.41	.14	-.27	.19	-.18	-.46	-.05	.06
Mother's salary (1=low)	.67b	-.54	.00	-.04	.58a	-.69b	-.49	-.21	-.27	-.34	-.46	-.28	-.65a	-.36	-.77b	-.11
Mother's involvement in community activities (low score=low involvement)	.25	.80c	.46	.51c	.33	.26	-.02	.12	.30	.74c	.00	.42b	.40	.26	.05	-.04
Grade in school mother desires child to complete (1=low)	.15	.23	.72b	.41b	.39	.25	.05	.37b	-.29	.37	.24	.31b	-.00	-.15	.22	.12
Grade mother expects child to finish	.52	.33	.74c	.54c	.37	.06	-.13	.19	-.02	.53b	.13	.37b	.01	.18	.09	.17
Hours on school day with mother	-.24	.09	.32	.02	-.39	-.15	-.25	-.23	-.23	.08	-.11	-.09	.21	.08	-.28	.02
Hours on weekend day with mother	-.19	-.15	.05	-.08	-.43	-.21	-.21	-.19	-.28	-.07	-.19	-.11	.28	.27	-.05	.12
Frequency of play with siblings (1=little)	-.86c	-.70b	.60b	.32b	-.11	.23	-.10	.10	-.14	-.17	.24	.17	.12	-.25	-.46	-.28
Frequency of child's visits to relatives (1=less frequent)	.53b	-.02	.12	.18	.54b	-.29	-.15	.00	.33	.15	.46	.29a	.43a	-.18	-.04	-.11
Contact with extended family (1=no contact)	.70c	.36	-.31	.18	.45a	-.05	-.46	-.11	.26	.21	-.69b	.00	-.12	.58b	.00	.22
Number of friends (1=fewer than average)	.42	-.27	.17	.09	-.27	.00	.15	.22	-.23	.20	.14	.08	.24	-.16	-.11	.23
Frequency of play with other children (1=rarely)	.25	-.44	.13	.07	.19	.31	-.55a	-.09	.54b	.00	-.21	.13	-.05	-.27	-.42	-.20
Child's report: Frequency of activities with parents, other adults	.08	.50b	.09	.24a	-.18	.24	.11	.24a	-.32	.85c	-.07	.35b	-.10	.22	.02	.22

Mother's report: Frequency to parks, museums (1=rarely)	.16	.13	.17	.25[a]	.06	-.28	.27	.14	.70[c]	.38	.28	.54[c]	-.31	.65[b]	-.25	.09
Mother's report: frequency of out-of-school activities (1=rarely)	.92[c]	-.27	-.50	-.13	.61[a]	.39	.73	.51[b]	.20	.00	.33	.07	-.11	.33	.98[c]	.34[a]
Mother's report: How well child gets along with adults (1=worse than average)	.35	.12	-.36	.07	.66[b]	.21	-.66[b]	.03	.24	.20	-.57[a]	.10	.03	-.15	-.50[a]	-.24
Mother's report: How good child is at getting grownups to help (1=poor)	-.03	.03	.39	.04	.26	.50[a]	.63[b]	.33[b]	-.48[a]	.25	.83[c]	-.03	.07	-.54[b]	.22	-.06
Child's report: Frequency child watches TV	-.36	-.55[b]	.20	-.15	.07	-.54[b]	-.52[a]	-.31[b]	-.20	-.16	-.26	-.15	.08	.27	-.41	.02
Mother's report: Frequency child watches TV	-.63[b]	-.30	.68[a]	-.06	-.88[c]	.01	.68[a]	-.12	-.47	.25	.74[b]	.01	.46	.12	.36	.06
Organization of physical environment	-.40	.30	.62[b]	.22	.08	-.11	.41	.13	-.18	.31	.44	.20	.22	.57[b]	.39	.29[a]
Rules and schedules in family	.43	.06	.29	.18	.02	-.34	-.08	-.23	.06	.29	.17	.13	-.05	.71[c]	-.33	.18
Reliability of mother	-.13	-.06	.47	.22	-.20	-.34	-.09	-.13	-.26	-.02	.22	.06	-.36	.06	.27	-.11
Reliability of father	-.28	-.07	-.01	-.10	-.18	-.37	.53	.06	-.57[b]	-.24	.25	-.20	.31	.68[b]	.21	.41[b]
Frequency child late to school (1=never)	.26	-.30	-.17	.00	.31	-.24	.47	.05	.80[c]	.11	.13	.36[b]	-.34	-.20	.12	-.30[b]
Family emotional stability	-.36	.37	.60[b]	.21	.16	.06	.15	.16	-.02	.76[c]	.19	.37[b]	.34	.70[c]	.47	.46[c]
Swanson child-parent relationship scale	.23	-.07	-.10	.20	.10	-.02	.33	-.09	.32	-.20	.15	.12	-.07	-.19	-.58[b]	-.51[c]
Punishment scale	.57[b]	-.10	-.16	.09	.12	-.05	.21	-.02	-.03	-.16	.09	-.11	-.22	-.15	.49	.02
Locus of control	—	—	—	-.16	—	—	—	.10	—	—	—	-.10	—	—	—	.21
Child's perception of mother's nurturance	—	—	—	-.07	—	—	—	.06	—	—	—	.09	—	—	—	.09
Child's perception of father's nurturance	—	—	—	.26[a]	—	—	—	—	—	—	—	.22	—	—	—	.07
Social stress score of mother	-.50[a]	.21	-.06	.03	-.26	.36	.06	.19	.03	.21	-.13	.16	.54[a]	.08	.15	.10

a. $p < .10$
b. $p < .05$
c. $p < .01$

References

Adult Performance Level Study. 1977. Final Report, Adult Performance Level Project, University of Texas at Austin.

Alexander, K., and D. Entwisle. 1988. Achievement in the first two years of school: Patterns and processes. *Monographs of the Society for Research in Child Development,* serial no. 218, vol. 53, no. 2.

Allington, R. L. 1980. Teacher interruption behaviors during primary grade oral reading. *Journal of Educational Psychology* 72: 371–377.

Anderson, R., P. Wilson, and L. Fielding. 1988. Growth in reading and how children spend their time outside of school. *Reading Research Quarterly* 23: 285–303.

Applebee, A., J. Langer, and I. Mullis. 1988. *Who reads best? Factors related to reading achievement in grades 3, 7, and 11.* Princeton, N.J.: Educational Testing Service.

Au, K., and C. Jordan. 1981. Teaching reading to Hawaiian children: Finding a culturally appropriate solution. In *Culture and the bilingual classroom: Studies in classroom ethnography,* eds. H. Trueba, G. Guthrie, and K. Au. Rawley, Mass.: Newbury House.

Ayllon, T., S. Garber, and K. Pisor. 1975. The elimination of discipline problems through a combined school-home motivational system. *Behavior Therapy* 6: 616–626.

Bachman, J., S. Green, and I. Wirtanen. 1971. *Youth in transition,* vol. 3, *Dropping out—problem or symptom?* Ann Arbor, Mich.: Institute for Social Research.

Baker, D., and D. Stevenson. 1986. Mothers' strategies for school achievement: Managing the transition to high school. *Sociology of Education* 59: 156–167.

Bales, R. F., and S. P. Cohen. 1979. *SYMLOG: A system for the multiple level observations of groups.* New York: Free Press.

Barnes, W. B. 1984. Sibling influences within family and school contexts. Ed.D. diss., Harvard Graduate School of Education.

Beavers, W. R. 1977. *Psychotherapy and growth: A family systems perspective.* New York: Brunner/Mazel.

Becker, H., and J. Epstein. 1982. Parent involvement: A survey of teacher practices. *Elementary School Journal* 83: 85–102.

Belle, D., ed. 1982. *Lives in stress: Women and depression.* Beverly Hills, Calif.: Sage.

Birnbaum, J. C. 1980. Why should I write? Environmental influences on children's views of writing. *Theory into Practice* 19: 202–210.

Blau, P., and O. D. Duncan. 1977. *The American occupational structure.* New York: John Wiley and Sons.

Bloom, B. S. 1976. *Human characteristics and school learning.* New York: McGraw Hill.

Bloome, D. 1980. Capturing the social contexts of reading. Paper presented at the Ethnography in Education Research Forum, University of Pennsylvania, Philadelphia, March.

———— 1981. An ethnographic approach to the study of reading activities among black junior high school students: A sociolinguistic ethnography. Ph.D. diss., Kent State University, Graduate School of Education.

Blyth, D., R. Simmons, and S. Carlton-Ford, S. 1983. The adjustment of early adolescents to school transition. *Journal of Early Adolescence* 3: 105–120.

Boston Public Schools. 1986. A working document on the dropout problem in Boston Public Schools. Office of Research and Development.

Boyer, E. L. 1983. *High School: A report on secondary education in America.* New York: Harper and Row.

Bradley, R. H. and B. M. Caldwell. 1984. The relation of infants' home environments to achievement test performance in first grade: A follow-up study. *Child Development* 55: 803–809.

Britton, J. N., T. Burgess, N. Martin, A. McLeod, and H. Rosen. 1975. *The development of writing abilities 11–18.* London: Macmillan Education Ltd.

Brookover, W., L. Beamer, H. Efthim, D. Hathaway, L. Lezotte, S. Miller, Passalacque, and L. Tornatzky. 1982. *Creating effective schools: An inservice program for enhancing school learning climate and achievement.* Holmes Beach, Fla.: Learning Publications Inc.

Cadoret, R., and C. Cain. 1980. Sex differences in predictors of antisocial behavior in adoptees. *Archives of General Psychiatry* 37: 1171–75.

Carnegie Foundation. 1986. *Report on higher education.* New York: Carnegie Foundation.

Carroll, J. 1987. The national assessments in reading: Are we misreading the findings? *Phi Delta Kappan* 68: 424–430.

Chall, J. S. 1983. *Stages of reading development.* New York: McGraw Hill.

Chall, J. S., and C. E. Snow. 1988. School influences on the reading development of low-income children. *Harvard Education Letter* 4, no.1, 1–4.

Chall, J. S., V. Jacobs, and L. Baldwin. 1990. *The reading crisis: Why poor children fall behind.* Cambridge, Mass.: Harvard University Press.

Chandler, J., and L. Hemphill. 1983. Models of classrooms as effective literacy environments for low-income children. Unpublished ms., Harvard Graduate School of Education.

Chandler, J., D. Argyris, W. S. Barnes, I. F. Goodman, and C. E. Snow. 1986. Parents as teachers: Observations of low-income parents and children in a homework-like task. In *The acquisition of literacy: Ethnographic perspectives,* eds. B. Schieffelin and P. Gilmore. Norwood, N.J.: Ablex.

Chomsky, C. 1972. Stages in language development and reading exposure. *Harvard Educational Review* 42: 1–33.

Clark, M. 1976. *Young fluent readers.* London: Heinemann.

Clark, R. 1983. *Family life and school achievement. Why poor black children succeed or fail.* Chicago: University of Chicago Press.

Coleman, J. S., E. Campbell, C. Hobson, J. McPartland, A. Mood, F. Weinfeld, and R. York. 1966. *Equality of educational opportunity.* Washington, D.C.: U.S. Office of Education, National Center for Educational Statistics.

Collins, J. 1986. Differential instruction in reading groups. In *A Social Construction of Literacy.* ed. J. Cook-Gumperz. Cambridge, Eng.: Cambridge University Press.

Cousert, G. C. 1978. Six selected home reading environment factors and their relationship to reading achievement. Ph.D. diss., Indiana University.

Csikszentmihalyi, M., and R. Larson. 1984. *Being adolescent: Conflict and growth in the teenage years.* New York: Basic Books.

Csikszentmihalyi, M., and J. McCormack. 1986. The influence of teachers. *Phi Delta Kappan* 67: 415–420.

Dave, R. 1963. The identification and measurement of environmental process variables that are related to education achievement. Ph.D. diss., University of Chicago.

Dornbusch, S. M., and P. L. Ritter. 1988. Parents of high school students: A neglected resource. *Educational Horizons* 66: 75–77.

Dougherty, E. H., and A. Dougherty. 1977. The daily report card: A simplified flexible package for classroom behavior management. *Psychology in the Schools* 14: 191–195.

Doyle, A. B., and D. S. Moskowitz. 1984. *Children in families under stress.* New Directions for Child Development, no. 24. San Francisco: Jossey-Bass.

Durkin, D. 1966. *Children who read early.* New York: Teachers College Press, Columbia University.

——— 1982. A study of poor black children who are successful readers. Reading Education Report, no. 33. Center for the Study of Reading, University of Illinois at Urbana-Champaign, April.

Eckert, P. 1988. Adolescent social structure and the spread of linguistic change. *Language in Society* 17: 183–208.

Eder, D. 1981. Ability grouping as a self-fulfilling prophecy: A micro-analysis of teacher-student interaction. *Sociology of Education* 54: 151–162.

Ekstrom, R., M. Goertz, J. Pollack, and D. Rock. 1986. Who drops out of high school and why? Findings from a national study. *Teachers College Record* 87: 356–373.

Epstein, J. L. 1983. Longitudinal effects of person-family-school interactions on student outcomes. *Research in sociology of education and socialization,* vol. 4, ed. A. Kerckhoff. Greenwich, Conn.: Jai.

——— 1984. Effects of teacher practices of parent involvement on change in student achievement in reading and math. Paper presented at the Annual Meeting of the American Educational Research Association, New Orleans, April.

——— 1985. Home and school connections in schools of the future: Implications of research on parent involvement. *Peabody Journal of Education* 62: 18–41.

——— 1986. Parents' reactions to teacher practices of parent involvement. *Elementary School Journal* 86: 277–294.

——— 1988. How do we improve programs for parent involvement? *Educational Horizons* 66: 58–59.

——— In press. Effects of parent involvement on change in student achievement in reading and math. In *Literacy through family, community, and school interaction,* ed. S. Silvern. Greenwich, Conn.: Jai.

Epstein, J. L. and J. M. McPartland. 1979. Authority structures. In *Educational environments and effects,* ed. H. Walberg. Berkeley: McCutcheon.

Evertson, C. M., C. W. Anderson, L. M. Anderson, and J. E. Brophy. 1980. Relationships between classroom behaviors and student outcomes in junior high mathematics and English classes. *American Educational Research Journal* 17: 43–60.

Fiering, S. 1981. Unofficial writing. In *Ethnographic monitoring of children's acquisition of reading/language arts skills in and out of the classroom,* vols. 1–3, ed. D. Hymes. Final report to the National Institute of Education. Philadelphia: University of Pennsylvania Graduate School of Education.

Fleming, M. 1985. *The effective-schools program, Project Perform Schools: Evaluation report.* Cleveland, Ohio: Cleveland Public Schools.

Flower, L., and J. Hayes. 1980. The dynamics of composing: Making plans and juggling constraints. In *Cognitive processes in writing,* eds. L. Gregg and E. Steinberg. Hillsdale, N.J.: Erlbaum.

Fowles, M. E. 1978. Basic skills assessment: Manual for scoring the writing sample—Analytic scoring and holistic scoring. Princeton, N.J.: Educational Testing Service.

Framo, J., ed. 1972. *Family interaction: A dialogue between family researchers and family therapists.* New York: Springer Publishing Co.

Fraser, M. 1974. *Children in conflict.* Harmondsworth, Middlesex, Eng.: Penguin Books.

Friedman, R. 1973. *Family roots of school learning and behavior disorders.* Springfield, Ill.: Charles C. Thomas.

Garmezy, N. 1981. Children under stress: Perspectives on antecedents and correlates of vulnerability and resistance to psychopathology. In *Further explorations in personality,* eds. A. I. Rabin, J. Aronoff, A. M. Barclay, and R. A. Zucker. New York: Wiley Interscience.

—— 1983. Stressors of childhood. In *Stress, coping, and development in children,* eds. N. Garmezy and M. Rutter. New York: McGraw-Hill.

—— 1988. Garmezy on genetics, moms, social support. *APA Monitor,* July, p. 13.

Gilmore, P. 1983. Spelling Mississippi: Recontextualizing a literacy-related speech event. *Anthropology and Education Quarterly* 14: 235–255.

—— 1986. Sub-rosa literacy: Peers, play, and ownership in literacy acquisition. In *The acquisition of literacy: Ethnographic perspectives,* eds. B. Schieffelin and P. Gilmore. Norwood, N.J.: Ablex.

Gilmore, P., and D. M. Smith. 1982. A retrospective discussion of the state of the art in ethnography in education. In *Children in and out of school,* eds. P. Gilmore and A. Glatthorn. Washington, D.C.: Center for Applied Linguistics.

Goodlad, J. I. 1984. *A place called school: Prospects for the future.* New York: McGraw Hill.

Goodman, I. F. 1983. Television's role in family interaction: A family systems perspective. *Journal of Family Issues* 4: 405–424.

—— 1984. The relationship between perceptions of family interaction and of television's role in the family. Ed.D. diss., Harvard Graduate School of Education.

Goodman, I. F., and L. Hemphill. 1982. Home factors associated with superior reading achievement among low income children. Paper presented at the Twentieth Congress of Applied Psychology, Edinburgh, July.

Gotts, E. E. 1984. *Communicating through the home-school handbook: Guidelines for principals.* Charleston, W. Va.: Appalachia Educational Laboratory.

Gotts, E. E., and R. F. Purnell. 1987. Practicing school-family relations in urban settings. *Education and Urban Society* 19: 212–218.

Grant, G. 1988. *The world we created at Hamilton High.* Cambridge, Mass.: Harvard University Press.

Graves, D. H. 1982. *Writing: Teachers and children at work.* Exeter, N.H.: Heinemann Educational Books.

Griffin, P. 1977. How and when does reading occur in the classroom? *Theory into Practice* 16: 376–383.

Griswold, P. A. 1986. Family outing activities and achievement among fourth graders in compensatory education funded schools. *Journal of Educational Research* 79: 261–266.

Gumperz, J. J. 1970. Verbal strategies in multilingual communication. In

Georgetown University Roundtable on Languages and Linguistics, 1970, ed. J. Alatis. Washington, D.C.: Georgetown University Press.

Hargreaves, D. H. 1974. *Interpersonal relations in education.* London: Routledge and Kegan Paul.

Hauser-Cram, J. P. 1983. A question of balance: Relationships between parents and teachers. Ed.D. diss., Harvard Graduate School of Education.

Heath, S. B. 1983. *Ways with words.* Cambridge, Eng.: Cambridge University Press.

Hemphill, L. 1986. Context and conversational style: A reappraisal of social class differences in speech. Ed.D. diss., Harvard Graduate School of Education.

Hemphill, L., and I. F. Goodman. 1982. Classroom factors associated with superior reading achievement among low income children. Paper presented at the Twentieth Congress of Applied Psychology, Edinburgh, July.

Henderson, A. T., C. L. Marburger, and T. Ooms. 1986. Developing a family-school partnership in every school. *Journal of Educational Public Relations* 9: 5–9.

Henderson, R. W. 1981. Home environment and intellectual performance. In *Parent-child interaction,* ed. R. Henderson. New York: Academic Press.

Hess, R. D. 1970. Social class and ethnic influences on socialization. In *Carmichael's manual of child psychology,* vol. 2. New York: Wiley.

Hess, R. D., and K. A. Camara. 1979. Post-divorce family relationships as mediating factors in the consequences of divorce for children. *Journal of Social Issues* 35: 79–96.

Hess, R. D., and V. Shipman. 1965. Early experience and the socialization of cognitive modes in children. *Child Development* 36: 869–886.

Hetherington, E. M. 1984. Stress and coping in children and families. In *Children in families under stress,* eds. A. B. Doyle, D. Gold, and D. Moskowitz. New Directions for Child Development no. 24. San Francisco: Jossey-Bass.

Hetherington, E. M., M. Cox, and R. Cox. 1982. Effects of divorce on parents and children. In *Nontraditional families,* ed. M. Lamb. Hillsdale, N.J.: Erlbaum.

Hewison, J., and J. Tizard. 1980. Parental involvement and reading attainment. *British Journal of Educational Psychology* 50: 209–215.

Hill, J. 1983. Early adolescence: A research agenda. *Journal of Early Adolescence* 3: 1–21.

Holdaway, D. 1984. *Stability and change in literacy learning.* Exeter, N.H.: Heinemann Educational Books.

Holmes, T. H., and M. Masuda. 1974. Life changes and illness susceptibility. In *Stressful life events: Their nature and effects,* eds. B. S. Dohrenwent and B. P. Dohrenwent. New York: John Wiley.

Hyman, H. 1953. The value systems of different classes: A social psychological contribution to the analysis of stratification. In *Class status and power,* eds. R. Bendix and S. M. Lipset. Glencoe, Ill.: Free Press.

Iverson, B. A., and H. J. Walberg. 1982. Home environment and school learning: A quantitative synthesis. *Journal of Experimental Education* 50: 144–151.

Jacobs, V. 1986. Use of connectives in low-income, elementary children's writing and its relation to their reading, writing, and language skill development. Ed.D. diss., Harvard Graduate School of Education.

Jeffers, C. 1967. *Living poor.* Ann Arbor, Mich.: Ann Arbor Publishers.

Jencks, C., M. Smith, H. Acland, M. J. Bane, D. Cohen, H. Gintis, B. Heyns, and S. Michelson. 1972. *Inequality: A reassessment of family and schooling in America.* New York: Basic Books.

Johnson, D., and E. Ransom. 1983. *Family and school.* London: Croom Helm.

Kean, M. H., A. A. Summers, M. J. Raivetz, and I. J. Farber. 1979. *What works in reading.* Philadelphia: Office of Research and Evaluation, School District of Philadelphia.

Lamme, L., and P. Olmstead. 1977. Family reading habits and children's progress in reading. Paper presented at the Annual Meeting of the International Reading Association, Miami Beach.

Laosa, L. 1978. Maternal teaching strategies in Chicano families of varied educational and socioeconomic levels. *Child Development* 49: 1129–35.

Lawrence, S. 1969. Ability grouping. Unpublished manuscript prepared for the Center for Educational Policy Research, Harvard Graduate School of Education.

Leichter, H. J. 1974. Some perspectives on the family as educator. *Teachers College Record* 76: 198–225.

Leitch, M. L., and S. Tangri. 1988. Barriers to home-school collaboration. *Educational Horizons* 66: 70–74.

Levine, D. U., and J. Stark. 1981. *Instructional and organizational arrangements for improving achievement at inner city elementary schools.* Washington, D.C.: Educational Resources Information Center, U.S. Department of Education.

Lightfoot, S. L. 1978. *Worlds apart: Relationships between families and schools.* New York: Basic Books.

———— 1983. *The good high school: Portraits of character and culture.* New York: Basic Books.

Longfellow, C. 1979. Divorce in context: Its impact on children. In *Divorce and separation: Context, causes, and consequences,* eds. G. Levinger and O. Moles. New York: Basic Books.

Malone, C. A. 1963. Observations on children of disorganized families and problems of acting out. *Journal of the American Academy of Child Psychiatry* 2: 42–49.

Marjoribanks, K. 1979. *Families and their learning environments: An empirical analysis.* London: Routledge and Kegan Paul.

———— 1980. *Ethnic families and children's achievement.* Sydney: George Allen and Unwin.

Marston, E. 1982. A study of variables relating to the voluntary reading habits of eighth graders. Ph.D. diss., Harvard Graduate School of Education.

McAfee, O. 1987. Improving home-school relations: Implications for staff development. *Education and Urban Society* 19: 185–199.

McDermott, R. P. 1978. Pirandello in the classroom: On the possibility of equal educational opportunity in American culture. In *Features of exceptional children: Emerging structures,* ed. M. C. Reynolds. Reston, V.A.: Council for Exceptional Children.

McDermott, R. P., S. Goldman, and H. Varenne. 1984. When school goes home: Some problems in the organization of homework. *Teacher's College Record* 85: 381–409.

McDill, E. L., and L. Rigsby. 1973. *Structure and process in secondary schools: The academic impact of educational climates.* Baltimore: John Hopkins University Press.

McGillicuddy-DeLisi, A. V. 1982. The relationship between parents' beliefs about development and family constellation, socioeconomic status, and parents' teaching strategies. In *Families as learning environments for children,* eds. L. M. Laosa and I. E. Siegel. New York: Plenum Press.

Medrich, E. A., J. A. Roizen, V. Rubin, and S. Buckley. 1982. *The serious business of growing up: A study of children's lives outside school.* Berkeley: University of California Press.

Miller, P. J. 1982. *Amy, Wendy, and Beth: Learning language in South Baltimore.* Austin: University of Texas Press.

Minuchin, S. 1974. *Families and family therapy.* Cambridge, Mass.: Harvard University Press.

Moll, L., E. Estrada, E. Diaz, and L. Lopes. 1982. Making contexts: The social construction of lessons in two languages. In *Cross-cultural and communicative competencies,* eds. S. Arvizu and M. Saravia-Shore. New York: Garland Press.

Murnane, R. J., J. D. Singer, and J. B. Willett. 1988. The career paths of teachers: Implications for teacher supply and methodological lessons for research. *Educational Researcher* 17: 22–30.

National Assessment of Educational Progress. 1981. *Reading, thinking, writing: A report on the 1979–1980 assessment.* Denver: NAEP.

———— 1985. *The reading report card: Progress toward excellence in our schools.* Princeton, N.J.: Educational Testing Service.

Norman-Jackson, J. 1982. Family interactions, language development, and primary reading achievement of black children in families of low income. *Child Development* 53: 349–358.

Osborn, A. F., N. R. Butler, and A. C. Morris. 1984. *The social life of Britain's five year olds.* London: Routledge and Kegan Paul.

Panton, K. J. 1986. Patterns of reading ability in the inner city: A study of London. *First Language* 6: 203–218.

Parkinson, C. E., et al. 1982. Research note—Rating the home environment of school-age children: A comparison with general cognitive index and school progress. *Journal of Child Psychology and Psychiatry* 23: 329–333.

Paschal, R., T. Weinstein, and H. J. Walberg. 1984. Effects of homework on learning: A quantitative synthesis. *Journal of Educational Research* 2: 97–104.

Pavenstedt, E. 1965. A comparison of the child rearing environment of upper-lower and very low-lower class families. *American Journal of Orthopsychiatry* 35: 89–98.

Pecheone, R., and J. Shoemaker. 1984. *An evaluation of school effectiveness programs in Connecticut: Technical report.* Hartford: Connecticut Department of Education.

Philips, S. U. 1983. *The invisible culture: Communication in classroom and community on the Warm Springs Indian Reservation.* New York: Longman.

Plowden Report. 1967. *Children and their primary schools: A report of the Central Advisory Council for Education.* London: Her Majesty's Stationery Office.

Powell, A., E. Farrar, and D. Cohen. 1985. *The shopping mall high school: Winners and losers in the educational marketplace.* Boston: Houghton Mifflin.

Prescott, B. L., C. L. Pelton, and S. M. Dornbusch. 1986. Teacher perceptions of parent-school communication: A collaborative analysis. Paper delivered at the Conference of Effects for Alternative Designs in Compensatory Education, Washington, D.C.

Reiss, D. 1981. *The family's construction of reality.* Cambridge, Mass.: Harvard University Press.

Rodman, H. 1963. The lower-class value stretch. *Social Forces* 42: 205–215.

Rodman, H., and P. Voydanoff. 1978. Social class and parents' range of aspirations for their children. *Social Problems* 25: 333–344.

Rosenthal, R., and L. Jacobson. 1984. *Pygmalion in the classroom: Teacher expectation and pupils' intellectual development.* Bridgeport, Conn.: Irvington Publishing, Inc.

Roswell, F., and J. Chall. In press. *The Roswell-Chall diagnostic reading test,* rev. ed. New York: McGraw-Hill.

Rutter, M., et al. (A. Cox, C. Tupling, M. Berger, and W. Yule). 1975a. Attainment and adjustment in two geographical areas; part 1, The prevalence of psychiatric disorder. *British Journal of Psychiatry* 126: 493–509.

Rutter, M., et al. (B. Yule, D. Quinton, O. Rowlands, W. Yule, and M. Berger). 1975b. Attainment and adjustment in two geographical areas: III. Some factors accounting for area differences. *British Journal of Psychiatry* 126: 520–533.

Rutter, M., B. Maughan, P. Mortimore, J. Ouston, and A. Smith. 1979. *Fifteen thousand hours: Secondary schools and their effects on children.* Cambridge, Mass.: Harvard University Press.

St. John, N. 1972. Mothers and children: Congruence and optimism of school-related attitudes. *Journal of Marriage and the Family* 34: 422–430.

Saunders, E. B. 1977. The nurturance scale. Stress and Families Project, Harvard University.

Scarr, S. 1981. Testing for children. *American Psychologist* 36: 1159–66.

Schachter, F. F. 1979. *Everyday mother talk to toddlers: Early intervention.* New York: Academic Press.

Schieffelin, B., and P. Gilmore, eds. 1986. *The acquisition of literacy: Ethnographic perspectives.* Norwood, N.J.: Ablex.

Scollon, R., and S. Scollon. 1981. *Narrative, literacy, and face in interethnic communication.* Norwood, N.J.: Ablex.

Scott-Jones, D. 1984. Family influences on cognitive development and school achievement. In *Review of Research in Education,* ed. E. W. Gordon, vol. 11, pp. 259–304. Washington, D.C.: American Educational Research Association.

Seginer, R. 1983. Parents' educational expectations and children's academic achievements: A literature review. *Merrill-Palmer Quarterly* 29: 1–23.

Sewell, W. M., and R. M. Hauser. 1976. Causes and consequences of higher education models of the status attainment process. In *Schooling and achievement in American society,* eds. W. H. Sewell, R. M. Hauser, and D. L. Featherman. New York: Academic Press.

Sewell, W., and V. P. Shah. 1968. Parents' education and children's educational aspirations and achievements. *American Sociological Review* 33: 191–209.

Shaughnessy, M. 1977. *Errors and expectations.* New York: Oxford University Press.

Shea, J., and M. Hanes. 1977. The relationship between measures of home environment and school achievement of Follow Through children. Paper presented at the Annual Meeting of the American Educational Research Association, New York.

Sheats, D. W., and G. E. Dunkleberger. 1979. A determination of the principal's effect in school-initiated home contacts concerning attendance of elementary school students. *Journal of Educational Research* 72: 310–312.

Silverstein, B., and R. Krate. 1975. *Children of the dark ghetto.* New York: Praeger.

Sizer, T. R. 1984. *Horace's compromise: The dilemma of the American high school.* Boston: Houghton Mifflin.

Snow, C. E. 1987. Factors influencing vocabulary and reading achievement in low-income children. In *Toegepaste taalwetenschap in artikelen,* ed. R. Appel. Amsterdam: ANELA.

Snow, C. E. and D. Dickinson. In press. Skills that aren't basic in a new conception of literacy. In *New conceptions of literacy,* eds. A. Purves and T. Jennings. Albany: SUNY Press.

Snow, M. 1982. *Characteristics of families with special needs in relation to schools.* Charleston, W. Va.: Appalachia Educational Laboratory.

Spenner, K., and D. Featherman. 1978. Achievement ambitions. *Annual Review of Sociology* 4: 373–420.

Stevenson, D. L., and D. P. Baker. 1987. The family-school relation and the child's school performance. *Child Development* 58: 1348–57.

Swanson, G. W. 1950. The development of an instrument for rating child-parent relationships. *Social Focus* 29: 84–90.

Tangri, S., and L. M. Leitch. 1982. Barriers to home-school collaboration: Two case studies in junior high schools. Final report to the National Institute of Education. Washington, D.C.: Urban Institute.

Tangri, S., and O. Moles. In press. Parents and the community. In *Educator's handbook,* ed. V. Koehler. New York: Longman.

Teale, W. H., and E. Sulzby, eds. 1986. *Emergent literacy: Writing and reading.* Norwood, N.J.: Ablex.

Thorndike, R. L. 1973. *Reading comprehension in fifteen countries.* New York: John Wiley and Sons.

Tizard, J., W. N. Schofield, and J. Hewison. 1982. Collaboration between teachers and parents in assisting children's reading. *British Journal of Educational Psychology* 52: 1–15.

Toomey, D. 1986. Home-school relations and inequality in education. Address given to Conference on Education and the Family, Brigham Young University, Provo, Utah, February.

Varenne, H., V. Hamid-Buglione, R. P. McDermott, and A. Morrison. 1982. I teach him everything he learns in school: The acquisition of literacy for learning and working in families. Final Report, contract no. 400-79-0046. Washington, D.C.: National Institute of Education.

Walberg, H. J. 1984. Families as partners in educational productivity. *Phi Delta Kappan* 65: 397–400.

Walberg, H. J., and K. Marjoribanks. 1976. Family environments and cognitive development. *Review of Educational Research* 46: 527–551.

Waller, W. 1932. *Sociology of teaching.* New York: John Wiley and Sons.

Wallerstein, J. S., and J. B. Kelly. 1980. *Surviving the breakup: How children and parents cope with divorce.* New York: Basic Books.

Ware, W. B., and M. Garber. 1972. The home environment as a predictor of school achievement. *Theory into Practice* 11: 190–195.

Weiss, R. 1969. Growing up a little faster: The experience of growing up in a single parent household. *Journal of Social Issues* 35: 97–109.

Wells, C. G. 1985. Preschool literacy-related activities and success in school. In *Literacy, language, and learning,* eds. D. Olson, M. Torrance, and A. Hildyard. London: Cambridge University Press.

Werner, E. E., and R. S. Smith. 1982. *Vulnerable but invincible: A longitudinal study of resilient children and youth.* New York: McGraw-Hill.

Wolf, R. M. 1964. The identification and measurement of home environmental process variables that are related to intelligence. Ph.D. diss., University of Chicago.

Wyne, M. D. and G. B. Stuck. 1983. Time and learning: Implications for the classroom teacher. *Elementary School Journal* 83: 67–75.

Zelkowitz, P. 1982. Children's support networks: Their role in families under stress. Ed.D. diss., Harvard Graduate School of Education.

Acknowledgments

The present volume constitutes one of two companion volumes being published by Harvard University Press. These volumes have a long and intertwined history. In December 1979, Jeanne Chall and Catherine Snow together submitted a proposal to the National Institute of Education (NIE) to carry out a study on factors affecting literacy achievement in children of low-income families. The proposal was originally written in response to an NIE request for proposals, which specified that the proposed study should focus on low-income populations and children in the middle elementary years and should generate information about out-of-school factors that relate to literacy. Our proposal included a detailed plan to collect such information, as well as information about the children's in-school experiences, and to document their reading, writing, and language skills at regular intervals during the course of the study. We proposed a three-year longitudinal study; we were awarded funds to carry out the study largely as proposed, with one unfortunate change—money for the third year of data collection, which would have enabled us to collect data on three groups of children at overlapping ages and thus to ensure the comparability of the groups, was not granted.

To carry out our ambitious research plan, we turned to faculty colleagues and to a large group of graduate research assistants for collaboration and help. Some of these former student assistants have been able to continue their interest in an association with the project to the stage of collaborating on the final manuscripts. Deserving of special mention is our colleague Marcus Lieberman, who carried out data analyses for all sections of the project.

Jeanne Chall supervised the collection of test data used to select the subjects and the two rounds of reading, writing, and language data used as outcome measures. Carol Chomsky advised us on the design of the language tests. Literacy and language testing was carried out by research assistants Rosalind Davidson, Barbara Eckhoff, Vicki Jacobs, Steven Stahl, and Judith Zorfass, and Luke Baldwin and Vicki Jacobs took on much of the work involved in more detailed analyses of the test data.

Courtney Cazden worked generously with classroom researchers Beverly Goldfield, Lowry Hemphill, and Jean Chandler to develop procedures for classroom observations, collection of interview and questionnaire data from teachers, and compilation of information from the children's school records. Lowry Hemphill and Jean Chandler took primary responsibility for the analysis of the classroom data.

Catherine Snow supervised the collection of interview and observational data in the homes. Debbie Belle helped with interview design, and Irene Goodman and Wendy Barnes collaborated in the piloting and final design of the parent and the child interviews, respectively. Catherine Snow, Wendy Barnes, and Irene Goodman carried out the bulk of the home interviews with help from Polly Wheeler, Luke Baldwin, James Day, and John Clarke. Jean Chandler also carried out some parental interviews and participated in all the home observations. Irene Goodman and Wendy Barnes worked with Catherine Snow to carry out analyses and data reduction for the home interview and observation data.

In December 1982 a final report that represented the first level of analysis of all these data was submitted to NIE. Chall and Snow coauthored this report in collaboration with Barnes, Chandler, Goodman, Hemphill, and Jacobs. Prepared in the few months directly after final data collection, this report (included in the Educational Resources Information Center as document ED 234345) reflects our first attempt to make sense of a very large and complex data set. Inevitably at that point, some of the analyses were more advanced than others. While the literacy and language test data had been extensively analyzed, more qualitative analyses of the writing data were still to be carried out. Similarly, though the basic analyses of the home and school data had been completed for the final report, later examinations of several aspects of these data have enriched our understanding of effects on literacy development. These later analyses have been reported in articles, chapters, and theses by various members of the original research team. Findings relevant to homework were reported by Chandler, Argyris, Barnes, Goodman, and Snow (1986). Snow wrote a summary of some of the home and school findings relevant to vocabulary development (1987), and Chall and Show together wrote a summary of recommendations to schools for the *Harvard Education Letter* (vol. 4, 1988). Barnes analyzed some of the data collected about the focal children in comparison with comparable data she had collected on their siblings for her thesis (1984). Goodman focused on data she had collected from the families about TV use and the ways that TV use reflected other aspects of family functioning in her thesis (1984). Jacobs carried out extensive additional analyses of the children's writing samples for her thesis (1986). Chandler and Hemphill received funding from the American Association of Publishers to carry out alternative analyses of the classroom data, and wrote a report of these analyses that focused on the predictive power of different models of classroom functioning (1983).

The first attempt to rework the final report to NIE and subsequent analyses into a publishable volume maintained the structure of the final report in presenting the findings as one large study. In this version of the manuscript (by Snow, Chall, Barnes, Chandler, Goodman, Hemphill, and Jacobs), the introductory and final chapters were primarily written by Chall and Snow together, chapters on the children's literacy development were written by Chall with Jacobs, and chapters on family and school data collection, findings, and analyses were written by Barnes, Chandler, Goodman, Hemphill, and Snow working collaboratively. This version of the manuscript was reviewed by many people, several of whom noted a shift in voice between the chapters reporting on literacy development and those reporting on home and school factors. In reflecting on these reviews, Chall realized that in a deeper sense we had carried out two studies on one group of children and thus proposed dividing the report into two separate volumes. One study (published as *The Reading Crisis: Why Poor Children Fall Behind* by Chall, Jacobs, and Baldwin, 1990) documented the literacy skills of a group of children from low-income families across a period of crucial changes in the literacy demands some of those children met. It derived from an academic tradition grounded in psycho-linguistic and developmental approaches to reading and writing, in psychometric approaches to literacy assessment, and in analysis of reading materials and procedures for reading instruction. The variables of primary interest were defined in the long period of preparatory work, during which instruments to assess reading, writing, and language had been developed by Chall and her collaborators.

The other study, reported here, relates individual differences among the children in literacy status and literacy gains to factors in their homes and classrooms. It shows the influence of qualitative, ethnographic research traditions, relying on methods traditionally used in studies of parent-child interaction as related to language, cognitive, and socio-emotional development, and in analyses of classroom discourse. In keeping with those methods, the variables of interest were allowed to emerge from the observations.

Obviously, though each of these companion volumes can be read on its own, there is no way in which they can be fully divorced. Both studies derived from a single set of theoretical starting points. The home and family analyses reported in this book rely crucially on data about children's literacy skills generated by Chall's research team. Conversely, interpretations of the children's literacy achievements in *The Reading Crisis* depend on information about instruction and classroom factors generated by the team of classroom researchers. Conclusions of both studies rely on the children selected—children who met our shared criteria both for literacy skills and for family demographics.

The authors of this book express their warm appreciation to all our collaborators, especially Debbie Belle, Courtney Cazden, Carol Chomsky, and Marcus Lieberman. Our deepest thanks are due to the families and teachers who let us observe their homes and classrooms and gave us so much time and access to their views on literacy, education, and their own lives. The project would not have been possible without the cooperation of the school system in the city we studied, especially its director of primary education, cooperating school principals, and the clerks and secretaries who facilitated our access to school records.

Index